KELLY ROWLAND

FROM DESTINY & BEYOND

Chloé Govan

OMNIBUS PRESS

London / New York / Paris / Sydney / Copenhagen / Berlin / Madrid / Tokyo

Exclusive Distributors
Music Sales Limited,
14/15 Berners Street,
London, W1T 3LJ.

Music Sales Corporation,
257 Park Avenue South,
New York, NY 10010, USA.

Macmillan Distribution Services,
56 Parkwest Drive
Derrimut, Vic 3030,
Australia.

Every effort has been made to trace the copyright holders of the photographs in this book but one or
two were unreachable. We would be grateful if the photographers concerned would contact us.

Typeset by Phoenix Photosetting, Chatham, Kent
Printed in the EU

A catalogue record for this book is available from the British Library.

Visit Omnibus Press on the web at www.omnibuspress.com

Contents

Chapter 1   Humble Beginnings   7

Chapter 2   A Little Faith   21

Chapter 3   Somethin' Fresh   48

Chapter 4   A Southern Girl's First Taste Of Success   65

Chapter 5   Moving On Up   84

Chapter 6   The Cut-Throat World of Showbiz   100

Chapter 7   Surviving Solo   122

Chapter 8   Cinderella Dreams   146

Chapter 9   No Future In The Past   169

Chapter 10   When Dance Takes Over   195

Chapter 11   Down For Whatever   218

Chapter 1

Humble Beginnings

Public service announcement: it's 2011 and Kelly Rowland is "down for whatever". And yes, she assures her audience – for those in any doubt – she could make love on the floor.

She wasn't talking about her boyfriend either. Earlier that year, she had openly admitted to having a "friend with benefits" – the kind of revelation that might have compelled furious former manager Mathew Knowles – the devout father of Beyoncé – to wring his hands in horror.

In today's hyper-sexualised music world where sex appeal equals sales, no-one questioned suggestive songs like 'Down For Whatever': they blended in with the background perfectly. In fact, compared to Rihanna's less than subtle lyrical shout-outs about whips, chains and the scent of sex, Kelly's track was almost tame.

But measure it against her clean-cut Christian background and a former manager who pledged to sack the girls of Destiny's Child if they either had sex outside marriage or were no longer virgins at age 20, and her transformation became that little bit more surprising. Kelly was a God-fearing girl, not a good-time girl. Hearing otherwise was, at that stage in her career, about as astonishing as finding a nun on stage at a strip club, taking a break from all the gyration only to throw her habit into the baying crowd.

Yet a couple of years after firing Mathew Knowles, Kelly had replaced R&B tracks with dance anthems and entered a world of candid confessions and topless photo shoots. No longer under the control of a strait-laced manager, she declared herself ready to reclaim her power and call her own shots.

It was time to shake aside the Beyoncé comparisons, step out of her more famous soul sister's shadow and show the world that she too had the confidence to come into her own. It was a formidable war cry – but it hadn't always been this easy.

Press rewind on the album of her life and her humble beginnings could be traced back to a day some 25 years earlier in 1986. It had been just another ordinary gathering at an Atlanta Baptist church that Sunday morning – except for the fact that there was a five-year-old taking centre-stage. All eyes were on the girl standing on tiptoes on a chair, her cheeks blushing bright red with excitement as she craned to reach the mic stand.

This was no insipid sermon – she was belting out the hymn 'I Want To Walk And Talk With Jesus'. After a stunned silence, murmurs of admiration echoed around the hall, along with the occasional cry of "Dang, baby!" and "You go, girl!"

If it had been any other child, listeners might have grimaced, shuddered and covered their ears whilst making an earnest prayer to God to guarantee this child never stepped foot on a stage again. But this was no ordinary little girl – and instead of tuts and glares, the entire congregation was cheering her on. It was Kelly's first live performance and, in fact – unbeknown to her or her audience – the first of many. She wasn't going to let being five years old and unable to reach the microphone properly deter her.

Named at birth Kelendria Trene Rowland, but better known by her more popular moniker – simply Kelly – even then this R&B singer to be needed little introduction. That day Kelly, born on February 11, 1981, had already started to set her sights on a career in the music business – and she was looking for a muse, someone to model herself on.

However at first glance, the Eighties weren't exactly inspiring for a black female artist with aspirations of chart domination. It was a decade when rock reigned, featuring stadium fillers performed by white male lead singers whose hair was often longer than their girlfriends'. Bands such as Van Halen, Poison, Bon Jovi and Whitesnake were all chart contenders.

At the time, female singers were in the minority – and those that did hit the top of the charts were predominantly white, often featuring an obligatory fair-haired leader. Dishearteningly for Kelly, all of the most successful girls really did seem to have one thing in common – their hair colour. The future was bright if you were blonde – and number one hits beckoned.

In the country corner was Dolly Parton, described witheringly by some critics as a cross between a country housewife and a wide-eyed real-life Barbie doll.

Meanwhile pop was illustrated with the colour yellow by the Scandinavian sweethearts of Abba, the bleached blonde chic of Madonna and, of course, the aptly named Blondie. For a girl like Kelly, who was already struggling to accept her dark skin colour, it was a little intimidating.

Thus, for some, the music scene was bleak, representing only the tastes of a white majority. That said, the tide was slowly turning – the Eighties was also the era when Prince and Michael Jackson stood tall, not to mention their black female counterparts such as Aretha Franklin and Janet Jackson. In 1986, the year that a five-year-old Kelly decided her destiny was to be a singer, the US charts made history when – for the first time ever – the three top spots were held by female artists. What was more, two of them – Janet Jackson and Tina Turner – were African-American. It seemed that finally singers were being rewarded on merit, regardless of skin colour.

However for Kelly, the most inspirational artist of all in the era was Whitney Houston. To her, Whitney was the much lusted-after glass of ice-cold water in a parched musical desert. "I used to drive my mommy up the wall trying to listen out for Whitney!" she later recalled to the *Coventry Evening Telegraph*. "I remember getting her first album as it was the first record I ever owned. I played it every day!"

To an impressionable young Kelly, she was the "pop queen" and someone who "defined beauty". More importantly, it was at this moment – watching the diva's 'I Wanna Dance With Somebody' video – that the missing puzzle pieces fell into place for Kelly. She wanted to be a singer.

She wouldn't be the first pre-teen to idolise Whitney, but it came as Kelly's second epiphany – the first being her church performance – and it left her in no doubt about her future. From then on, she wasn't just listening to music, but singing along loudly – and she had allies in her parents. "Momma, I remember when you'd clap your hands and listen as I sang along every week to the theme song for the show *Amen*," Kelly reminisced years later in an open Mother's Day letter printed in *Essence*. "You'd look at me like I was the sun and the moon and say, 'Sing up baby, a little louder!' It meant so much that you believed in me."

Her father, Christopher Lovett, had equally fond memories, telling *The Daily Mirror*: "I remember as clear as day Kelly and I singing together, from the moment she could talk. Our favourite songs were by Stevie Wonder. I would put one headphone in my ear and the other in hers and we would sing and sing, so happy to be together."

He added: "She was just this joyous, happy smiling girl who could melt my heart just by looking at me. She was a real daddy's girl. My heart would burst with pride when she belted out Whitney Houston songs. I saw her jumping around the front room singing like a pro, when she had barely just learned to walk!"

Although she had a brother 10 years her senior, Orlando, to compete with for his attention, Kelly was the apple of her father's eye. The two quickly bonded over their shared love of singing. Her mother, Doris, on the other hand, didn't instantly warm to her miniature Whitney Houston concerts – especially when she was trying desperately to put her feet up and concentrate on the TV.

For her, while Kelly might have had a voice, so did every other boisterous five-year-old. In fact, it wasn't until she saw her daughter perform in her second-grade school play, *The Sound Of Music*, that she realised what she was working with.

The story was set in a Salzburg Abbey just prior to the Second World War and Kelly played Mother Abbess, the head nun. Maria, a young nun in training whom she is mentoring, plans to become a fully-fledged woman of God, but she is also showing signs of wanderlust. Sensing she's having second thoughts about where her life is headed, Mother Abbess suggests Maria should leave the abbey temporarily to get some perspective on her future.

She duly takes a job as a governess for a widowed captain's seven children but, instead of disciplining them, a mischievous Maria ends up teaching them music. Gradually, she falls in love with their father and believes the affection is mutual, only to discover that he is betrothed to someone else. Heartbroken, Maria flees back to the abbey, pledging to give him up and take her vows of celibacy there and then. However Mother Abbess urges her to turn back and tell the captain how she feels. To emphasise the point, she launches into the song 'Climb Every Mountain'.

After Maria has the courage to finally confess her love, he calls off his other engagement and marries her instead. The play ends with Maria and her new husband fleeing over the Austrian Alps as war breaks out around them in a bid for happiness and freedom. Their escape is played out by a second and final rendition of 'Climb Every Mountain'.

The song – which was also sung by Michael Jackson at a school show when he was Kelly's age – was a metaphor for pursuing one's destiny, no matter what. Its words struck a chord with Doris, whose own dreams of a fulfilling career had long since fallen down.

Doris had dreamed of going to university but didn't get the grades and – fearing the humiliation of failure a second time round – didn't want to go back to school. Long legged and slim, she had also aspired to be a catwalk model, but had come up against racism and intense competition. In her teens, she had envisaged herself flying first class and sipping champagne before taking on *haute couture* fashion in London, Milan and Paris – but it wasn't to be. It was like the storyline of the Fergie song 'Glamorous' – but its chorus, advising those with empty wallets to make their way home, was the stark reality for Kelly's mother.

As time passed, somehow she found herself working in a pharmacy for the minimum wage, sticking labels on drug prescription bottles for a living. The only highlight of each monotonous day was making small-talk with a stream of sickly customers. Her own dream might not have come true, but now she was determined not to let history repeat itself where her daughter was concerned.

That night, as the sound of Kelly's voice rang in her ears, she vowed that somehow she would find a way to help her daughter climb whatever mountain stood in her way and live out the words of the song. "I said, 'Lord, how am I going to help this child to achieve her dreams?'" Doris recalled to *Vixen* magazine.

Her prayers weren't answered straight away. In fact the train of destiny was derailed for a moment when husband Christopher lost his job as a driver for a transportation company. Raised in a traditional African-American culture that expected the man of the house to step up and provide for his family, Christopher was engulfed with shame. What was more, Doris's income was almost non-existent – and, without his wages to supplement it, the family was in trouble. "I sank into a depression about money and began drinking more and more," he later told *The Mirror*. "I am a proud man and wanted the best for my family, so when I lost my job I was utterly ashamed and hid from that shame with drink… It fuelled an anger that I will be ashamed of until my dying day."

As time went on, he lost all hope of finding new work and, as a coping mechanism, his drinking increased. It was having a damaging effect on Kelly already, who later commented that her most vivid memory of her father was of "an alcoholic".

But while he was drowning his sorrows, Doris had no such defence. She became increasingly distressed, begging him to put down the bottle. She felt disrespected as it seemed he was no longer even trying to find employment. Yet Christopher already felt inadequate and emasculated – after all, he wasn't contributing a penny to his children's welfare – and faced with what he perceived as taunts, he snapped. That was when the verbal war began.

"When Doris challenged me, I would just lose it," he confessed. "No parent should scream and shout in front of their child and I am sorry to say there were too many times that Kelly heard me screaming abuse at her mother. Sometimes she would run to her bedroom screaming, others she would cling to my trouser leg begging me to stop."

He claimed that the fights were "never physical", although Doris remembered things differently, telling *Vixen*: "He was abusive to me verbally, mentally, physically. All of it."

Whatever the truth, by all accounts it was psychologically distressing – and it left lasting scars. "There were many days and nights when Kelly would be bawling her eyes out, clutching my leg, begging me, 'Please daddy, stop shouting at mummy!'" Christopher continued. "That image of her howling, begging me to stop will haunt me forever."

The trauma went both ways. When her fear subsided, Kelly found herself overwhelmed by resentment towards her father, later claiming, "All my dad ever did for me was help me to exist. That's all the credit he deserves and I don't want to give him any more than that."

Eventually, the moment came that Doris had been both dreading and half-expecting – she found herself homeless. Her daughter was just seven years old.

"She tried her best to protect me so that I wouldn't know how bad off we were," Kelly recalled. "But one day I came home early from school and there was an eviction notice posted on our door. It said that we would be evicted from our apartment if we didn't immediately pay the overdue rent. My mama is a strong woman. She never wanted me to see her cry, but that night, I thought the tears would never end. It was the worst thing in the world."

The following morning, Doris rose from her bed with a lump in her throat and a hardened heart, only to find that there was no electricity powering the flat. Straining her eyes through candlelight, waiting for the inevitable knock at the door from the bailiffs come to take away everything she owned was not an option for Doris. What was more, it was the final nail in the coffin for her relationship with her husband. That day, she packed her bags and moved into her sister's house 20 miles away.

"Little did I know the day they left would be the last time I would see my wife and daughter ever again," Christopher remembered.

Ironically, being by herself – the one thing she feared the most – ended up making Doris stronger. She regained a little of her confidence and soon managed to secure better-paid employment as a nanny, looking after a succession of wealthy women's children.

The transition was an eye-opener for Kelly. Before, she had been cooped up in a tiny flat with a clinically depressed, alcoholic father for company; but the homes her mother worked in introduced her to another world.

These families lived in detached houses, carried handbags with conspicuous designer logos emblazoned on them, wore diamond rings and spritzed themselves with the latest perfumes. By observing these families, Kelly was given a glimpse of how things could be.

She also learned from them. Seeing her mother doubled over in floods of tears after losing the house had provoked a lifelong fear in Kelly's heart of poverty – a fear that would inspire and shape her work ethic for the future. She hoped to watch the wealthy families around her carefully and try to emulate them.

"I'm thankful to [my mother's] job for showing me a different way," she later told *Stylist*. "She worked for doctors, lawyers, people who worked in finance. I was like, 'That's a nice car. Woo, this is a great house. Wow, that woman smells good!' My mom had perfume, but it came from the drug store, not Neiman Marcus. But I also saw how hard her bosses worked to have these nice things. I saw the time they spent away from their children. I saw that when they came home, they were still working. I understood what kind of work ethic it took to be a success."

There was another bittersweet lesson to be learned from her mother's employees: they often had devoted husbands. She saw children her own age grow up in families where they were hugged and kissed goodnight by their fathers – but that was one luxury which, for Kelly, was just a distant memory.

It provoked questions in her about where her own father was. She longed to ask her mother the truth, but feared upsetting her. Had Doris been at fault for continually nagging her husband and perhaps driving him to seek solace in alcohol? Had she been too harsh for walking out on a penniless man about to lose his apartment? Or was it justified to leave someone who it seemed hadn't lifted a finger to raise the children he should have loved?

Whatever the answers to Kelly's painful questions were, it didn't

14

change the fact that she felt abandoned. "I would go to school and see kids holding the hands of their moms and dads and I'd feel very much alone," she recalled. "I would put my head down on the desk and wish that I could disappear."

Her pain was the most prominent at school parents' evenings. While some of Kelly's classmates had seen their families split down the middle with divorce, every single one of them still had their parents – and, at meetings with teachers, they would be flanked by one on either side of them. Children would taunt her with cries of "Where's your dad?" When a shamefaced Kelly confessed she had no idea, they would demand to know why not. It was an experience that, time and time again, left her feeling like "an outcast".

"He left me and my mom and I was angry," Kelly explained to *Cosmopolitan*. "I wanted to be a daddy's girl so bad. God damn *The Cosby Show* because that made me think, 'Why isn't my family like that?'"

In fact, her father had been desperately trying to get in touch but her protective aunt, sceptical about his intentions, was reluctant to connect him. "Every time I phoned her aunt's house, she told me Kelly and her mum were out," Christopher later revealed to *The Mirror*. "I had no job, no money, no car and just no way of getting the 20 miles to where they were staying."

However, his track record with Kelly wasn't exactly blemish-free. He proudly told the world that he had loved her "from the moment she took her first breath" – but he hadn't always reflected those words with his actions. Before she had moved out for good, Kelly had seen her father flit in and out of her life, sometimes staying away for almost a year at a time before returning to the family home. Unable to forgive his inconsistency, let alone believe he had changed, Kelly's aunt fobbed him off with new excuses each time he called.

Doris had moved not just because the bailiffs were breathing down her neck, but to remove her children from an environment she believed was, at the very least, emotionally violent. Her family was wary about putting her through that again – and, even worse, worried that she might be tempted to return to Christopher. In their eyes he was incapable of supporting her emotionally or financially – and there was little left for him to offer. "My grandmother used to say when I was little, 'Don't settle for nothing because you'll fall for anything,'" Kelly later admitted to *I Like Music*.

There was always a faint possibility that Kelly would be reunited with her father, but the death knell for their fraught relationship came when she and her mother left the state for good.

Doris had started working as a live-in nanny for a wealthy doctor in the area, but no sooner had she and Kelly settled in than a bombshell was dropped – the family was planning a move cross-country. They would be moving to Houston, Texas – over 800 miles away.

Orlando – by now in his late teens – objected to being uprooted and opted to stay with his grandmother in Atlanta. Doris and Kelly, however, were keen to make a fresh start – and, by 1990, they relocated to Houston, splitting their family three separate ways forever.

Texas didn't instantly live up to a fickle Kelly's expectations. At first, she imagined clichés of cowboy territory with vintage-style rodeos and yodelling, but the reality was very different. "When I got there, I was like, 'What is this?'" she recalled. "I mean, honestly, it was just a big ol' land with dirt!"

Sadly, it was also somewhere Kelly would experience racism – by now an age-old tradition in the South. America's race-relations history was dismal and in her mother's youth, those of African origin were regarded as little better than the slaves of previous generations. It was an era of total apartheid, with separate areas in restaurants, schools, trains, buses and even public toilets.

Laws were strictly enforced, too – at one point, something as simple as sharing a park bench with a stranger of a different race could see offenders convicted and imprisoned. On rare occasions, lovers reached beyond the race barrier to brave secret affairs – but with disastrous consequences. In a world of white supremacy, mixed-race babies were all too often seen as filthy secrets and disowned or drowned at birth.

Racial tension was so ingrained into the fabric of American society that even catching a glimpse of a black visitor in an upscale white neighbourhood could spark full-blown riots.

However, blacks were fighting back. By 1954, a court challenged the policy of segregation in schools, claiming that it reinforced "the inferiority of the Negro group" and had "a detrimental effect on the coloured children". The following year, legendary activist Rosa Parks made her mark in the history books by refusing to surrender her seat to a white passenger on a public bus in Alabama. It was a brave act that shook up the status quo, challenged the automatic superiority of white travellers and ultimately saw Rosa arrested and convicted for flaunting the law. The protest that followed in her honour involved almost 50,000 people and led to the desegregation of public transport. Then the ban on mixed-race marriages – not just taboo but strictly forbidden – was lifted in 1967.

Yet while laws had changed, attitudes had not – and many black people felt they were still treated as second class citizens. Segregation might have formally ended and all traces of slavery might have faded away, but invisible lines still divided the races. Stereotypes dictated that blacks were doomed to live in cramped tenement-style flats in the 'hood, while whites inhabited spacious pads in the suburbs. Blacks were condemned to poorly paid roles as subordinate domestic staff, while for whites the only limit for employment opportunities was their imagination. While they might inherit daddy's lucrative family business or be welcomed into the ranks of top doctors, lawyers and salesmen, their black counterparts seemed to be battling an impenetrable glass ceiling.

The occasional hip-hop star who'd made it big would defiantly flaunt his "young money", using his new-found wealth as a middle finger up in the face of white rule; but for the most part, black music hadn't yet found its place in the mainstream. It was a difficult, transitional time – one when many white people would still glance fearfully when passing a dark-skinned man on the street and maybe even clutch their handbags a little bit tighter.

It was this world that Kelly walked into when she first enrolled at Briargrove Elementary School in 1990. "I remember the teachers sitting me in the back," she recalled. "One teacher made it known that he was superior and I was inferior."

What was more, there were few people that she could share her predicament with. "I had an identity crisis," she confessed to *Heat* magazine. "I went to a school that was predominantly white and I was the only black girl. I remember thinking, 'I don't want to be as dark as I am, I want to be a little fairer.' I didn't want to be me."

As she approached double figures, so began a painful stage of self-consciousness – and Kelly felt anything but beautiful. She became so ambivalent about her reflection that she would shudder and squeeze her eyes shut every time she walked past a mirror. In America at that time, the culture was to be brash and shamelessly immodest. People were seen as straight-talking and fearless and they would brag about everything from their earnings to their sexual conquests to their looks and much more besides. Yet despite being a beautiful girl, Kelly didn't feel she had much to brag about.

The USA had been slow to acknowledge black beauty, with *Vogue*'s first African-American cover model hitting the newsagent shelves in 1974. Unfortunately few had followed in those footsteps and the model, Beverly Johnson, had complained bitterly that she felt like "the token black". She claimed that she would habitually earn less than her white counterparts in fashion catalogue shoots, even though many times her photographs had demonstrably sold more product. Plus, according to the complaints of some models, black women rarely appeared at all, and when they did, it was for photo shoots featuring clichéd tribal scenes and "patronising" ethnic prints.

True, in 1990 a black female won the Miss USA beauty pageant, but she had been the first to do so. As a rule, popular culture was dominated by white faces. It didn't help that most of the role models at Kelly's school were blonde haired and blue eyed, leaving her with few women to identify with. Instead, she turned to magazines to catch a glimpse of alternative beauty. "Halle Berry is one of the most beautiful women I've ever seen," she told *Essence*. "Same thing with Whitney Houston and Janet Jackson – especially as a kid, because they have brown skin like me. I remember looking at magazines and television and [finally] seeing someone that looked like me and seeing a piece of myself in them."

She later revealed that chat show host Oprah Winfrey had been a 'beauty icon' and an inspiration to her too. "I love the fact that she's so comfortable with herself," Kelly explained. "One of my favourite episodes of her show was when she showed millions of people how she woke up in the morning with no make-up on. That was so selfless and so revealing."

Role models like these empowered Kelly to feel more comfortable about herself, secure in the knowledge that if she looked outside her immediate circle of school friends, she would find plenty of successful black women to look up to.

Although Kelly was still described as "painfully shy" and at times still felt marginalised for her race in the classroom, she began to hold her head a little higher. What was more, she discovered that she wasn't the only black girl in school after all – she had company in one Ms. LaTavia Roberson. She didn't know it at the time, but the pair's chance meeting in the school playground was about to change her life.

LaTavia, whose aunt would later employ Kelly's mother as a nanny, had been recruited as a dancer in local band Girl's Tyme. The two quickly became friends and she was keen for Kelly to join the all-female line-up. "She was just as sweet as pie," LaTavia later told *The Daily Mirror*. "We would play Barbies all the time. Kelly loved Whitney Houston and would sing her songs. I was like, 'Hey, I'm in a band, you should come over and rehearse.'"

The group consisted of lead singer Beyoncé Knowles and backing vocalist Ashley Tamar Davis, along with sisters Nikki and Nina Taylor who, like LaTavia, were dancers. Other girls came and went, but most of the time the group was packed full to capacity. Overall, since it began in 1989, more than 65 girls had auditioned: only Beyoncé had been there from the beginning.

With that in mind, Kelly felt as though she had been plunged in at the deep end. Desperately nervous, she took to the stage in front of the group's members, its two founders, Denise Seals and Debra LaDay, and its manager Andretta Tillman.

"Kelly had a whistle," Beyoncé recalled to *Vixen* magazine of her first audition. "I told her I liked her whistle. She said, 'It's my lucky whistle!' She was so cute and had the sweetest disposition. She sang the bridge for 'I'm Your Baby Tonight' by Whitney Houston, which is really fast. I was so excited because her voice was so beautiful."

Fortunately those in authority agreed and, aged just 10 years old, Kelly had won herself a place in Girl's Tyme. "There's a power and a presence groups have that solo artists don't," Beyoncé would tell *The Times*. "As soon as I met Kelly, I knew it was right."

Chapter 2

A Little Faith

The day that Kelly had been invited to audition for the group, she had been lounging in LaTavia's back garden, soaking up the sun and playing with Barbies – but that was the last time that she would experience anything even close to an ordinary childhood. Back then, Girl's Tyme had been all about Beyoncé – and her very involved father, Mathew, had a reputation as a notorious slave driver. By hook or by crook, he planned to make sure his daughter made the big time.

It had all begun back in 1989 when the group was a mere thought in a music manager's mind. There were very few girl groups on the market at that time, but, cheered by the instant success of four-piece En Vogue, certain people felt that there was a market for them.

Enter Beyoncé, the Houston girl who had already acquired a formidable mountain of trophies by the tender age of seven after winning just about every pageant, beauty show or singing contest in town. News travelled fast – and when it reached the ears of entertainment-business moguls Denise Seals and Debra LaDay, they were interested immediately.

It wasn't hard to love Beyoncé. She had strikingly good looks, a talented voice and – the ultimate on every manager's wish list – a perfectionist streak and a high work ethic. Most notably, she had sung a note-perfect version of John Lennon's 'Imagine' at her very first talent show – and dozens more winning appearances would follow. Before the days of *The X-Factor* and *American Idol*, talent scouts had needed to work a little harder to track down the next big thing – but, convinced Beyoncé had star quality, Debra and Denise had made an appearance at her mother, Tina's, aptly named hair salon, Headliners, to ask for her daughter's hand in musical marriage. They asked Tina whether a group could be created around Beyoncé, positioning her as the informal leader of the pack. Her family agreed and multiple auditions followed to find appropriate accompaniments.

While the group had been a seven piece when Kelly had first joined, Beyoncé was the star of the show and the band became a Team Knowles operation. Mathew was co-managing the group with Andretta Tillman, although his presence had been an informal one at that early stage, while his wife, Tina, was a mother figure to the girls, styling their hair and clothes and occasionally creating hand-sewn costumes for them to wear on stage. Unsurprisingly, with all of this action going on, rehearsals were often held at Beyoncé's house. What was more, a few months after Kelly joined, Mathew turned his home into a summer boot camp to train the girls in the art of fame.

Acclaimed opera singer David Lee Brewer was recruited as a live-in tutor, training the girls in everything from grace and poise to perfecting their pitch in the studio. In exchange for his mentoring, he received a rent-free room at the back of the house. "I trained them vocally," David recalled. "I taught them how to do interviews, I taught Beyoncé how to build chords, I taught them about etiquette in the studio, how to go into the studio, how to work in the studio. I... did everything."

However, this gentle training was child's play in comparison to what Mathew had in store for them. Although David insisted that Mathew had come in "only as a parent whose daughter had been selected for the group", Mathew asserted his control early on – and his role model was the notoriously strict Joe Jackson.

Joe had watched over his children, The Jackson 5, as they painstakingly rehearsed their routines, beating and berating them if so much as one dance step was even slightly out of place. Michael Jackson would later reveal he was so fearful of his father's punishment that he would vomit in terror.

Yet to Joe, old-fashioned discipline was "the African way" and something that, while at times excruciatingly painful, was the best way to maintain focus. He was later criticised for denying Michael and the others a childhood, but to him his methods were synonymous with success.

Mathew was listening carefully – and he soon developed a rigorous routine that would leave Girl's Tyme exhausted. "We used to call him Joe Jackson," LaTavia later confided to *The Mirror*. "It's not like he beat us with his belt or anything, but he was very strict. Beyoncé was the only one brave enough to stand up to him. We worked really hard. It was rehearse, rehearse, rehearse. It would be the four of us and he was like a drill sergeant. When summertime came, he would wake us up early in the morning and take us to Hermann Park. There was a three-and-a-half mile track and we would sing while we jogged around it. Then we would go to the house and rehearse. That's what our days consisted of, seven days a week. Working that hard did cost us our childhood."

Mathew reasoned that part of being a pop star was having a toned, trim body that could make love to an unforgiving camera. The girls also needed to be in tip-top shape to master complex dance routines. What was more, they couldn't allow a several-mile run to zap their energy as they knew a relentless routine of vocal training would follow. Kelly would later recall, "We would hold rehearsals at two o'clock on Saturday afternoon and wouldn't be done until 11 or 12 at night."

When the exhausted girls finally crashed on the sofa, there were no cartoons – instead they watched 'motivational' videos of other groups that had trained since childhood and look at them for inspiration. "We weren't allowed to leave the house except to go jogging," LaTavia later added to *Touch* magazine. "We had to watch old videos of people like The Supremes and The Jackson 5. It was crazy."

Not only were they prohibited from going out, snack food was strictly forbidden too – not that the already weight-conscious children needed much encouragement to stay away from that. Beyoncé, in particular, claimed she piled on the pounds if she so much as looked at her favourite treat, fried chicken. There were no KFC bargain buckets for this group – they were served up salads and lean cuts of grilled meat instead.

"At school all the other kids in the cafeteria would be eating Ho Hos and I'd have to sit there and sip soup," Beyoncé grimaced of that era in her life. "It's a shame that a kid would have to worry about her weight, but I was trying to get a record deal and that was a reality. My mom tried to still let me eat normal food, but she would cook a non-fat version of it. She would fix me soup and crackers and cut up fruit for me when I got home from school. I would walk in the door and she would have turkey made or skinless chicken breasts ready for me to snack on. I didn't really eat any sweets and I love sweets [but] anything fattening I liked. Everything I wasn't supposed to have."

However that was the price of fame. Believing the age-old adage that a moment on the lips equated to a lifetime on the hips, she practised self-restraint. Fortunately Kelly had a little respite from the healthy eating regime, as she was naturally slim and could snack on pizza with few regrets.

However that didn't earn her a pass from the daily jogging sessions: the girls would sing while they ran, something which would train them not to lose their breath on stage or let strenuous dance routines impact on the quality of their voices in the future.

Boot camp night might have been a headache but, little by little, the group was learning what went into becoming a pop star. "Mathew would bark out orders at us and tell us if we didn't like it, we could leave," one anonymous former group member told the author. "He felt like anyone who could survive his boot camp was the kind of singer he was looking for and if you weren't prepared to do any of those things, he'd tell us there were other girls who'd be happy to take our place. It was never-ending!"

Yet for those who could cut it, it was an opportunity to learn. "We were rare nine and 10-year-olds, wanting to rehearse all day," Beyoncé later admitted to *Vibe*. "[But] we wanted a record deal, we wanted to be singers, we wanted to be stars."

That said, Mathew wasn't for everyone. While he'd never resorted to physical violence with any of the girls, he delivered ever harsher critiques which would leave some of the girls fighting back tears. It would take a specific temperament not to fly into a rage or withdraw into depression, but to take every verbal lash as constructive criticism instead. Tender loving care took a back seat to tough love. When Mathew began looking after the group he wasn't apologetic – rather, he saw it as an investment for the future.

"I continually work on being a better father," he would later confess. "But... I've had to compromise being a father to be a manager."

One possible reason for Mathew's attitude of unrelenting discipline was his background. He had been one of the first black children to go to a desegregated school back in the Fifties and had benefited from a better education than that of his parents. But at one point he had to be taken to and from school under the protection of state troopers.

With those humiliating memories still vivid in his mind, he felt he couldn't afford to slacken. He was a man on a mission to eradicate African–American stereotyping and raise his children above the confines set by that backdrop. As far as he was concerned, the battle against racism had not yet been won. Anger was a motivating force for Mathew and he refused to take his liberty for granted, knowing that it had been denied to his ancestors. He wouldn't sit back and relax until his daughter and her group had shown the world what black Americans were capable of and become the best that they could possibly be.

Yet they would battle against both racism and sexism for that coveted status. The pop music scene was populated with boy bands such as Another Bad Creation, New Edition, New Kids On The Block, Jodeci, Hi-Five and Boyz II Men. Most of these names would be virtually unrecognisable a decade later, but at the time it was the boys who were ruling the roost.

One radio programmer would point this out, declaring: "I don't know if it's because [the boys] have more opportunities or they have more appeal." Kelly and the others were unsure exactly how many opportunities a young black pre-teen girl group might have, but they were ready to find out.

Their persistence paid off when, in August 1992, *The Houston Chronicle* published a full-page feature on the group, describing them as an up-and-coming band that could "blend soaring harmonies, deliver gritty rap solos and pump out grooving dance moves".

Ashley Tamar Davis told the newspaper, "We hope to be the number one girls' group and send positive messages and bring people to see what we're talking about and make this world a better place."

By that point, they had performed at Astroworld – one of their favourite weekend hangouts when not working – the Miss Black Houston Metroplex Pageant, a Dallas high school where they were the support act for a rapper by the name of Yo Yo and, the week before their feature in the newspaper, a concert at the local Sammy Davis Junior annual award ceremony.

However their most important show that year was the Black Expo, an event which was littered with music business executives who had the power to change their lives. Daryl Simmons of the production company Silent Partner was in the audience with his wife, Carey, and they were both impressed: the group would later perform a showcase for them, leading to their very first record deal. The group had even won the interest of Prince, who phoned twice and expressed a desire to sign them.

Things were moving fast, but one member of the group wasn't keeping up: Kelly. She was starting to miss rehearsals left, right and centre. After so many years of hardship with money, her mother was desperate to maintain financial security and that meant working all hours as a nanny, at the mercy of her employer's ever-changing schedule. Work hours weren't always sociable and sometimes they altered by the day. Yet one of Mathew's bugbears was a singer who wasn't committed. Would Kelly get cut from the group?

"My mom was going back and forth from home to practice and I missed rehearsals waiting for my mom to finish her job," she later told *Vixen*. "That was so depressing to me as a child. I was like, 'I want to go to rehearsal!'"

Things came to a head one day when Doris's employer suddenly announced she was making her homeless. "I worked for this doctor and one day she came home and told me without any prior notice that she no longer needed me," she explained. "I said, 'Well, why didn't you give me notice so I could have been looking for a place to live for me and my child?' And she just looked at me. I had to think fast."

After a few frantic phone calls, she found a friend to stay with – but moving there would wreak havoc on her daughter's rehearsal schedule. Doris wanted to give Kelly a fighting chance, knowing that making it as a singer could be a way out of the unstable, unpredictable and poorly paid lifestyle she was suffering. Beyond that, she wanted her child to be happy, even if her singing career came to nothing in the end. "I didn't want her to be going from pillar to post," Doris continued. "I wanted her to be stable because this was something she needed in her life. I didn't want her to look back and say she didn't have an opportunity."

Reluctantly, she called Mathew and Tina – and within days, Kelly was moving into her new home. Now, rehearsals were no further than a flight of stairs away: she was sharing a room and a house with Beyoncé.

It was eye-opening for Kelly. The Knowles family had financial stability on a level she simply had never known before. Tina had a successful hair salon in South Houston, while Mathew was receiving a comfortable six-figure salary as a salesman for Xerox. The couple's combined incomes had afforded them a large house and mortgages and loans weren't on their radar.

Beyoncé had enrolled at a succession of private fee-paying Catholic schools while Kelly had continued to attend the local state school. There was a world of difference between Kelly and her more privileged room-mate – but in spite of that, they quickly became the best of friends.

While some children might have been fazed by the emotional upheaval and succumbed to homesickness, Kelly was resilient, insisting that God had blessed her with three parents. "I was a very happy child," she told *Vixen*. "People look at that whole situation and don't understand, but everybody has a different way of growing up. I was OK because when I came into the Knowles's home, they made me feel like I was one of their own kids and I was happy. I felt lucky to have three parents instead of just one." In fact, Kelly would later describe the move as "the only way to make sure I had stability".

Her mother's presence loomed large, too, in spite of living in a separate home. Doris had keys to the family's house and car and an access-all-areas pass to her daughter's life. "Doris spent the weekends, Christmas and Thanksgiving with us," explained Tina. "We all went to church on Sundays [and] ate together afterwards. Doris spent the night a lot of the time."

In fact, her role was just like any other parent – and that included reprimanding Kelly if she hadn't finished her homework or nagging her to remember her gym kit for school. Then of course, there was the consistent affection. "It was like a big ol' happy family because my mom came over every night to kiss me goodnight," Kelly remembered.

Not only did she have a mother who visited regularly, but she had a new aunt to mentor her and provide guidance. Ever since discovering she was one of the few black faces in a white majority school, Kelly had been plagued with insecurity about her colour and at times had an inferiority complex. Yet Tina, who had endured cruel comments herself for being mixed race – Native American, Creole and Jewish – wasn't having that.

"She sat me in front of the mirror and said, 'Girl, look at how pretty you are!'" Kelly recalled to *Heat*. "She made me feel comfortable in my own skin." She added, "[Now] I think that it's important to instil that in our girls, to know that they possess something special, that not everybody's meant to be the same."

Thanks to Tina, Kelly felt she could shake away her fears about her appearance. She also began to feel more confident about her singing abilities. On occasion, she would become carried away and boast to her classmates that she wanted to be "bigger than Whitney Houston", prompting retorts from a couple of the other girls that she couldn't sing. However, not only did Tina restore her confidence about that, but she spent time coaching her to make her vocals the strongest they could be.

"Mama T, you took extra time to rehearse with me when I got my first lead song at 12," Kelly wrote in an open letter published in *Essence*. "My voice was so small then, and you'd tell me to sing up, just the way my momma did!"

However, there was still sadness in her heart that her father wasn't there to do the same. As a pre-teen she'd been suspicious of the male gender generally. As far as boys were concerned, she had never been interested, while her father's absence left her feeling awkward about how to relate to men and often fearful and distraught.

"Kelly was painfully shy. She was just like a little mouse," revealed one acquaintance to the author. "Especially around men – they were her Achilles heel. She was scared to get close to anyone in case they let her down again."

There was an emotional roadblock in her heart until one man disarmed her and coaxed her into putting down the shield – and that was Mathew Knowles. Little by little, he became a surrogate father figure, someone who – along with God – slowly began to fill the void that her absent father had left in her heart.

"One day, I just said, 'Dad, can I go to the mall?'" Kelly recalled. "He was like, 'I love that name, I like you calling me dad,' and that was just one of the most beautiful days of my life… it just felt like I was home at last."

She added, "I feel like God sent Mathew into my life for a reason. He's taken the place of my dad and I also have God as my father, so I really have nothing to worry about any more."

Then there was her new sister. Kelly and Beyoncé sang together constantly and, once the pair had got past the awkwardness of having to share a wardrobe and intimate living space, they would spend hours laughing together so loudly it would echo through the walls and irritate Tina.

The pair also shared a fascination with Mickey Mouse, turning their bedroom into a shrine to the cartoon character, with matching duvet covers, pillows, alarm clock and lamp. Much to Tina's horror, they improvised on the rest of the room to make it fit the theme – she once walked in only to catch Beyoncé red-handed with a magic marker, daubing the walls and floor with mouse ears. Needless to say, the custom-designed Mickey Mouse wall art wouldn't remain a fixture for very long.

When they weren't working on their singing – almost a full-time job – Kelly and Beyoncé were partners in crime for limitless mischief. According to Kelly, they would run riot around the house and treat it like their own private "amusement park".

They would rip their mattresses off the beds and use them as sleds to slide down the staircases. At sleepovers, they daubed their unsuspecting friends' faces with toothpaste and mustard, or – if they were especially unlucky – slide ice cubes down their pyjamas.

Even rehearsal time proved chaotic, when unrestrained dance moves led to breakages on a near weekly basis. Expensive fine art from the family collection would end up smashed to pieces and the pair once broke a table and shattered a glass cabinet. Tina's reaction would vary from a wry smile to untamed fury. However, the upside was that they were perfecting their dance routines - and one day their work would put them in a position to pay off the damages.

Kelly was now living in the largest house she had ever set foot in and had privileges like a season pass to SeaWorld and visits every weekend – a luxury her mother could never have afforded. She had gained an aunt, a sister and a replacement father all at the same time – and without sacrificing her relationship with her biological mother, who was a constant fixture in her life.

However, that wasn't to suggest that life with the Knowles family was plain sailing. Beyoncé had struggled sometimes to share her parents with a new arrival. When her biological sister, Solange, had been born, she remembered becoming quiet, withdrawn and consumed with jealousy towards the newcomer. Her parents had been so concerned by her reaction that, at age seven, they sent her to a child psychiatrist. Solange later reciprocated the jealousy when, one by one, she smashed into tiny pieces every single trophy her talented sister had won through pageants and singing contests over the years. More than 30 awards were destroyed in the space of a few minutes, but Beyoncé merely laughed.

Clearly the sisters were not immune from sibling rivalry. Yet, while no-one had a family portrait that was blemish free, how would Beyoncé handle sharing her room, her life and even her parents with a newcomer who wasn't even her biological relative?

"Young kids are selfish with their parents... you want to be the favourite child," Beyoncé would later explain of their situation. "It took some getting used to."

Kelly also had to swallow her pride when Beyoncé got the lion's share of the attention as a singer. She'd initially had designs on being a solo performer, admitting: "When I saw Whitney Houston, a solo artist, I asked God if I could be like her, but instead He put me in a different setting – a group."

However, many of those who heard the pair in action had other ideas. "Beyoncé was the only one that came with this phenomenal voice," vocal coach David Lee Brewer revealed of his work with the two. "Kelly's voice was little more than air."

To him, Beyoncé was a natural born talent, while Kelly was little more than a beginner. Not only was she left feeling humiliated by his unforgivingly honest critique of her vocals, but it quickly became apparent that other challenges too stood in the way between her and success. She would need to turn to her soul sister for some lessons in how to dance.

Years later, Kelly could laugh about her shaky moves, confessing to *Rolling Stone*: "I'm telling you, I couldn't dance. It took some work on Kelly to get her where she is today." However back then, as a clumsy child, it had felt as though she would never get better.

"Kelly was just plain uncoordinated," one friend chuckled to the author. "Every dance rehearsal was like purgatory for her because she felt like she had two left feet and everyone could see it. Beyoncé was always the first to pick up dance moves and Mathew wasted no time in critiquing Kelly when she wasn't just as good."

As someone who took his cues from legendary slave driver Joe Jackson, Mathew just wanted his girls to succeed. Even before they were teenagers, he had a vision of them topping the charts as the next female super-group, one that would put The Supremes and En Vogue to shame. Yet Kelly, who lacked a father figure to look up to, was very sensitive to his criticism. As the only man in her life, she was desperate to win favour with him and, in her eagerness to please, she could become over-emotional.

"He would yell at her non-stop," her friend continued. "He took his role in coaching the girls super seriously and I feel like at times he struggled to juggle being a parent with being a mentor in the beginning. Off duty, he was the kindest guy – tender, even – but when his girls were performing, he really stepped up his game. Beyoncé was always reluctant to stand up to her father and lose her position as the golden girl, so there was no-one to really defend Kelly's awkwardness. There'd be times when he'd be shouting at her about focus and concentration and Kelly would literally flee in floods of tears. It was more than she could take."

It wasn't just on stage that Kelly felt insecure and inadequate, either. Living with the wealthy Knowles family had been a rags to riches tale. While sometimes she felt as blessed as Cinderella, at other times she definitely felt like one of the ugly sisters. Beyoncé, with her long flowing hair, was the pale-skinned beauty Kelly had wished she could be when she was growing up in an all-white school – at a time when her chocolate complexion had been a curse to her rather than merely something which set her apart. Not only was Beyoncé a couple of shades lighter, but she commanded the majority of the attention from the opposite sex too, attracting wolf whistles from her peers even when she dressed inconspicuously. In their pre-teen years, neither had more than a fleeting interest in boys – and yet the constant reminders that Beyoncé was the beauty of the pair bruised Kelly's already fragile ego.

Years later of course, each would establish their own meaningful identity within the group. Beyoncé's caramel skin colour would complement Kelly's ebony tones. Beyoncé's curvaceous rear would become synonymous with the word "bootylicious" – but Kelly would stand out for her slim figure, the product of much self-discipline and many hours in the gym.

Back then, however, as a child who was yet to find herself and identify what made her special, life was tough. When she looked in the mirror, all she could see were flaws. Two left feet that didn't live up to their owner's enthusiasm. A weak vocal that didn't reflect her burning desire to succeed. A shyness that saw her eclipsed by her more bubbly surrogate sister. A face that in her darkest moments she felt that only a mother could love.

And even worse, when Kelly opened her mouth, all she wanted to be was Whitney Houston Junior, but her nerves paralysed her vocal chords, and the pitiful croak that rose in her throat was miles away from the note-perfect tune she heard in her head.

At a tender age, Kelly was already beginning to experience self-loathing. Beyoncé's now constant presence in her life reminded her of the disparity between who she was and who she wanted to be – something which seemed to grow by the day. She wasn't to know that Beyoncé too had her issues, that she was mortified by her "huge Dumbo ears", deliberately picking out huge hoop earrings to disguise them, or self-consciously pushing her hair in front of her face.

Everything that Beyoncé had that Kelly didn't – a loving father, a large house, a conspicuous talent – magnified Kelly's anxiety about herself. She was pleased that the Knowles family had given her such a warm welcome, but she didn't always feel she could live up to expectation, or even that she deserved to be there. "When Kelly started out, she was this shy little person who wouldn't open her mouth," confirmed family friend Vernell Jackson.

What was more, there was another knock-back to come. Girl's Tyme had attracted the attention of renowned producer Arne Frager, someone who already had a catalogue of hits under his belt courtesy of artists like Mariah Carey. He was instantly intrigued by what he heard – so much so that he booked a flight from California to Houston to see them in person. So far, so good, but when the day they had been waiting for came, it emerged that he had a clear favourite: Beyoncé. Scheduling a meeting with the girls' management, he put forward Beyoncé as a potential lead singer due to her talent for the spotlight. He claimed that she should be given the lion's share of the lyrics and, owing to her distinctive personality, also become the spokesperson for the group.

These nuggets of information were also passed on to other key players in the music industry and word spread quickly about the power bias in the group. When Arne invited the group to his studio to record some demos, it was Beyoncé who sang lead vocals there too. Yet, in spite of what a young Kelly might have regarded as favouritism, it was Arne who secured them a spot on TV talent show *Star Search*.

It was America's first-ever televised talent contest. Its first episode was screened in 1983 – within six years, a then 10-year-old Aaliyah would take to the stage, and by 1994 she would be in the Top Five in the US charts. Proving there was no age limit on becoming a serious performer, LeAnn Rimes then took to the *Star Search* stage at age eight and went on to earn herself a number one album by the age of 13.

Cementing its status as a fast-track to success for the talented, the show also saw Christina Aguilera, Britney Spears, Justin Timberlake, Alanis Morissette and Usher make their performance débuts. Was Kelly about to become the next pop-star statistic?

On hearing the Girl's Tyme demos, impressed producers booked the group first-class tickets on a flight to Orlando, Florida, where they were to compete against a rival group at Walt Disney World. Unlike most children, the rides were the last thing on Kelly's mind – she wanted to get on the stage. With the exception of a few beauty pageants and local shows around Houston, she had very little experience of the pressures of performing to a crowd live and she was keen to start learning. This time, her audience was the entire nation – anyone in America who happened to turn on their TV.

The show would also bring them attention not just from the general public but also from record labels scouting for talent. The thrill of Disney and the VIP treatment of first-class travel – despite both being luxuries the cash-strapped Rowlands had never experienced before – paled in comparison to the promise of nationwide fame. Plus, the winner of the series would receive a career-boosting $100,000. Unlike *American Idol* and other later shows, there was no guarantee of the winner getting signed, but most previous winners had been offered a contract within weeks.

The first show, in September 1992, saw Girl's Tyme pitted against Skeleton Crew, an acoustic-based pop-rock band from Detroit, whose members were heavily influenced by The Beatles. It seemed to be a mismatch from the start – a seasoned soft-rock group in their thirties with years of experience and who wrote their own songs versus a pre-teen R&B group whose oldest member was 12.

At first, Skeleton Crew weren't exactly taking their rivals seriously. "The morning of the show, the producer called for two band members to meet our competition and we were introduced to Mathew Knowles," bassist Chris Badynee told the author. "I thought it was a joke at first. We, grown men, were to compete against little girls?!"

"We mostly hung with other solo singers and groups that played actual instruments," lead singer William Pilipchuk added dismissively. That said, the girls were keeping Skeleton Crew on their toes – and when he heard them in action, William had to hastily re-evaluate his preconceptions. "After watching the girls' rehearsal, I told the boys to pack their bags and get ready to go home," he added. "There was no way we were going to beat them as they were just too cute!"

Not only that, but Girl's Tyme were on the musical warpath and ready to take prisoners. Their appearance as cute, demure girls might just have been deceptive. "They were politely rude," Chris recalled, "but were probably warned about being psyched by us, so I felt that they had their guard up."

The two groups were scheduled to perform for the judges one after the other. Each would score points on a number of criteria and would be rated from one to four stars. In the case of a tie-break, the studio audience would vote for their favourite. Skeleton Crew had done their research and, seeing that previous audiences had always warmed to power ballads, they marketed themselves with the biggest one in their repertoire, 'Sentimental'.

Girl's Tyme, on the other hand, had been warned by judges that they were in the hip-hop category. With those criteria in mind, the girls chose the only track they had which featured a rap – the Alonzo Jackson song 'All About My Baby'. After LaTavia delivered a rap with a childlike twist, referencing the children's book *Green Eggs And Ham* by Dr Seuss, Beyoncé, Kelly and Ashley broke into song.

It quickly became apparent, however, that their song choice was inappropriate. "We rapped… and it was shameful because the judges looked at us as if to say, 'What are y'all *doing*?'" Beyoncé later groaned in frustration.

Not only that, but one magazine would later joke that they suspected the judges they were performing to could barely distinguish hip-hop from a pelvic operation. One thing was for sure – they were the first ever group to rap on *Star Search*.

Skeleton Crew singer William Pilipchuk was also sceptical about the song. "Their ability to exhibit a performance on such a professional level in front of a global television and in-studio audience at that age of innocence was impressive to say the least," he told the author. "[But] their weakness at that particular moment in time was their choice of material. Our song was simply better than their song."

There were personal agonies as well as professional failures. Kelly was also struggling with being demoted to background vocals. Beyoncé had dominated the song almost from the moment LaTavia had finished rapping and, aside from harmonies, Kelly didn't feel she had a chance to shine. "Beyoncé took charge," confirmed William Pilipchuk. "You could tell they went to a lot of trouble to make them look like a group with matching boots and colourful plastic macs. But once Beyoncé started singing, you immediately knew who was the focal point and that the other girls were clearly the back-up singers and dancers."

For someone who wanted to be the next Mariah Carey, it sounded like a dubious privilege. It was also frustrating for a boisterous, energetic young girl full of enthusiasm to step back from her big TV moment and submit to offering another girl the microphone.

To make matters worse, some criticised the performance for being overtly sexual and age-inappropriate. One of those concerned onlookers was Skeleton Crew bassist Chris Badynee himself. "I thought Girl's Tyme dressed too sexy for their age," he told the author. "One girl danced right up to the judges in a kind of twist and grind. To me, the judges looked a little uncomfortable at that moment."

No judge would want to be seen condoning precocious pre-teen sexuality, but was the dancing as salacious as it seemed – or was it simply the efforts of a nimble-footed, athletic group keen to be on-trend and show off their physical agility? Those were questions that would undoubtedly be asked when it came to critiquing a group so young that its members hadn't even entered secondary school.

In any event, something about the performance hadn't captivated the judges – and they were booted out of the competition. "The audience liked Girl's Tyme and was entertained," mused William Pilipchuk. "They just liked Skeleton Crew better at that moment in time."

That wasn't much of a comfort to Kelly, who had her mind set on success. Backstage, she was inconsolable. "Even when it hurt so bad, we were still smiling," she recalled to *The Guardian*. "But when we walked off stage, everyone just broke down. Imagine [us] just breaking down and crying. Now that I'm thinking about it, I want to cry [again]!" According to Beyoncé, the green room had turned into a "baby nursery".

Not yet mature enough to disguise their emotions, the whole group was in floods of tears – and even the presence of Skeleton Crew didn't sober them. "I remember the girls crying and the father was saying, 'It's OK, it's OK, we're still going to enjoy the parks'," Chris Badynee recalled.

The following day, as promised, Mathew took them back to Disney World – but this time for play. The girls went on every single ride that there was and by the end of the day, were almost smiling again. For all his tough posturing, that day did seem to distinguish Mathew from his role model, Joe Jackson. While Joe might have furiously beaten his boys for failing to make the grade, and punished them by withdrawing their privileges, Mathew was showing a tender side to himself. He was not just a musical mentor, but also a parent, and the trip to Disney World wasn't about tough love but was more a case of TLC.

Knocked out in the very first round, the girls went back home to Houston. Although in those days there were no caustic Simon Cowell sound-alikes on-hand to deliver step-by-step putdowns, it was still hard to accept defeat. The girls had been coached in taking failure graciously but, as the self-confessed "sensitive" member of the group, Kelly hurt a little harder than most.

In January 1993, just as the wounds were starting to heal, their *Star Search* performance was televised across America. It made it pretty hard to forget. A proud Tina Knowles invited her entire extended family to the house to watch the girls, marking the occasion with a pot of gumbo, but even her legendary home cooking didn't comfort them – and before long, the tears began all over again.

After dinner, Mathew took Beyoncé and Kelly to one side. "So you lost on *Star Search*," he exclaimed. "That's just one TV show. Do you still want to be performers? Is that what you really want more than anything? Because if you decide the answer is yes, are you going to just give up?" He added, "You worked so hard... think about the way that you feel when you're on stage. Think about your dreams. Think about if it's worth giving up on all of that because you lost just one show."

For a pair of girls who adored performing, it was a persuasive argument. It gave birth to a period of reassessment about why they had failed in the first place. Unlike those on subsequent shows such as *The X-Factor*, the judges on *Star Search* offered nothing by way of constructive criticism or feedback for the performers. Their only contribution was to hold up a star rating.

Not only that, but the show had pitted them against a much older group with years of performance experience and a very different musical style. LaTavia denounced it as "unfair" while Beyoncé made a new golden rule. "Quit watching *Star Search*. What kind of TV show puts small children against adults who are twice their age?"

Then there were the stringent guidelines the show's producers had handed to the group, pigeon-holing them as hip-hop artists and forcing them to change their style for the show. "We weren't mainly rap, we had one song that was rap," Beyoncé told *Black Beat*. "They told us that we were in the hip-hop category, so we had to do the song. It wasn't our best song, but we did it... after *Star Search*, we threw the whole rap thing out."

The girls came to the conclusion that with mentors to guide them – people who saw them as talented works in progress, rather than mere accessories for entertainment – and songs that reflected who they were instead of who others wanted them to be, they reasoned they could go far.

But they also had to confess to and work on their weaknesses. For example, why else hadn't they won? As hard as it was for the girls to admit it to themselves, their performance just hadn't been perfect. As Beyoncé would later comment, "We needed some work. We were good for our age, but that's not good enough to make it in the real world."

They began to watch themselves with critical eyes, noticing an off-key vocal here or an unsynchronised dance routine there. Now they could see where they had gone wrong, there was hope of rectifying it. The girls arranged a pow-wow in Beyoncé and Kelly's bedroom to discuss the fate of the group – something which ended in a quick and unanimous promise to keep fighting until they scored their place in the music business. As if to remind the world that they were still 11-year-olds – albeit unusually focused ones – they followed up with a pillow fight.

However, one question remained: were the girls ready to be placed under the microscope? Were they equipped to deal with the scrutiny of their faults at such a young age? The symbols of childhood in Kelly's life were both countless and poignant. After losing the contest, Kelly had recalled soaking her Mickey Mouse pillow with tears each night she forced herself to relive her failure.

That she was crying into a Disney pillow betrayed just how young she was – and yet emotionally she was growing up so fast. Her determination to succeed belied her true age, but she admitted herself that she had the potential to be very sensitive and easily wounded. Was entering the limelight a recipe for disaster?

Take any number one artist of any genre and any era, and the evidence reveals that even the most popular multi-million selling artists aren't just fending off praise. They're also inundated with internet death threats from the public and, on occasion, jaw-droppingly bad reviews in the media. It's happened to Madonna, to Michael Jackson, to Britney Spears, to Amy Winehouse – all stars who stood the test of time and were no strangers to platinum-selling CDs. History dictated that it didn't matter how talented or indeed how popular Girl's Tyme might have been – they would still be criticised.

For 11-year-olds, words could cut deep. As a child, would Kelly have the emotional strength to take the backlash without tipping over the edge? There was great potential for a child star to go off the rails. There could be a time when it would be heroin and self-harm that shielded a former young star from pain instead of the innocent theme park rides that had been an 11-year-old Kelly's salvation. Until the times when so-called business meetings ended with play fights, or Kelly would pick up a Barbie doll between rehearsal slots, it was easy to forget how young she truly was.

The world of child stardom is often a sinister one, particularly for young girls, with Botox and cosmetic enhancement sometimes becoming the norm for children as young as eight. There is a never-ending pressure to have that perfect Hollywood smile, extraordinarily synchronised dance steps, a body that is red-carpet ready and an ability to eclipse every other girl in the room just with a flutter of her false eyelashes.

Psychologists cite pushy stage parents and the pressure of the limelight as a cause of meltdowns, as well as childhood anxiety, depression, cosmetic surgery addiction and eating disorders. The website *Minor Con* would go on to publish a special feature entitled "Children As Chattels" about the twisted nature of the fame game. "It seems that every era produces a consistent stream of child performers who end up dead, addicted, depressed, in financial distress or in trouble with the law," it read.

One doesn't have to look too far to find some prime examples. Britney Spears, who had enjoyed both a pre-teen TV career on *The Mickey Mouse Club* and a subsequent teenage singing career, had gone from bad to worse. She attempted to assault a photographer, bashing his car with an umbrella; suddenly shaved her head in an LA hair salon; lost custody of her children; and, on one occasion, was involuntarily admitted to a psychiatric ward. Being manhandled out of her own home for her own safety was one of Britney's lowest points – and her career hit rock bottom.

Michael Jackson, whose entire young life had been filled with rules and restrictions and the fear that there would be hell to pay if he wasn't at his best on stage, first climbed to the top of the charts at age 11 as one of The Jackson 5. His mental health was later called into question, not least when he confessed to sharing a bed with children – including a cancer-stricken pre-teen who might have had just months to live. Even his sister La Toya publicly turned against him, raging: "Forget about the superstar, forget about the icon. If he was any other 35-year-old man who was sleeping with little boys, you wouldn't like this guy."

Then there was actress Lindsay Lohan, who hit the public eye aged 11 and who also hit the skids later in her career. There were car crashes, theft charges, drug-possession charges, rumours of cocaine addiction and seemingly endless stints in rehab. She was photographed injecting an unknown substance into her arm in a public nightclub, and it wasn't uncommon to see Lindsay not just intoxicated but extremely distressed on a night out, with eyeliner-streaked tears running down her cheeks.

It might have seemed that Lindsay had everything she could want, but her childhood in the film industry had left scars that a bank full of money and a wardrobe packed with designer items couldn't fix. Rumours of bed-hopping and lesbian love affairs – played out against insistence that she was straight – added to the sense of confusion.

Meanwhile fellow actress Drew Barrymore entered alcohol and drug rehab at just 13.

Kelly herself, like actor Macaulay Culkin before her, also faced the possibility of becoming her family's sole breadwinner if she became famous. Her mother still had no stable job and no permanent home, and was reliant on the kindness of the women who intermittently employed her for childcare. The pressure of potentially supporting her mother at Kelly's age might have triggered psychological damage. Macaulay had financially supported his family throughout his film career and, ironically, even footed the bill for the legal fees of a bitter custody battle following his parents' divorce. It became such an expensive pursuit that one lawyer commented there was "a real possibility of this millionaire and his family being evicted and left without any home". A more extreme case involved actress Shirley Temple, who supported a household of 12 people with her earnings – and was left with just a few thousand dollars to show for it when her fame was over.

The full-throttle pressures of childhood fame and mini-celebrity misbehaviour came into focus at *Star Search* that year, too. Skeleton Crew bassist Chris Badynee saw a 13-year-old girl trying out the rides at Disney World, ironically the same day that Girl's Tyme was there. "I asked the girl if she was having fun," he told the author. "She snapped at me, 'We're not going to have fun until we beat you!' Then she put her hand up to her mouth and did a little curtsey thing. I saw that the father really pumped the girls up with specific expectations. I went back to the father and said it was terrible how he's missing the point of the show and the father said back to me, 'They're already signed to Disney' and he smiled and shook my hand. I was upset at the pressure these little girls were exposed to."

Few child stars seemed able to grow up without succumbing to the pressure and suffering some kind of psychological meltdown. If Kelly was to be the exception, she had to tread carefully.

The track record of other youthful performers showed that nothing was certain, but Kelly seemed grounded enough to deal with whatever the music business threw at her. One way that she handled the rejection, pressure and uncertainty associated with early fame-hunting was by turning to God.

Prayer became an important part of the group's life after losing *Star Search*, as the still somewhat disheartened girls sought salvation and guidance. Kelly was soon a regular visitor at St John's United Methodist Church, the Knowles family's local.

The church itself was a respectable place of worship, but its pastor, Rudy Rasmus, was about the most unlikely candidate for God's work imaginable: he was the former co-owner of a brothel.

At the age of five, Rasmus had been party to his father's plans to get rich quick in the sex industry, and by the time he was 22, his father had made the plans a reality and opened a "borderline bordello" next door to the family home. "It was all about making money," Rudy reflected. "It was all about going to the bank. Money was God."

That all changed when wife-to-be Juanita entered his life. Living up to his reputation as a callous money-maker – a former self whom he said possessed no conscience – he claimed: "[As soon as I saw her] I really forgot what was going on at the front of the room."

There was one complication: Juanita was a devout Christian. But despite Rasmus's line of work, she reached out to him and encouraged him to attend her church. What he saw there had a profound effect on him. "There was definitely something missing in my life," he explained, "and I think the one thing that was missing was fulfilment. [My soul] was just an empty place. I had cash, but there was a hole in my spirit, in my being, that I couldn't fill up with money… I knew something was missing, but I didn't know what. I never figured it to be God that was missing."

Rasmus began attending Bible study group, and found the idea of the family business increasingly unsavoury by the day. "In a sexually oriented business, it is a dark environment," he said. "In these dark places, a lot of unseemly activity takes place. I remember my heart being really calloused, not really caring – as long as it was profitable. That's what we did every day. We profited from darkness. We profited from other people's misery and other people's pain."

Within months, he stepped out of the business altogether. "My pops really thought I was losing my mind," he chuckled. "I really had. I lost my mind to Christ." And his next step was to volunteer as a pastor at a downtrodden inner city church on the verge of closure – St John's. When he arrived, the congregation consisted of just nine people; it would go on to exceed 9,000. He fondly described his church as being like "a small town" – and it was this close-knit environment that Kelly would enter, along with Beyoncé, Solange, Mathew, Tina and LaTavia.

Entering the chapel for the first time it struck an emotional chord in her. It reminded her of her first-ever musical solo, which had taken place in church back in Atlanta, the day she discovered music was her life's passion. "Music was infectious just from being in church," she would later recall to *The Scotsman*.

The experience afforded church a place in her emotional memory – it became a retreat in which she felt safe and could call home. She didn't formally join the church until a few years later, at age 14, as her mother had previously insisted Kelly attend regularly at her church in a different part of the city – but the "positive and affirming atmosphere" of St John's was one she wouldn't forget.

Lost and alone, it was in this church that she would ask God to console her or offer insight at times when her musical journey seemed to have arrived at a dead end.

It was also at the same church that she would find the courage to confess her jealousy towards Beyoncé. "Kelly was humbled by what the Knowles family had done for her," one friend confided, "but she could not shake off this horrible, horrible jealousy. She felt inferior and didn't think she deserved what they'd done for her. At the back of her mind, I guess she was thinking that if she was anything at all, why had her daddy left?"

Indeed, this early loss had been horrible for Kelly's self-esteem. Most other children without a parent had a reason – they might have been parted by death or divorce. They were reassured that even if their parents didn't love each other any more, it didn't break the bond that they shared with their beloved children. Yet Kelly was no man's beloved child. She couldn't even rationally explain why her father had gone, let alone where he had gone.

"She felt vulnerable," her friend explained. "She could play fantasy happy families with Beyoncé's parents becoming her own, but she wasn't Mathew's real child, she was an imposter. To her, Bee was the perfect package – and to get to what she had, she had to be more like her. She wanted Beyoncé's looks, her voice, her hair, her clothes – even her exact same personality."

At that moment, it seemed that Kelly was living vicariously through Beyoncé, seeing everything in the second-hand light of her friend's glowing star. But the situation was unsustainable: the combination of having her own life put on hold and living in the shadow of her soul sister – while also enduring a dizzying rehearsal schedule aimed solely at becoming good enough to prove the *Star Search* producers wrong – led to a total loss of identity. "She worked so hard in the group that she lost sight of who she was," her friend continued. "What did Kelly want, think and feel? Who was Kelly and what made her different? How did she define herself as an individual? These were the questions she could never answer."

Kelly knew who she wanted to be, but she was so caught up in trying to get there that she didn't know much about herself any more. In an interview several years later, she confirmed this private dilemma. "One time Beyoncé asked me, 'What are your favourite things?'" Kelly recalled, "and I had to say, 'I don't know.'" After a few moments of contemplating, all she could come up with was that she despised the colour pink.

Kelly's hunger for fame threatened to swallow her identity altogether. It was time to make a change. As hard as it was at such a young age to accept a place lower down in the pecking order, Kelly knew she wanted to work with Beyoncé, not against her. Instead of giving into the green-eyed monster, she looked for a way that her envy could inspire her constructively – and prayer and confession saw her through.

"Beyoncé and Kelly were like sisters," her friend elaborated. "Kelly didn't want to be no poor man's Beyoncé, she wanted to be Whitney Houston, but at the same time she didn't want to get in a funk about what her sister had. She wanted to learn from her instead. When Kelly got a bit more confident in her own skin, she realised that she had something to offer too and that she and Beyoncé could learn from each other. Both of them had something unique to give – and if the Knowles's didn't believe in what she was working with, they would never have signed her up, let alone offered her a place in their home."

From then on, it was all about working as a team and filling in each other's weaknesses. After confiding in her church's youth pastor, Kelly realised each of the group had something significant to offer.

Shaking off her pride, she also grew to believe that it was God's will that she was, for now, just a backing singer. In Kelly's eyes, her creator made no mistakes – and she was going to follow the path He'd set out for her. "He put me in a group... because He knew I couldn't handle being a solo performer yet," she would later assert. "I wasn't prepared to be on my own even though I thought I was ready."

Ironically Beyoncé claimed she originally never saw herself as a solo artist – and that she yearned for the support of having other group members to lean on. Cynical bystanders might have seen her stance as merely a way to share the blame when things went wrong. However, far from just being a crutch to prop up the main attraction, Kelly believed – after much soul searching – that the group complemented each other. Plus, to her, there was nothing to match the camaraderie of group laughter and companionship.

Beyoncé seemed to share Kelly's new-found sentiments when in a later interview she claimed they all had different strengths. "God gives everybody gifts," she had told *Cosmo Girl*. "You just have to realise what yours is and work on that. [One of the other girls] may be more articulate than me and I might do the snake dance better than her. Instead of being jealous, she'll say, 'Girl, you do that bounce dance good, can you teach me how to do it?' and I'll say, 'Teach me how to pronounce this word.' That's how you have to look at it."

Beyoncé had learned precisely that lesson as a shy seven-year-old at her first ever talent show: that her competitors were not enemies but inspirations. Their performances taught her as much as textbooks could an academic. "You can't hate people who perform better than you," she would later confirm. "If another girl got higher marks from the judges, I tried to learn from her act instead of allowing myself to get consumed with envy. If you dwell on [jealousy] it will make you crazy... Sometimes you can still win even when you lose – you just need to be able to look at it the right way."

With the help of her church, that was exactly what Kelly had begun to do. The message was clear – as inexperienced 11-year-olds, they were far stronger united than they ever could be apart.

The same lesson could be applied to the humiliating defeat on *Star Search*. It had taught them not to be complacent and envious of the ultimate winners, instead learning from watching them. Replaying the tape repeatedly might have seemed like a bad case of emotional masochism, but in fact they were profiting from their pain. They came away from the show with a new strategy and a resolve to raise their game. Kelly had also profited on a personal level when she promised to rid herself of her burning jealousy towards Beyoncé.

While it was a few more years before Kelly was baptised at St John's Church, an experience that she would describe as an "opportunity to wash all your sins away and start over again with a clean slate", it seemed as though the group was already embarking on a brand new beginning.

Chapter 3

Somethin' Fresh

Girl's Tyme had entered *Star Search* desperate to be discovered and had come home empty-handed – or so they thought. It turned out someone had discovered them after all – and that was Mathew Knowles. He was about to take the next step from informal coach and mentor to full-blown manager.

Deep in conversation with veteran *Star Search* producer Alfred Masini, he had been given some heartening advice. "For those who lose, something happens," Masini had reassured him. "They go back and rededicate themselves, reorganise and some of them go on to make it. For some reason, those who win don't go on."

If Justin Timberlake was anything to go by, this advice was true. He lost on *Star Search* after appearing on the show dressed as a cowboy, but he would soon transform himself into a multi-million seller, reaching out to an ardent teenage audience. Then there was Britney Spears: the year before Girl's Tyme had taken to the *Star Search* stage, she had lost out by just a quarter of a star. Not content with a silver medal, she had – like Kelly – fled backstage in a sea of tears. Six years later, she had a number one single. Perhaps the loser tag wasn't so bad after all.

Mathew took heart from Masini's advice. He knew his girls – who had got a disappointing but nevertheless above average score of three stars on the show – had the talent. They simply needed good guidance and someone to stand up for their interests, he reasoned. To his wife, Tina's, open-mouthed astonishment, he announced his intention to quit his job selling MRI and CT scanners and other neurosurgical equipment in order to invest his time in the group's career.

But Mathew, who retrospectively described himself as "the number one salesman at Xerox in the country", was taking a plunge into the unknown. How did he know Girl's Tyme could succeed?

"Him leaving his corporate job was very scary for me," Tina admitted to *Rolling Stone*. "I don't know many people who would give up a job making the kind of money he made. I thought he had gone a little nuts." She added: "I had a large [hair] salon and it was generating good money, but we were accustomed to two incomes. All of a sudden we had to totally alter our lifestyle."

In spite of his wife's protests, Mathew was determined to resign. "I think part of the reason my dad decided to become our manager was because he couldn't stand to hear [us] bawling any more," Beyoncé would later joke. "We almost went crazy from crying."

Once Tina realised she was outnumbered, she warmed to the group's ambitions. No matter how distressed they might have felt about things like their first-round defeat on *Star Search*, she would give them emotional backing. "When Beyoncé and I were at our lowest, my aunt Tina would come into the room and say, 'No, we're not going to sit around in a funk today,'" Kelly recalled. "'We're going to get out and be positive and we're going to make this situation better.'"

Bringing Mathew on board – as well as Tina as the resident counsellor – was just one way that the band hoped to start afresh. However the move wasn't without its difficulties. Firstly, the group already had a manager. According to someone closely involved with the girls who declined to be named, Mathew had secured co-management rights by threatening to withdraw Beyoncé – by now the star attraction – from the group.

"He insisted that it was his group and that he wanted either to be involved as the manager or he would take Beyoncé out and start his own group," the source told the author. "That was out of the question.

Beyoncé was the favourite among the record labels and producers who we'd introduced to the group. There were labels who expressed interest in ditching the other performers and signing Beyoncé solo. Without her, the group was nothing, so Mathew had manipulated us into a headlock."

The source added, "We believed in every single one of those girls, though. We were on the edge of the knife waiting to see what Mathew would do next because he could be so unpredictable. We lived in angst that we would lose everything we'd worked so hard for. He just took over and it was the last thing we expected."

In the end a deal was brokered giving both Mathew and Andretta Tillman equal rights as managers. The other women involved retained their positions working with the group. A keen fashionista, Tina also found her place, creating costumes and customising them with glitter, beads and patterns. Now that Mathew was involved, the girls seemed to be on stage more than ever before, singing at a public venue almost every week.

What was more, Mathew also had a strategy to increase their chances of a record deal. Labels liked them; but the major criticism, almost invariably, was the number of girls in the group. It was suggested that those who danced could be demoted to the role of back-up dancers, leaving just three singers – Ashley, Beyoncé and Kelly.

This prompted some internal shifts within the group. LaTavia was desperate to be a fully fledged singer, despite allegedly lacking the vocal prowess of her peers. Until that time, however, she had only rapped and danced; and, owing to the disastrous reception Girl's Tyme had faced for the rap on 'All About My Baby', the girls had sworn off rap altogether.

It seemed as though LaTavia's days in the group were numbered. However, she was Beyoncé's best friend at the time and was also close to Kelly, as the two attended the same school. They were willing to fight for their friend's rights and – with the help of intensive sessions with vocal coach David Lee Brewer – LaTavia became a vocalist too.

"LaTavia was not a singer," David explained. "They were going to kick her out of the group. I told them, 'This girl has been there from the beginning and she deserves a chance.' I asked them to give me six months – just six months – to work with her. She worked the hardest out of all of them because she was the weakest. I built her into a singer."

David taught her how to adapt her breathing techniques when making the transition from a throaty rap style to vocals sung from the chest. He also coached Beyoncé first on how to recognise chords herself and then how to "instruct" LaTavia and the others.

Beyoncé's leadership was very apparent to the other three vocalists, but each girl had a meaningful place. There was one member, however, whose enthusiasm for the new line-up was muted – and that was Ashley. Not only was she keen to stay in school a few more years, she was also becoming increasingly disenchanted by the prospect of a career as Beyoncé's backing singer.

Ashley, who had inspired interest from chart-topping soul singer Prince, wanted to try to make it on her own. Prince had initially approached the entire group, but then expressed interest in signing Ashley as an individual to his label, Paisley Records. Emboldened by the way he had singled her out, Ashley began to think she could stand alone. (She would later achieve moderate mainstream success in the USA as an R&B singer.)

Despite assuring *The Houston Chronicle* in 1992 that her heart lay with the group, just months after the feature containing her sentiments was published, she left.

When it became clear she wouldn't be returning, she was replaced with 11-year-old LeToya Luckett, an aspiring singer Beyoncé had met at her girl scouts' group. In fact, they had briefly encountered each other before when, aged five, LeToya asked a teacher at the pair's earliest primary school to "remove" Beyoncé from her assigned seat. Six years later, they were firm friends.

"It was a really good chemistry," LeToya would later tell MTV. "We were like sisters immediately. Of course, it was harder for me because I just stepped into the group like that, but they had bonded for like three years before that. But, as soon as I got in, it was magic!"

So Kelly, Beyoncé, LaTavia and LeToya were the revised group – and to mark the new chapter in their lives, Girl's Tyme changed its name to Somethin' Fresh. "Fresh" was the teenage buzz-word of the early Nineties – a more fashionable way of saying "cool". However it was also an apt way of describing the girls' total transformation.

It wasn't just the line-up and the resolve to succeed that was new, either. How could Kelly and co reinvent themselves? What *was* fresh about the group – and how could they live up to their name? Firstly, Mathew was keen on setting defined goals so that his group knew what they were working towards. He asked them to think about their influences in the music world and then what set them apart, so that they could both match their idols and add something extra.

"En Vogue were the biggest inspiration," Beyoncé would later explain to *The Washington Post*. "They all had their own individual look but they also looked like a group." These were the terms in which Skeleton Crew would describe their rivals' appearance on *Star Search*, so perhaps Somethin' Fresh was halfway there already. "They all had wonderful voices," Beyoncé added, "but they also had great harmonies. They had great songs, great routines. We would sit and watch and pretend to be them."

It wasn't just sitting either: the group would buy the same wedge heels they saw their idols in and spend hours trying to emulate their dance moves while wearing them. As one friend told the author, "Their feet were covered in bruises and blisters, but they persevered."

Their other influences of choice included Sixties girl group The Supremes, led by Diana Ross. "[They] showed us the glamour, the hair and all the little moves," Kelly said to *Blues & Soul*. "I guess we basically took what was admired and made it our own."

Later the group would also commend the Spice Girls for teaching them how to be credible "businesswomen" – a rare title to be used in conjunction with an all-female group in those days. Within months of first hitting the charts and public consciousness, the Spice Girls had a range of dolls in their images and a series of business ventures that would ultimately make all five of them millionaires. While some surmised that media-savvy manager Simon Fuller was behind their success, other saw them as independent, business-minded women in their own right, using their trademark term "girl power" to back up that belief.

Opinions were clearly divided but, if it really was just a second-hand version of Fuller's business acumen that the Spice Girls boasted, then Somethin' Fresh had found out what set them apart – they were keen to get their business brains on by themselves.

Now aged just 12, Kelly was already wary of the opposite sex, fearing that they would seduce her into losing her focus. Even worse, she suspected that, later, they could swoop in and try to control both her business affairs and her life. Knowing that they could only enter her world if she let them, Kelly listened to Mathew's warnings about men and declared herself "totally disinterested" in dating.

Her mind was on the music, and – although it would be easy to dismiss girls so young as manufactured pop puppets on account of their tender ages – Kelly was keen to avoid those comparisons and to be involved with every aspect of business.

She was also protected somewhat by Somethin' Fresh being a family venture. Tina was now referring to Kelly as her "daughter" and, living side by side with the family, she had a bird's-eye view of any business that was being planned or conducted on her behalf. Mathew's emphasis on hiring family was something he attributed to being African American, explaining: "Other cultures keep their business in the family, rather than having too many outside influences."

In fact, he took his main inspiration from soul bands who had done exactly that, and the man who had made it happen: Motown mogul Berry Gordy. "He had everything in house," Mathew told *Ebony* magazine admiringly. "He had his choreographers, stylists, producers and writers. He taught his artists etiquette. He had real artist development – and his artists were glamorous. That's really what the music world is all about."

Inspired by this type of role model, Mathew was now heading a family-run enterprise – and it was one Kelly was proud to be part of. By now, Mr Knowles was working so hard to get the girls noticed that the group had even started to name him after a mail centre. "We used to call him Mr Kinko," Kelly chuckled to *Blues & Soul*, "which was a coffee place and a mail centre where he'd send off all our pictures and bios and put packages together to send to every record label. He'd always be up there making sure all our stuff was sent out so he could get us our record deal!"

He was also working to counter the preconceptions of record labels that Houston yielded only country-and-western singers. "When me and Beyoncé first started out, it was hard being from Texas," Kelly continued. "No-one came to Houston in those days besides country groups... Mathew worked his butt off when it came to shopping deals and putting packets together [on the rare occasions that] record labels came through."

While he was doing this, he instilled in the group a sense of humility, telling them that no venue – no matter how small or seemingly insignificant to the bigger picture, was below them. The mission was to put themselves out there, no matter what, whether the audience was a group of bemused-looking primary school children or a collection of bored teenagers waiting for a more established rapper who was that night's headline act. Gigs at shopping centres, beauty pageants, schools and even up close and personal performances to clients of Tina's hair salon would follow, where the girls got to fill up their tip jars: nothing was too much trouble.

It was an era of humility, where the girls were compelled to swallow their pride and follow the small-fry circuit. However, their attitude ultimately paid off, as – once they had paid their dues and gained a little attention – the offers to tour with "real" bands came flowing in.

One such group was Immature, an R&B boy band who were touring their second album when Somethin' Fresh joined them. The album had reached number 26 on the American R&B chart, so it was a good opportunity to win over a pre-made audience.

Another group they would tour with, Dru Hill, shared their humble beginnings: all four members had started out working together at a Baltimore fudge factory while trying to make it big. The group achieved moderate success and one member, SisQó, would later rise to fame after the group appeared on Will Smith's 'Wild Wild West'. He went on to release the infamously cheeky 'Thong Song', which – before explicit songs by artists like Rihanna flooded the radio waves – was considered a little controversial.

However, perhaps the biggest honour yet for the fledgling performers was their role as support act for the all-female group Sisters With Voices, also known as SWV. In 1992, their début album had gone triple platinum and produced several Top 10 hits. The song 'I'm So Into You' sampled Michael Jackson's 'Human Nature' and went to number two in the US chart, while subsequent release 'Weak' made the number one spot.

SWV loved Somethin' Fresh and their affection was reciprocated, with Beyoncé seeing them as "big sisters". "SWV adopted us," she would later remark. "They brought us on their bus and, after that, we were hooked. We knew what we wanted."

Indeed, mingling with people who had already made it increased the group's sense of enthusiasm and ambition, channelling them towards what they wanted and – most importantly of all – giving them the determination they needed to succeed.

That sense of determination was now common to both the group and its management. "Dad did everything for us," Beyoncé would later marvel to *The Times*. "He rehearsed us, produced us, paid for studio time, photo shoots and packaging our demos – because of En Vogue, who were huge at the time, there were lots of young girl groups trying to break through. My father made sure it was us who made it."

However, arguably, the pressure was now close to overwhelming for Mathew. In his keenness for the girls to succeed, he became an even tougher task-master than before – and one who, at times, seemed totally devoid of mercy.

He had given up a job many white-collar workers would give their eye-teeth for and, with so much as stake – not least his reputation – he wasn't about to let the girls slacken on his watch. If his early boot camps had seemed strict, that was nothing compared to the draconian regime that followed. Once Mathew was in a managerial role, things stepped up a notch. In fact, according to one woman who knew the girls well during that period, he would take out his frustration on Kelly and the others with verbal abuse – and sometimes even with slaps.

"There was *no* room for bad behaviour," she revealed to the author. "Kelly got slapped at least once if she stood up to the family or tried to act like a diva. On another occasion that I recall, she was ordered out of the house. She had to go to where her mother was staying. If she hadn't been such a timid little thing, she might have been thrown out for good, but she'd always go back and apologise and say she'd been in the wrong."

She added, "To say it was hard for her was an understatement. Mathew wasn't exactly a bad person, but he was an incredibly dominant character who, let's say, didn't stand for nonsense. He wasn't sensitive because he was focused on the goal in front of him and hurting someone's feelings was secondary. If it happened, it happened."

Mathew even encouraged the girls to look out for their bandmates' flaws and then point them out, before reporting back to him so that the offender would work on their faults. For a group of young girls, it could have been a recipe for resentment and confrontation – but when Mathew was around, no-one raised their voice.

"They knew the consequences," the source continued. "There was no talking back – that was unthinkable. And there was no complaining about hard work – he saw that as ungracious. Believe me, Mathew was big on etiquette. His attitude was, if a girl was willing to complain about it, she didn't deserve to be in the group because she might drag the others down. That happened to Kelly. She was typically one of the best behaved, but she nearly got thrown out of that group."

She was also subjected to public appraisals. "He'd call Kelly up on something she'd done wrong – a wobbly note, a clumsy dance step or an incorrect pitch and he'd make her stand aside from the rest and ask the others what they thought – and they'd get brownie points for singling out whichever was her fault. Then he'd ask Kelly if she thought she deserved to be there. It was a shame because Kelly was so fragile. She looked up to Mathew but he was so damned hard to please. I can't count the number of times she went crying in despair."

However there was one persistent rumour that emerged in later years that the source was quick to address. "There is absolutely no truth in allegations of sexual abuse," she insisted. "That's the most ridiculous thing I ever heard. He would snap his fingers in her face, yell at her – but beyond that, there was certainly no funny business."

In spite of that, the source would hold Mathew responsible for overworking the children. "Like I said, it was hard work, but no-one was ever allowed to complain," she said. "Their workload was something grown women would baulk at. There was no balance or moderation in their lives. These girls were expected to work for hours and hours straight, and sometimes so hard that they would crumble into tears of exhaustion at the end of a hectic day. Some people would call that child abuse. Mathew called it discipline."

As an afterthought, she conceded: "Obviously his techniques worked because look where Kelly and Beyoncé are today… But at what cost?"

That was a tough question. Through Mathew, Kelly seemed to be living out her fantasies of being a "daddy's girl" – the one she always wanted to be before her father's disappearance thwarted that ambition. It also seemed she would do anything not to lose the love of a male mentor the second time around. However, as a man who was not her biological father, could Mathew bestow on her the unconditional love a daughter might expect of someone in that role? By accepting him as her father figure and calling him "daddy", Kelly might have been fulfilling a previously unsatisfied fantasy of family life, but was she out of her depth?

She seemed to be finding it hard to accept the gaping difference between the side of Mathew that had been a loving surrogate father, on hand to wipe away her tears and take her on every ride Disney World could offer as a consolation prize after losing *Star Search,* and the side of him that was harsh, that felt he had to be cruel to be kind. Since he had become formally involved in her life, the boundaries between personal (family) and professional (music) were rapidly burning.

In his eyes, if Somethin' Fresh were to succeed, sweet, sugar-coated words of praise were never going to cut it. He wasn't there to massage their egos, but to give them a taste of the work that went into becoming successful. Tender loving care would have to take a back seat to tough love, and he wasn't apologetic, seeing the work as an investment for their futures. He might feel differently in his down-time; but when the girls were on stage, he was running a business – and he was as ruthless as the word might imply.

He invested his life savings into promoting the girls and paying for studio time while they produced demos. He crossed the country, flying them to meet record producers, radio stations and labels. The money he spent in the group's early career was a sum Beyoncé would later claim amounted to "hundreds of thousands of dollars".

A TV documentary the girls watched about the Jackson family offered them an insight into Mathew's mindset. "The Jackson dad had spent all the family's money to buy musical instruments for his kids, and his wife was saying something like, 'What are you doing, Joseph? That was our savings!'" Beyoncé recalled. "And he was like, 'I've got to get my kids out of the ghetto!'"

While Mathew's situation was nowhere near as extreme – peaceful, leafy, suburban living could hardly compare to tenements, tower blocks and crime-ridden estates – he was still making huge personal sacrifices to keep the group's dreams alive. Over time, every aspect of the family's lifestyle was downgraded. They went from a large detached house to a much smaller one and sold one of their cars to keep the family's bank balance healthy. Kelly was forced to share a tiny annexe-like room with Beyoncé, while Beyoncé's sister, Solange, went from having a bedroom of her own to the indignity of sharing with her mother. Tensions were running high and there was very little privacy, no haven to escape to. It was perhaps unsurprising that by 1994, Tina and Mathew had undergone a trial separation. Everything was on the line to make the foursome international stars.

Needless to say, hanging on to his finances, family and relationship with his wife by a thin – and, at times, invisible – thread piled pressure onto Mathew - and then onto his girls by proxy. Like Macaulay Culkin, Somethin' Fresh was now Mathew's sole source of potential earnings. Yet they weren't just a product – they were real people. It would be hard for Mathew to avoid anger towards the girls if they failed to live up to expectations, because he had given up a steady income and his livelihood, and future earnings were at stake. While it did open a window into why he was so strict, potential resentment, depression and anxiety could all be on the cards if the group didn't succeed – all heady emotions that could keep a psychoanalyst's couch warm for hours.

One prominent psychologist anonymously revealed to the author, "Whilst every child star can by no means be tarred with the same brush, there *is* a concern about the effects of early stardom and all the associated pressures on a child's psychological well-being. So many child actors, singers and beauty queens have been victims of suicide, drug addiction or death by misdemeanour. Many children in these situations are prone to anxiety or depression in later life and are often left with chronically low self-esteem.

"They value themselves only as a product, a marketable commodity, because experience has taught them that's what their role is in life. Many are objectified by the consumer world to such an extent that they lose their sense of self. Off-camera, they don't know who they are – they struggle to accurately distinguish between what is acting and what is reality.

"They are expected to live up to so much and to satisfy the often unsatisfiable demands of a fickle public and yet their self-worth is defined by exactly that. Many believe that it stores up trouble for the future. However the biggest concern in this case is that the children are holding up their father, that all his aspirations for the future are focused on them.

"The children can become products, not loved human beings in their own right, and statistics would seem to suggest that being a child star is correlated with an unusually high level of psychological disorder in later life. At an age when children should be free to play, learn and make mistakes without fear of repercussions – least of all, losing a parent's love – the weight of other's expectations can stifle them."

Meanwhile, the source who was close to Kelly in her childhood concurred: "She turned out well because she made it in the music business, but you have to ask what these kids might have grown up to be like if they hadn't made it. Could they have coped with the burden of being nothing more to their parents than a disappointment? It just ain't healthy to pin your hopes and dreams on kids that way."

Similarly, there was also a risk that Mathew, who had been a singer and piano player and entered numerous talent contests in his youth, could be a frustrated performer living out his fantasies of fame vicariously through the group. Interestingly, Mathew had also gone on to achieve a joint honours degree in Economics and Management while studying at Fisk University in Nashville, Tennessee, during his teens. Inspired by the heights of the Motown era, he applied the business techniques he learned there to the music industry, indicating a strong interest in moving into music management. Was there a chance that the group provided a convenient stepping stone by which Mathew could enter that world?

That possibility would seem particularly poignant in light of the psychologist's description of the despair and emotional damage a child might suffer if perceived as a product – even unintentionally.

However, Beyoncé fiercely defended her father, declaring: "This was our father's dream because it was our dream." Plus, although Mathew was honest, straight-talking and strict, the group valued those traits as much as they feared them because it kept them on their toes musically. With him around, there was no chance of becoming complacent. Rather than pandering to the girls' egos or, as Kelly would describe it, "butt-kissing", as a stranger might, to keep his management role, Mathew was part of her family. That meant he knew Beyoncé and Kelly like no-one else in the industry, wasn't afraid to point out their flaws and, in a cut-throat music world, probably had their best interests at heart. Surely for inexperienced young girls just about to break into music, there was no better mentor than someone they already knew and trusted?

Kelly made it clear that she held no grudges about his passion and drive in the early days when she later revealed to *Ebony*, "He's my hero. Mathew has sacrificed so much for us. He didn't have to take me in. He didn't have to sell his house and his cars for us. He didn't have to give up his life for Destiny's Child."

Clearly there were both pros and cons to Mathew's involvement with the group – but, as co-manager Andretta began to suffer more and more with the auto-immune disorder lupus, perhaps his intervention had come at the right time.

That wasn't to say that gate-crashing the music world was fast – or indeed easy. Kelly, despite having a naturally slim physique, decided to join the other girls on a weight-loss regime. Before *Star Search*, it had been just Beyoncé and LaTavia – the ones that felt they struggled to control their body weight – who had taken part. Now it was everyone.

The regime consisted of gymnastic exercise and jogging and singing simultaneously. The group was focused on daily rehearsals too, trying to build the confidence and skill to sing a cappella – not to mention liaising with producers to create some new songs. The humiliation of the earlier rap they had been persuaded to perform on *Star Search* still loomed large in their minds, meaning that the collection of a repertoire of high-quality songs rated highly on the to-do list. But then again, what didn't?

There was more vocal coaching, learning how to read music, developing an ear for chords so that they recognised each one by sound, familiarising themselves with the recording studio and mastering grace, elegance and etiquette. It was very much like the girls' original schedule when they first started – but the workload was now even more intense.

The group was finally able to showcase their new skills to an industry-based audience when Beyoncé's father landed them a meeting with Columbia Records. Unfortunately, their nervous energy sent them into self-destruct mode. The night before their first ever showcase with a major label, they could hardly sleep a wink – and ended up going for an ill-advised night-time swimming session at a local producer's house. Needless to say, when they took to the stage at the local Jewish Community Centre the following morning, they failed to impress.

Mathew interrupted the group mid-song to ask incredulously, "Did y'all go swimming last night?" When they all begrudgingly admitted they had, he had some stern words for them. "I could tell, because y'all look tired and you aren't performing as good as you can. So you girls need to focus and do it again. Start over from the beginning."

With the group trying to disguise chlorine-clogged noses and bad cases of swollen sinuses, it wasn't looking good. However, their off-par performance didn't detract much from their appeal, and A&R employee Teresa LaBarbera Whites was full of praise.

Back in Houston, by another twist of fate, a performance at an event called Black Expo introduced another key player in the music world to their sound. Daryl Simmons at the production company Silent Partner was in the audience with his wife, Carey. Both were impressed – enough to warrant a special mention to Sylvia Rhone, the same woman who had signed En Vogue.

Sylvia, who was working for Elektra Records, was interested in the group too; but, at their audition, she singled out Beyoncé as someone extra special. As she envisaged working with Silent Partner Productions on the new recruits if she was to sign them, she told Daryl she had designs on Beyoncé as the lead singer and asked him to orchestrate that through the songs he chose for the group.

It was another blow to Kelly's ego and, to make matters worse, soon afterwards she would be denied entry to a performing arts course that all the other girls had been accepted for. The reason for rejection was that she failed to impress in her audition. If she was to have a chance in the music business so early on, it seemed she had to bite the bullet and bow down to Beyoncé's leadership.

She did, and soon after the group was faced with two deals on the table. It wasn't the worst dilemma a group of aspiring performers could have, but even so they were relieved to have been spared that difficult decision. Mathew chose to sign with Elektra Records – and the deal was sealed in 1995.

That was where the real adventure began. The magnitude of the opportunity was obvious, but taking advantage of it meant sacrifice. First of all, the girls would have to switch states to Atlanta and pull out of school at just 14. It also came at a time when Kelly had relaxed her 'no boyfriends' rule a little – and she would be leaving behind a beau. It had been a short relationship and they formally separated before Kelly left the state, but there were hopes between the two that they might one day get back together.

That said, the relationship hadn't been without its troubles. For one thing, her lover was white. It had just been an ordinary boy-meets-girl scenario, where Kelly had innocently fallen for a guy who happened to be of a different race. However, inter-racial dating was still a sensitive issue in America's Deep South, with the nation's painful history of slavery being something many of the older generation found impossible to forget.

Consequently, she found herself the victim of sniggers, stares and at times downright hostility. "I remember being in public with him and getting the dirty looks and the whispering," she groaned to *Cosmo Girl*.

Yet undeterred by the trifling of small minds, Kelly had rebelled, turning romance into a forbidden love affair, *Romeo and Juliet* style. Although it had ended a little prematurely, that wasn't necessarily unusual for someone in the so-called 'puppy love' era of their lives. In any case, Kelly had little time for romance – she was now heading to Atlanta to record her debut album.

When they arrived, however, reality set in. They no longer had their own home, but were instead crammed into a tiny studio room in the basement of Daryl Simmons's assistant's house – hardly the most glamorous location for big stars to be. At just 14, they were also separated from their families. Kelly was 800 miles away from her mother and Mathew and Tina, with LaTavia's mother representing the only familiar adult in their party.

The girls had to forfeit the simple pleasures of spending time with family and friends to move into a tiny apartment with people they barely knew. It was lonely and nerve-racking – and their only confidantes were each other.

It wasn't all bad of course – Beyoncé would later boast of the freedom they enjoyed and the feeling they had of finally being 'cool' and 'grown up'. They received an allowance of $150 per week each from the record company – and for a group of 14-year-olds in the early Nineties, this seemingly small amount was a princely sum.

They shook away the blues of being alone with some retail therapy – spending their entire allowance each week on clothes. Plus it was a slightly less alien experience for Kelly, who even had faint memories of the place "where I would've grown up". She found herself coming face to face with landmarks she recognised, which was a comfort – and she still had aunts living in the area.

Yet another curve ball came in the shape of the memories Atlanta triggered about her father. She couldn't help but wonder, now that they might be sharing the same city again, where he was. In fact, given that her only memories of him were as an out-of-control alcoholic,

someone with an addiction to dangerous living, she even wondered –
with a lump in her throat – whether he was still alive.

The bittersweet experience of living in Atlanta soon came to a
premature end, however, when Elektra Records showed them the
door. It wasn't something Kelly had been expecting. As Beyoncé had
later remarked, "All we cared about was the contract, not realising that
contracts could be terminated."

However, the group had been signed under a development deal. That
meant that there was no cast-iron guarantee that the label would even
release an album. All the label was committing to was giving them a
shot at recording – and, when it called their studio time to a halt, there
wasn't even a further chance of that. Just eight months after signing on
the dotted line, the group was officially "on the shelf".

"They still had us signed," Beyoncé would later lament, "but they
would never put any money behind us or do anything for our career."

ly in Waiting: No longer in Beyoncé's shadow, Kelly strikes a pose for a promo shot in a hotel bedroom as she prepares for her first
te of solo fame. JOSEPH CULTICE/CORBIS

A five-year-old Kelly is all smiles as she clutches her kindergarten diploma. In the days before she was parted from her father, her twinkling eyes look care-free. SM

A barely recognisable Kelly poses with the pre-fame Destiny's Child, sporting a street look with long dreads and a baggy sweatshirt. Focused fully on 14-hour training days and chasing the then elusive record deal, fashion wasn't at the forefront of her mind. WENN

ly and the girls don matching outfits carefully crafted by Beyoncé's mother for a promo shot capturing the early Destiny's Child.

riking Gold: By now rather more glamorous, Kelly steps out with her girls in leather trousers and a matching bralet to celebrate her st gold CD.

With outstretched arms, Kelly shakes off her well-documented shyness to be the centre of attention in a 2000 Destiny's Child promo shot. JOSEPH CULTICE/CORBIS

ly and co claim a trophy at the 2000 MTV Video Music Awards in honour of the promo video for 'Say My Name'.

Unconventional Family Portrait: Kelly with her two mothers – Doris Rowland, the one who gave birth to her, and Tina Knowles, e one who raised her in the Destiny's Child days.

Going It Alone: 'Dilemma', Kelly's first song away from Destiny's Child, which saw her duet with Nelly, wins the award for Best Rap/Sung Collaboration at the 2003 Grammy Awards. STEVE AZZARA/CORBIS SYGMA

Kelly has her hands full as, clad in an elegant peach gown, she shows off two trophies at the 2005 American Music Awards in LA. LISA O'CONNOR/ZUMA/CORBIS

Feel The Fear And Do It Anyway: Kelly betrays her phobia of horror movies as she steps out for her first ever film role in the blood-thirsty thriller *Freddie vs. Jason.* THE KOBAL COLLECTION/NEW LINE

...ly mixes business with pleasure as she steps out socially with super-producer Rodney Jerkins for the 2005 opening of the 40/40 Club ...Atlantic City, co-owned by band-mate Beyoncé's husband Jay-Z. SHAREIF ZIYADAT/FILMMAGIC

...ve In A Hopeless Face: A loved up Kelly anticipates the ...ry-tale wedding that wasn't to be with football player Roy ...illiams, her then fiancé. JASON NEVADER/WIREIMAGE

Ignoring heavy rain in Hollywood, Destiny's Child brave the brutal weather conditions to step out and receive a star in LA's legendary Walk of Fame. It would be one of their last formal outings as a group. MARIO ANZUONI/REUTERS/CORBIS

Soul Sisters Reunited: After two years, Destiny's Child get together again for the 2007 BET Awards. That night Beyoncé would duet with Kelly on forthcoming single 'Like This', while she would return the favour on her band-mate's solo effort 'Get Me Bodied'.

Chapter 4

A Southern Girl's First Taste Of Success

Kelly's first reaction to the news was to turn to Mathew, her eyes welling up with tears, and wail: "What are we going to do now?"

"Don't worry," he replied simply. "I'm going to get another showcase for you girls. Everything is going to be fine."

Kelly didn't exactly share his confidence. Everyone she knew was reassuring her with promises that things would work out just fine, but that didn't change the devastating reality that she had just received a letter of rejection – before she had even made her first album. They were just 14 and already rejects.

However, while stoicism might have been an alien concept for the average disappointed teenager, Kelly was working with adults now. Where the music business was concerned, she would have to cast aside the teenage angst, reapply herself and start acting like an adult before her time.

In fact, with a more mature perspective, Kelly would realise that rejection could even work in the group's favour. Persistence and refusal to give up could be interpreted as signs of a true professional, someone dedicated to their trade. Not giving up at the first hurdle would show record labels they weren't merely spoilt children, squandering daddy's money on a whim, but that they were truly serious about their chosen career.

Katy Perry had made herself immune to a whole string of rejections and kept going – and ultimately, Capitol boss Jason Flom would report that was one of the factors that attracted him to her, citing as a personal motto the phrase: "True stars persevere!"

As a source close to Kelly would later remark, "Rejection separates the weak from the strong – and, unfortunately, in this industry, the weak need not apply!"

Kelly wasn't to know these words of wisdom so young, though – and, at the time, she was a little hysterical. After a pow-wow, the group decided to take action in the way they always did in times of trouble – they reinvented themselves.

For Somethin' Fresh, this meant going through a series of name changes. After all, times had changed. The word 'fresh' had become chronically unfashionable. They had to choose a timeless, classic name that would stand the test of ever-changing trends.

After much deliberation, they christened themselves Borderline, only to scrap the idea a week later. Then there was Cliché, based on the concept that they would create marketing slogans that were mini-clichés as a means to describe themselves and their style. However, the word had negative connotations and was seen as something to be sneered at. Clichés were usually deemed meaningless, empty and stereotypical and greeted with a roll of the eyes. Within a month, all four girls would unanimously describe the idea as "terrible".

Their next name wouldn't earn them much respect in the feminist quarter – the Dolls. According to Beyoncé, it depicted them as "little dolls come to life". It was under this new moniker that they invited aspiring R&B artist Keke Wyatt to join their line-up.

However Keke wouldn't stay. She later found fame as a solo artist with a début album that went gold; a collaboration with Avant – a singer who also worked with Kelly later in her career; a signing to Cash Money, the same label as Drake and Nicki Minaj; and – notably – co-writing the Pussycat Dolls track 'Stickwitu'. But she also went on to develop a questionable reputation. One of her most ill-advised PR moments was hitting the headlines after stabbing her husband and manager with a steak knife, leaving doctors to remove parts of it that were embedded in his back. Her one-year-old son was in the house at the time.

It was as The Dolls – still a four-piece – that the group would hear the good news. Mathew had followed through on his promise and landed them a new showcase – again with Teresa LaBarbera Whites of Columbia Records. He had sent out dozens of new demo tapes to publicise his girls and alert labels to the fact that they were back in town, so it was ironic that they would end up in the same place they had auditioned before.

Potentially, there might have been some awkwardness about Mathew's decision to turn down Columbia's deal the first time round, but ultimately he was dealing with professionals – people for whom it was all about the music.

They accepted an invitation to fly to New York and perform for Teresa, hardly daring to hope for too much. On arrival, they were shown into a conference room in the label's office, inside the city's iconic Sony building. Although the term "conference room" might have suggested a capacity of perhaps several hundred people, they were in for a surprise. There was a stage, but not as they knew it. An intimidated Kelly found herself performing so close to the record execs that she was within touching distance.

The format was unforgiving too – they were asked to sing a cappella, without microphones. Opting for one of their own tracks, 'Are You Ready?', followed by a version of the Bill Withers recording 'Ain't No Sunshine', the group was up for the challenge.

The latter was a song about life no longer being warm every time a lover went away and the lyrics were a fitting metaphor for how Kelly and the others felt about performing. For her, it wasn't a romance with a man but music that controlled the sunshine in her world – and things wouldn't be right until she'd bagged herself a new deal.

Fortunately, their passion shone through. "I think they saw our hunger right away," Beyoncé was to comment following their audition. Kelly was equally confident, remarking, "I think they were so impressed that they decided to sign us almost on the spot."

It seemed as though the music industry had already toughened a formerly timid Kelly up, giving her the first flickers of confidence she needed in her career. However, back in Houston, she was permanently on tenterhooks. After two weeks of jumping out of her skin in anticipation every time the phone rang, her prayers were answered.

It had started out as just another day in Tina's nail salon. However Tina knew something they didn't. She sneaked the group's contract into an envelope imprinted with the logo of a local café where they ate every Sunday, hoping to fool them into thinking it was something as benign as a gift certificate. They weren't under that illusion for long.

"When we saw it was a recording contract, we started screaming and crying right in the middle of the salon," Beyoncé remembered fondly. "The ladies with their heads under the dryers looked at us like we were crazy, because they couldn't hear what all the yelling was about."

The girls were too thrilled to have many of their usual inhibitions that afternoon. They ran maniacally around the salon, jumping up and down and waving those precious sheets of paper above their heads – ready to celebrate a day that Kelly would, years later, still acknowledge as "the best of our lives".

This time, there were no false promises or misleading starts: they would be going straight into the studio to work on their debut album.

Before they could begin, however, Mathew insisted that – in addition to the co-management deal he shared with Andretta Tillman – all the girls had to sign a contract binding them to a production company he had set up known as Music World Entertainment. LeToya and LaTavia were reluctant to sign at first, with LaTavia point-blank refusing. There was a minor drama when Mathew expelled her from the group for not co-operating; but, after a battle of wills, she finally signed, leaving The Dolls free to focus on their creative output instead.

The group had never expected that their early demos would amount to anything. In any case, they were now in the studio for real, voiding their previous attempts, which they scoffed at as merely "practice".

In early 1997, however, they were proved wrong. Producers of the soundtrack for the forthcoming blockbuster *Men In Black*, starring

Will Smith, happened upon a demo they had recorded in Oakland, California, back when they were still known as Somethin' Fresh.

They fell in love with the track 'Killing Time' and asked to use it on the album. A then unknown Alicia Keys, a label mate on Columbia, was also selected to appear. This was a perfect way for The Dolls to promote themselves without touring, which had proved impossible when they were locked in the studio.

The only problem was how to refer to themselves on the soundtrack as, unbelievably, they still didn't have a formal name. Up to that point, they had been free to change their name as often as they changed clothes, but – for a song that was being released to the public – they needed to choose one fast. It had to be powerful, defining, something that would be memorable to listeners long after the fanfare around the film had died down and the soundtracks ended up as donations at the local charity shop. What they were looking for was longevity.

The Dolls, they mused, might objectify them – and, in any case, the name had originally been suggested by their former label Elektra, with whom they had cut all ties. They wanted to move on from that era, but were agonising over the perfect way to define themselves.

Finally, in what Tina Knowles described as a "twist of fate", inspiration struck. She had been unwittingly using a picture of the band as a bookmark and, when she went to pick up the Bible one day, it fell open to the chapter of Isaiah. The picture fluttered out and landed underneath a bold subheading titled "Destiny".

"At the top of the picture was the name in bare-face print, Destiny," Kelly told *Freebase* magazine. "We were like, 'This is sent from God' and that really freaked us out because it came from the Bible."

Tina concurred that the message had meaning and was from God – a sign that not only were the girls destined for a career on stage, but that they were destined to be called Destiny. However, they hit a brick wall in legal terms when they discovered that they weren't alone in their choice – a handful of groups were already using their name.

"So we called ourselves Destiny's Child, which is like a rebirth of destiny," explained LaTavia. "We just wanted a name that was different and representing our music through our name."

In July 1997, when the movie hit cinemas, Destiny's Child hit public consciousness for the first time ever. Yet they weren't around to appreciate the fruits of their labour, because – nearly 18 months after they were signed – they were still locked in intensive studio sessions. In fact, it would take almost two and a half years before their CD was complete. "It was our début album," Kelly would later explain simply, "and we wanted it to be perfect."

Loathe to stick to one style, this was also a period of experimentation for the group as they searched for their signature style. They would collaborate with numerous musical talents on their first album – from gangsta rappers to R&B hit-makers and, it seemed, everything in between.

Insatiable perfectionists, the group would agonise over their sound, analysing the impact of every breath and taking their time to painstakingly record and re-record.

The best example of this was when they were paired with Haitian singer Wyclef Jean, formerly of The Fugees, who was remixing the track 'No No No'. The label was paying special attention to this song as one of the catchiest in their repertoire and earmarking it as a possible single.

In the studio, however, there were time pressures. "We were already over budget with the album," Kelly would recall, "and recording time can cost more than a hotel room at The Four Seasons – it's thousands of dollars an hour."

If they were established artists who had just banked the profits of a multi-million-selling album, perhaps they could afford to take their time, but in reality, the clock was ticking and they were running out of resources fast.

Lingering over their vocals annoyed not just the record company but the cash-rich, time-poor Wyclef. "Hurry up, girl!" he joked to Beyoncé. "How's this?" she responded, transforming the slow, sensual ballad into a super-speed one. Peals of nervous laughter sounded out around the studio, but they needn't have worried. Wyclef, using what the star-struck girls saw as his infinite wisdom, deemed it "hot".

Yet an exhausted Beyoncé had initially speeded up the lyrics for a joke. The lesson was clear – when they relaxed, had fun and – counter-intuitively – let down their guard, that was when they produced some of their best material. Too much performance anxiety, on the other hand, could block out their creative responses. It taught them not to pile too much pressure on themselves. Try telling that, however, to a cash-strapped record label which, as yet, had seen no return whatsoever on Destiny's Child.

In spite of the pressure, the group was keen to work with Wyclef again. His voice loomed large on 'No No No (Part 2)', which was also livened up by a sample from the track 'Strange Games And Things' by Love Unlimited Orchestra.

Wyclef had the type of confidence and cheeky borderline arrogance that only established artists could bring. If the song and subject matter – berating a shy guy for not approaching and warning him he may lose out altogether – was anything to go by, confidence was something that eluded Destiny's Child.

"I would never make the first move," an alarmed Kelly insisted later. "I guess it's because I'm a southern girl." These traditional southern values, somewhat incongruent with the image of Destiny's Child as exhibitionists and go-getters destined for the stage, extended to their performance in the studio as well.

Wyclef also joined them on 'Illusion', where he and fellow Fugee, Pras, were on hand to boost the young apprentices' confidence. Boasting in the opening line that the group had gone from "a dream" to "the new Supremes", Wyclef then prompts the girls to search for their own musical destiny.

The metaphors about illusions of the mind and confusing tricks, however, illustrated how careful they needed to be not to get caught up in a tricky industry. As the group's resident rapper, LaTavia did the honours by rapping along with Pras on the track, successfully flying in the face of their previous promise to each other never to record another rap.

Meanwhile, 'Second Nature' was a slow jam with the sensual elements of Beyoncé's later solo song 'Speechless'. The lyrics described a relationship so absorbing that the girlfriend cannot distinguish herself from her lover – being entwined in the romance has become second nature. In fact, giving her love now seems as natural and instinctive as breathing. Unless you could count childhood crushes and a few chaste first dates, none of the girls had yet been in serious relationships – and yet they projected such intense adult emotions with conviction.

"Even if you're young, you can still experience the things we sing about," Beyoncé would later defend to *Touch* magazine. "You can experience love at any age, whether it's your parents, your dog or a toy."

Other love songs included 'Bridges' – originally intended as the title track of the album. The song begins with elements of jazzy reggae, before showcasing lyrics about being a bridge to a loved one.

'Birthday' was a soft, romantic safe-for-radio number containing a promise that the girls will do whatever their partners want in celebration of their birthdays, while the Alicia Keys-style 'Show Me The Way' urges a lover to take the lead.

However, it wasn't all child's play. 'Killing Time' is a slow, sad song which opens with Beyoncé slumped miserably on the staircase of her home playing the waiting game for her lover. Her vision and common sense clouded over by love, she promises to wait for him willingly if there's the slightest chance that the one she wants will be hers faithfully. The song's themes of suspense and loneliness were what attracted the producers of *Men In Black* to the track and prompted them to use it.

Other examples of love turned sour were displayed in 'Sail On' – originally written by Lionel Richie in the Seventies – where a girl accepts that she isn't right for her man and that, realistically, they are doomed to be no more than passing ships in the night to each other.

Then there was 'Tell Me', another slow song with aspects of gentle gospel and the dramatic crescendos of the average soundtrack for a Disney film. Despite giving her all, the girl in this track ultimately still fails to please.

'Know That' is a catchy track where the girls promise they will always be around for someone special. Notably, it features prominent vocals from other members of the group rather than Beyoncé.

Then there was 'With Me', a very special song for the group. Along with 'Birthday', it was one of just two tracks for which the girls could boast co-writing credits. Inevitably, they'd later go under the media microscope, confronted by people keen to know whether the temptress depicted in the lyrics – who seems to steal another woman's man before insisting it was destiny – was modelled on any of the girls' real-life experiences. As they co-wrote the song and were partially responsible for its lyrics, they didn't have much defence. However, they were quick to counter allegations of relationship theft, assuring journalists that the track had just been misunderstood. "Actually we're the guy's best friend," LeToya would clarify to *Freebase*. "Like a shoulder to cry on, because she was playing with him and doing him wrong and he didn't want to be in the relationship any more... We were just his friend, someone to comfort him. We ain't trying to take the girl's man or anything."

However, tellingly, the group would later claim that 'With Me' was their answer to Usher's 'You Make Me Wanna'. In the latter, a man is gradually driven away from his unkind girlfriend and seduced by the female companion that comforts him. Perhaps there were romantic motives behind 'With Me' too.

Two versions of the song were produced – one featuring the rap-lite vocals of producer Jermaine Dupri (known under his rap moniker as JD) and the other featuring a slice of "hardcore hip-hop" courtesy of gangsta rapper Master P. Both versions had the same uptempo beat, which sampled the latter's tune 'Freak Hoes'.

Finally, recording 'My Time Has Come' was a bittersweet moment for the girls. On one hand, it was a jubilant ode to finally finding career success, with lyrics of empowerment that talked of turning fears into strengths, refusing to turn back and touching the sky.

On the other hand, the track took on a new meaning when the group's much loved co-manager Andretta Tillman – who had always been on hand for guidance – died of the lupus that had been ravaging her immune system. The disease, often characterised by a T-shaped skin rash on the face, causes the victim's immune system to attack not just bacteria, but the tissues of his or her own body.

Andretta had only recently reached her thirties and, with a promising career in music management and two young sons at home to take care of, her life seemed to have been cut cruelly short. The lyrics represented not just the dawn of Destiny's Child's time to conquer the music industry, but also the time for Andretta to pass over into the afterlife.

It provided a poignant double meaning almost too sophisticated for an album fronted by girls so young. Kelly would dedicate the track – and the album – to Andretta, and as there were new beginnings all round – some good, some bad – the rest of the recording process was tinged with sadness.

Another issue that may have proved difficult to swallow was Beyoncé's total domination of the vocals. While Kelly accepted her position as a backing singer, some parts on the album didn't feature her vocals at all. As for LaTavia and LeToya, they rarely appeared on any of the songs either. Did it make the prospect of being in a band seem a mere façade?

According to vocal coach David Lee Brewer, who was a key figure behind the scenes, the decision for Beyoncé to sing on all four harmonies at times, leaving Kelly and her other two bandmates to watch longingly in the background, had been made purely to save time and money.

"If you've got $100 left and the studio costs $150 an hour and you're running short on time, you get someone in there who can do it quickly," he claimed. "I found that the producers wanted to get it done as quickly as possible to save time. When I was in the studio, I felt that the girls should at least be given a chance to do the tracks, but it was not their choice. They had nothing to say about it."

He added, "Beyoncé [often] laid down the background tracks [but] all four girls learned the tracks in order to perform them live… It wasn't that they weren't capable."

In spite of his reassurances, mutely standing behind Beyoncé while she commandeered the studio and received not only the lion's share of the work but – arguably – the lion's share of the praise might not have been easy to write off as a "learning experience". With the backdrop of Kelly's rejection from a performing arts course's audition that her bandmates passed with flying colours, Kelly might all too easily have started to lose confidence in her abilities again.

What was more, one thing that was distressing for all of them was the waiting game they had to play for producers. Perhaps if they'd been seasoned divas, they'd have had the right to complain, but as novices, there was no such option.

"I can remember sitting in the studio waiting for producers for 10 or even 12 hours," shuddered David. "They were supposed to be there at noon and showed up at ten at night."

Life as recording artists was as exhausting as it was fulfilling and Kelly would later describe the experience as "all-consuming". Becoming professional singers was everything they wished for – but where was the glamour? By the time the recording process drew to a close, the girls hadn't been to school or out with their friends for what seemed an eternity.

However, the long awaited first flashes of glamour finally came when they were flown to Cancun, Mexico, to shoot their first music video. The decision proved an auspicious one. The video they shot, featuring Wyclef Jean, would be released to promote their first single, 'No No No (Part 2)'.

Despite a slow start, the single, released on November 12, 1997, began to turn heads. Wyclef's constant name-checking of The Supremes was a clever marketing strategy, as fans of the Sixties super-group became curious about a modern group associated with their name. Being pigeonholed as a younger version of The Supremes would be both a blessing and a curse for Destiny's Child in those early years, as they saw themselves "lazily" categorised by the media. Magazines would demand to know whether Beyoncé was the new Diana Ross – and, of course, whether she matched her in the diva stakes.

However, they couldn't complain: the intrigue of that association was in part responsible for the fast-growing sales. In the USA, the single would make the *Billboard* Top 40, while it would peak in the UK charts in the Top 5. All in all, their début single would sell more than three million copies around the world.

Meanwhile Kelly was thrilled just to hear it on the radio. The first time it aired, she and Beyoncé had been driving to pick Solange up from school when they shifted the dial to their favourite radio station and – to their shock – heard the familiar sound of their own voices. By the time they pulled up at the school car park, they had totally forgotten where they were. They pumped up the volume, screamed raucously and started jumping up and down and running in circles around the car.

Appalled at this sudden display of emotional incontinence, a waiting Solange was furious with the pair for embarrassing her in front of her friends. "She was looking at me like she was going to beat me up," Beyoncé would later chuckle.

Then, as she approached the car, demanding to know what was wrong with them, she too twigged the magnitude of the moment. "We screamed and laughed and cried and danced and sang," Beyoncé told *Launch*. "My sister was so embarrassed – she was like, 'What's wrong with you?' Then she heard the song and she's like 'Aaaaahhhh!' and she dropped her bag and started running around the car too."

That was just the beginning. As the group's fame rose, so did their access to perks and privileges. Each new success seemed to be redeemable for bonus points in the diva department – and that included taking control of their image.

Columbia had previously ordered them to have an entire image overhaul almost from the moment that they were signed. In the record company's eyes, they were works in progress – and far from perfect. At first they suggested that Kelly needed a haircut, then that Beyoncé needed to glam up and wear more of the colour green – and the list went on. There was no aspect of how they appeared to the public that would be their decision. From then on, every aspect of the group's look would be manufactured by a stylist of the record company's choice.

Privately, Kelly was dismayed. Almost every fashion item picked out, whether it was too trendy or too trashy, just wasn't her. For this reason, the group's earliest official photo shoot, to publicise 'Killing Time', had been a disaster. All four were dressed from head to toe in white, with matching platform sandals. The group's horror showed on their faces – Beyoncé looked nervous and awkward, while LeToya and LaTavia seemed sulky. Kelly looked downright terrified.

The string of photo shoots that followed produced equally mediocre results, with the girls at times looking less like they were promoting the album of their dreams and more like someone had just killed their pet kitten.

Call it a twist of fate or a happy accident, but a trip to Jamaica to film a show for MTV with Wyclef Jean would cement Tina's role in styling the group instead. The suitcase containing the group's outfits was mislaid by the airline, leaving Tina to step in. She averted their fashion disaster in the making by quickly customising four outfits of her own with a theme of military chic.

These were no designer threads – the costumes had been converted from oversized men's outfits, found at an army surplus store. However, they didn't fail to impress.

Wyclef admiringly took one look at the girls in their camouflage costumes and asked who had styled them. On hearing it was Tina, he urged: "She needs to style you all the time!" Now that the outfits had the Wyclef seal of approval, it paved the way for Tina to start working with them as a designer and stylist full-time. This would satisfy the band's desire both to dress in a way that reflected their individual personalities and to set fashion trends instead of just following them.

Meanwhile the group decided to release 'With Me (Part 1)' as a single. Beyoncé produced it in Japan and it was then released exclusively in the EU on January 19, 1998, achieving success in both the UK and the Netherlands. The album followed on February 17. It would spend 26 weeks on the US *Billboard* Top 200 chart, before peaking at number 14 in the R&B chart. In the UK, it would sail into the top 75 the same day it hit the radio waves. In the short few years before it went out of print in 2002, it would stack up over three million sales around the world.

Most artists would have been thrilled with the instant success of the album but – compared to the expectations the girls had – it had under-performed badly. Ever the perfectionists, Beyoncé and Kelly were not happy.

Why had the album failed to make the number one spot they had been crossing their fingers for? There were many reasons – and countless early mistakes. "The first record was successful, but not hugely successful," Beyoncé would explain to *The Guardian*. "It was a neo-soul record and we were 15 years old. It was way too mature for us."

Indeed, despite defiantly insisting that "no matter how old we are, we still have to do the same things that people aged 30 and 40 have to do", she had come to realise over time that the intensity of the tracks – especially those that detailed the desperation of losing a long-time love – could be overwhelming for younger listeners. The group's look, style and youthful energy was relatable to teenage audiences, but – when they got to buying the album – they found the lyrics and the sound didn't reflect the preoccupations of the average teenager.

Not only was their young target audience struggling to relate to them, the older generation found it difficult to take women so much younger than themselves taking on intense love ballads seriously. "When older people look at you, they just dismiss you because you're so young," Beyoncé lamented to *Touch*. Keen to please all camps, Destiny's Child had ended up in a barren no-man's-land between the two.

They also struggled to nail a trademark sound. The two tracks they released as singles were fast, catchy and uptempo, but the rest of the album couldn't have been more different – and some listeners might have found that misleading. Those expecting a continuation of the youthful, uptempo sound were met instead with a collection of low-key ballads and would quickly realise that the singles were simply not representative of Destiny's Child's primary output. What was more, by mixing soul ballads with rap and hip-hop interludes, the group was coming no closer to finding their own self-defining signature sound. For better or worse, the debut album was a pick-and-mix bag of musical all-sorts.

If the girls' sound was hard to define, their attitude was even more so. Destiny's Child were the archetypal good girls – God-fearing, parent-respecting virgins who intended to stay that way until marriage. They were even willing to risk their contracts and go against their record company's wishes to stand up for the values they believed in.

For example, Beyoncé told *The Sun*: "Our label didn't like us talking about God on stage because they think it ruins our image. They say, 'That's not cool, don't do that.' But we don't care – we strongly believe in God and we want to let everyone know about this love."

Kelly added: "We see ourselves as spokesmen for the church and for God, spreading an important message wherever we go. We're introducing people to God that might not go to church and we reach people that may never read the Bible. That's very important to us. We are acting like missionaries, trying to get the message of the Bible as far as possible."

However, these missionaries were collaborating with some distinctly unholy rappers on the album – and their lyrical output was, at times, far from squeaky clean. In Wyclef Jean's case, it was merely a tame reference to a woman shaking her thighs, or to a man trying to survive in the 'hood, gangsta style. However, Master P was a different story. With titles like 'Pervin'', 'Dana You Can Bang Her' and 'Dope And Pussy And Money', his tunes made the likes of Rihanna, Eminem and Dr Dre seem as tame as a children's nursery rhyme or lullaby.

One track was dedicated to a prostitute; another saw him claim all he cared about was money and, predictably, "bitches". There were graphic descriptions of killings, knives, guns and gang warfare, as well as tales of his own colourful exploits out on the town – it wasn't exactly politically correct. Summarily, his songs featured two predominant themes – sex and violence – topics that weren't technically on the Destiny's Child radar.

This was a group so serious about God that all four members had been baptised together. They prayed daily and, no matter how much was packed into their showbiz schedule, had always made time to attend church on a Sunday. They were the angels of the pop world, and, by design, cookie-cutter role models for young children – which made their collaborations with gangsta rappers all the more surprising.

Asked by *Freebase* to explain their decision to invite someone widely regarded as a misogynist onto their CD, all LeToya would say by way of explanation was, "He knew that he would not be doing any cussing or talking about sex. He knew that wouldn't be on the song and that we wouldn't allow him to do that, so we weren't worried."

It was true that he toned down his profanity and subject matter; but the rap was still littered with sexual connotations. He boasted he could tell a real girl by the way she held him, as Beyoncé seemed to moan appreciatively in agreement.

Real killers liked to ride, he boasted, and if a girl truly wanted to be with him, she had to be willing to do anything. The message seemed strikingly incongruent with the God-fearing manifesto of four 15 and 16-year-old virgins. Perhaps a naïve LeToya's denials indicated that she didn't even realise the rap was about sex.

Either way, who was Destiny's Child's audience? They marketed themselves to devout Christians by refusing to let their love of God be censored; but they also risked the wrath of religious parents with their album's extra-curricular rap sideline. Beyond who the group's audience might be, who were the group? Could fame change them?

"As kids we were on fire for God," Kelly reminisced. "Then you grow up, travel and experience things and stop reading the Bible every day. You don't realise that you're taking important things away from yourself."

With that in mind, would spending time around colourful characters like Master P, breaking out from the group's close-knit sheltered unit – one which was centred around the Knowles family – and meeting more streetwise people change who they were? Could it lead them astray?

Or was Mathew strategically capitalising on the notion that sex sells, while paradoxically still trying to preserve the innocence of a group whose members he now regarded as his children?

Clearly, just being in Destiny's Child was complicated. However, the group wasn't about to analyse its blessings too much – they were headed for the road. They started out small, touring radio stations. Unlike the UK where Radio 1 is dominant nationally and breaking the whole country can mean something as simple as visiting London, making a mark on a country the size of the US is infinitely tougher.

In the States there was no such thing as nationwide radio play: each city's major stations would need to be visited on a one-by-one basis. "When we first came out we did a free radio show in just about every big city in America," Beyoncé would later reveal.

Yet, although they were broke, fatigued and yet to see the fruits of their labour, according to one record company exec, they acted like seasoned professionals – even at unglamorous locations in small-town Virginia.

"They were in a parking lot in front of a department store on a one-foot riser with a stage," he told *Billboard*. "Yet those girls came prepared like they were playing Madison Square Garden. They were doing their own hair and make-up [and] there were no lights and cameras. Just them and a crowd of people, [but] they killed it."

The humility they learned early on seemed to stand them in good stead for shows like these. "Most people see the fierce, glammed up, gorgeous Kelly living what they think is the lifestyle of a princess and they don't realise how tough it was to start with," revealed an anonymous friend. "They think she was always that immaculate and it was always that easy. But the truth is, no amount of money or even talent can get you to the top if you're not willing to work insanely hard."

That sentiment would prove to be Kelly's mission statement as she launched her career. The group toured as support acts for entertainers such as Wyclef Jean, Boyz II Men, K-Ci and JoJo and Uncle Sam throughout the year. Another showbiz lesson for Kelly was "audiences may vary". If she was booed, she simply swallowed her pride and smiled. If women scowled jealously from the front row, she would "kill" their negativity with "kindness". She reasoned, making the best of a bad situation, that nothing could be a better response than a smile.

Beyoncé also came in handy to hide behind. "[She] was simply a great leader," Kelly told the *Daily Mail*. "She took the reins if bad stuff was happening. I remember one show in New York when the crowd booed us. They were a really negative crowd, a hip-hop crowd who wanted to hear rappers, and we were the only R&B act on the bill. We were terrified but Beyoncé just ran on stage and faced the crowd."

Yet the worst audiences would be the ones who said nothing at all. "Most audiences would be good," Kelly's friend explained, "but sometimes they'd be totally silent, as if someone had pressed the mute button – until the final song. Then when they figured out the girls were leaving, there'd be a big roar of applause. That was kind of worse than being booed."

Another problem with being an opening act – aside from audience indifference or even hostility – was creative censorship. Some headline acts, fearful that their tour mates could upstage them, would refuse anything they deemed too fancy. Fireworks, elaborate show-stopping costumes and complicated choreography were all things that a headliner could ban. "If they worry that it might even halfway upstage their act, then they can say, 'Sorry, no way,'" Beyoncé confided. "They don't want you to look or sound better than them, so they don't allow you to have anything special."

Whilst that might have seemed a little mean-spirited to most performers, it was a rational business decision. After the heartache of lethargic crowds and stubborn fellow singers, some shows pleasantly surprised the group, confounding all of their expectations.

One concert, a four-song set at the UK's biggest HMV store on London's Oxford Street, was packed to the rafters with fans. A few even asked the group to sign their recently born babies, something which Kelly described as "scary".

"The people got really into it," she told *Freebase*. "We had to stop performing because they didn't have security and we kind of got mobbed." The group declared it their most enthusiastic crowd of all that year – if also the craziest. During their set, there was a rampage of more than 180 teenagers who looted the shop of CDs. Hundreds of displays and CDs were damaged or stolen and the performance had to be cut short to just two songs, for fear it might incite the crowd to riot further. For the girls, however, the experience was an exciting one, and their first taste of something akin to Beatlemania.

Things were about to get even crazier in August 1998 when Destiny's Child was invited to New York to attend Whitney Houston's 35th birthday party. "We got some money and put our happy butts on that plane," Beyoncé enthused to *Launch*. "[We] went straight to that party. We even dressed alike, like we were going to perform. And Whitney came and hugged us and she said that she loved us. We were just in awe."

Later, they got an even more public declaration of love at a Black Entertainment Television (BET) award ceremony when Whitney punctuated the words of her smash hit 'I Will Always Love You' by pointing at them. According to Kelly, some of the song's uplifting lyrics were also sung directly to the group.

And now, finally, life *was* treating them kind. Kelly had come face to face with her top childhood idol and won her support and approval. It didn't get much better than that. To top things off, that year the girls won their first award – Best R&B/Soul Artist at the Soul Train Lady of Soul Awards for 'No No No'.

It was a good start, but – as far as Kelly and the other three were concerned – it was just the beginning.

Chapter 5

Moving On Up

B ack in the studio, the girls had finally earned the right to make their own decisions. "The label people said, 'Do whatever you want,'" Beyoncé revealed to *The Miami Herald*. "That's why we were so vocal in the next album. We learned that us doing what we wanted was better than people telling us what to do."

These girls were growing up. Making the transition into womanhood meant more independence and freedom, but also more wisdom – and Destiny's Child wanted to convert that combination into music and make it deadly.

"There's a huge growth between 16 and 18 when we recorded the album," Beyoncé continued. "It was natural for us to mature and you hear it in the music."

Indeed, Destiny's Child had reinvented themselves as feminists, taking the Spice Girls' 'girl power' slogan and combining it with TLC's penchant for empowerment anthems – "creeping" if they weren't getting enough love and banishing "scrubs" from their speed dial. While there were still songs built around the theme of being desperately, dangerously, irredeemably in love, the majority of second album *The Writing's On The Wall* was less about unconditional devotion and more about setting boundaries in relationships and realising their value as young women.

Prior to this album, some music fans felt there was a dearth of successful singers that teenagers could connect with. Most of America's biggest soul and R&B singers up to that point had been older women – awe-inspiring but unrelatable. With the rise of feminism, the younger girls were seeking a new voice for their generation – role models who could work society's changes into their songs. With *The Writing's On The Wall*, many felt that their prayers had been answered. They believed that, instead of churning out bog-standard love songs, the group was now speaking directly to the fans and addressing meaningful issues in their lives.

And because the subject matter meant so much to them, inspiration came instinctively. Instead of agonising over every last detail, taking two and a half years to do so, the second album was completed in just three weeks.

The theme of the album is summed up in the very first song, the title track 'The Writing's On The Wall'. Here, Destiny's Child intone that times have changed and that relationships can no longer be played out in the same way as the old days. Subverting Moses's 10 commandments, they announce their own guide for life.

The next song, 'So Good', introduces the first commandment – "Thou shalt not hate". It saw a return to the speeded-up singing first showcased in 'No No No (Part 2)', signalling that the girls had found their signature sound at last.

Some thought Destiny's Child would never sell, but the purpose of the track was to remind the cynics of their mistakes and prove them wrong. Kelly – who had come from poverty – understood that sentiment more than most – she really had made it out of the 'hood.

Kelly knew that there were a myriad of reasons why haters might be on the warpath, but none of them were her fault. Perhaps a man was insecure in his relationship and, in the fear that his girlfriend might leave, wanted to lower her confidence with putdowns to make her believe she was lucky to have him. Or, perhaps, a woman was jealous because she felt threatened by someone's potential or because she had failed to achieve the same level of success.

"When people pick on you, it's usually because you have something they don't have," Kelly told *Cosmo Girl*. "If you're smart and they're not, they're going to dog you. If you've got pretty hair and they don't, they're going to try and tear you down."

In fact, Kelly had been taunted from day one by rival girls who told her she would never amount to anything. "When I was in elementary school, this one girl was always telling me I couldn't sing," she continued. "Now she sings too, but she doesn't have a career. I know she sees that I'm blessed with one and she hates that." Adding a spiritual message about karma, she warned, "You have to remember that the things you do to people are going to come back."

Kelly's priorities were to keep her circle of friends tight, not to heed the petty jealousies of those outside her trusted inner group of confidantes, and to stay down to earth and focused. She recognised that never taking her eyes off the ball was what had led to her success in the first place.

Yet, casting aside humility for just a minute, the all-prevailing message of 'So Good' was that success truly was the best revenge.

'Bills Bills Bills' was another example of the girls taking their power back. Like 'So Good', it was produced by She'kspere and – as someone who'd just produced the TLC track 'No Scrubs', this was a man who was very familiar with the whys and wherefores of feminism.

She'kspere worked with his girlfriend Kandi Burruss of the girl group Xscape to create a storyline based on gold-digging partners. Kandi recalled a man she once dated who would run up mobile phone bills without permission and then plead ignorance to her when an astronomically high bill came in.

While Kelly had little experience of swindling partners, she could relate. In Tina's hair salon, she would regularly hear disgruntled customers letting off steam about their other halves and their unreasonable behaviour. Kelly's life at that time was quite sheltered – revolving purely around the Knowles family and the group – but the salon, which at times seemed to double as a counselling service for wronged women, was her link to the wider world.

While some women had an equal balance of financial power in their relationships with men, that wasn't the case for everyone. Plus Destiny's

Child were no ordinary women – now they were earning serious money, making it all the more important for them not to give in to the persuasion of a cajoling boyfriend keen to borrow some cash or drive their car. Not only that, but they were delivering empowering lyrics to listeners, encouraging women not to be doormats in their relationships.

So far was the message that Destiny's Child wouldn't tolerate haters or time-wasters and weren't about to foot the bill for their boyfriends' lifestyles, but more revelations were to follow.

In 'Confessions', the girls spill out what they regard as shameful secrets and weaknesses. In this song, in an unprecedented turnaround, they're the ones borrowing money without asking – and, if the furious victim was wondering where it went, it was spent on a shopping spree for clothes and a road trip. In other confessions, they talk of going a little further than intended with a man or lying about being young, free and single when in fact only one of the three applied.

Meanwhile if 'With Me' had been an answer to Usher's 'You Make Me Wanna', perhaps 'Confessions' was a precursor to another Usher song by the same name. On that track he admits to his girlfriend that he is about to have a baby by a woman that he barely knows, despite her being oblivious to the fact that he had even cheated.

Some listeners of the track would scoff at his belief that his partner would appreciate him for being brave enough to tell her, asking incredulously whether he really thought his honesty absolved him from his sins.

Destiny's Child on the other hand are not asking for redemption – they're merely laying themselves bare and, feeling the age-old need to confess, are trying to tell the truth. In a major coup for the girls, tough cookie Missy Elliot would feature as producer and guest rapper.

'Bug A Boo' was another hit in the making, berating a man for his borderline stalking – and it would later become an R&B radio classic. When they first heard it, however, the girls were far from convinced. In fact, an embarrassed Kelly would later dub it the worst song of all time.

However, in the studio, they gradually warmed to its straight-talking lyrics. In the track, they make it clear that buying a pair of shoes does not buy an admirer the right to stalk them. The constant flood of texts, calls and emails leave the girls infuriated and ready to cut the cables of the phone pole. The lesser action of blocking the offender's number only leads to him resuming the bombardment from his friend's phone.

The song, although Kelly would eventually dismiss it as "stupid" – an embarrassing memory of her youth – reflected the changing scenery of gender-typical behaviour in modern America and set new standards.

In the past, it had stereotypically been the men who were trying to prise themselves out of the clutches of 'clingy', possessive women who they all too often accused of fawning over them. Plus, back in the Nineties, the girl groups who were compared to Destiny's Child – such as En Vogue and The Supremes – often came across as somewhat masochistic in their love lives and not very often in control.

Arguably the closest thing there was to a conspicuously feminist anthem at that moment in musical history was Gloria Gaynor's vintage disco classic 'I Will Survive' – so the girls were already standing out as different.

Independent women accusing their men of bugging them instead of choosing to sing about love? People didn't expect this from a girl group.

There were more expectation-defying moments in 'Temptation' when the God-fearing girls stepped out to confess that they too suffered from irresistible urges - and that the electricity in the air when a sexy man walks in the room is unbearable. They talk of biting their lips and swivelling their hips for a man who's caught their eye, forgetting for a moment that they have a boyfriend waiting at home.

It wasn't a typical theme for Destiny's Child and – to add to the dichotomy of a track on which sexual urges were balanced by innocence and God-fearing moderation - the groove was based on an old children's nursery rhyme 'This Old Man (Knick Knack Paddy Whack)'. However in this case, the girls wouldn't be giving the dog a bone – they were resisting temptation and going back to their boyfriends.

Meanwhile 'Now That She's Gone' sees Destiny's Child railing against the indignity of being on a man's speed dial again simply because another girl he dated has walked away. Noting that the other woman was always number one in his life, being treated to shopping sprees while they get nothing, the girls order the offending man off their radar altogether.

'Where'd You Go' is another uptempo song with the by now distinctive Destiny's Child beat, but the subject matter stands in stark contrast to the other tracks on the album. Embroiled in an all-consuming love affair which knows no logic or reason, the girls talk of pining away after someone who hasn't kept in touch, insisting that living life is impossible without the man around. Meanwhile, the vocals are reminiscent of a love-song veteran – Whitney Houston.

'Hey Ladies', however, sees a return to a theme that would become synonymous with the group – standing for no nonsense from men. However, listeners might do a double take at complaints of a man running off with a 'tenderoni' – street slang for a delectable younger woman. Coming from a group of 18-year-olds, talk of being usurped by a more youthful replacement would doubtless raise a few questioning eyebrows.

Regardless, something that's never in doubt is that the man featured is far from perfect, even cheating on his partner with prostitutes. In spite of that, there's still a temptation to take him back, a forlorn hope that one day he might change. Questioning why many women struggle to leave bad love behind, the song acts as a shout-out to those disrespected lovers not to accept anything but the best. Kelly would later tell *Cosmo Girl*: "[A man] is likely to be gaining your attention, that's the way I see it."

She would also reveal that her inspiration in all matters romantic was a book called *The Rules*. On its release, the title stirred up controversy for being "old fashioned", "outdated" and "irrelevant", with its assertions that a woman should under no circumstances call a man or appear too keen.

However, for a girl with traditional Texan values about relationships who swore off ever making the first move, it was a dating bible. "If he's interested, he'll call," Kelly recited.

For now, of course, while her life revolved around the studio, *The Rules* would have to be purely a theoretical reference book. However, in the meantime, 'Hey Ladies' was her take on how to handle the relationship game.

'If You Leave', featuring Next, was Kelly's fantasy of the perfect romance. It spoke of a girl and a guy leaving their respective partners, packing their bags and running away together. She's also bidding a bad relationship farewell, ominously singing that he knows when she packs her bags it will be for good. The girls respond to the velvety-voiced male vocal by asking for reassurance that he won't cause the pain previous men have – but Next promises to be a true gentleman.

However, not all Destiny's Child-sponsored commandments are as wholesome. 'Jumpin' Jumpin'' – the first track in which Beyoncé, on behalf of the group, would play a major co-writing role – was described by one journalist as "a crusade to convince all happily married women to have as much adulterous sex as possible". The lyrics were unmistakable – the club was teeming with eligible "ballers" (in other words, players who were keeping their options open) and so ladies looking for a good time needed to leave their men at home.

While the girls would later develop 'young lady' personas, this song captured a raw, fun side to the early Destiny's Child. For this incarnation of the group, a night out is all about immaculate hair and nails teamed with Fendi shoes, eyeing up a crowd of men just as exquisitely turned out and a commitment to partying as much as possible. The evening's main attraction? The club full of "ballers".

As mischievous as it might be, it all seemed to be purely artistic licence. In fact, if Tina Knowles was to be believed, the closest these girls would get to a party any time soon was singing about it. "Sometimes you have a performer with the attitude, 'Well, I'm an artist so I should enjoy the parties!'" she told *Ebony*. "[But] the girls today are focused enough that they realise they can't stay at a party until two o'clock in the morning and then get up at six o'clock for a radio interview... We can't stop them from going to a party. They can go anywhere and do anything they want to. We can't slave drive them. So why are they working so hard? Because they understand what goes into being successful."

If the party wasn't going to stop, the girls could at least experience it vicariously by writing a song about the other life they didn't choose.

Then there was 'Say My Name', produced by Rodney Jerkins. When Destiny's Child first hired him, he had recently entered the business, although he would later go on to become one of pop's super-producers. The previous year he'd worked on Whitney Houston's 'It's Not Right (But It's Okay)' and Jennifer Lopez's 'If You Had My Love' – both of which would be huge hits. He also went on to work with TLC, Britney Spears, Michael and Janet Jackson, Katy Perry, the Pussycat Dolls and even Lady Gaga on 'Telephone'. He would also be a judge on the talent show *American Idol*.

However, in spite of the fact that he had just helped Whitney to achieve a number one hit, the group was far from convinced when he played them the backing track for 'Say My Name'. According to Beyoncé, it sounded like "a big, ugly jungle". This song reportedly inspired the girls' first ever diva moment, with all four refusing to work with the mix until he revised it.

Rodney obliged and, a little later, Mathew gate-crashed an official photo shoot, consumed with excitement about the new version, and demanded they take a listen straight away. The group shared his enthusiasm, later claiming they were so excited that they could barely focus on anything else until they had laid down the vocals.

The lyrics challenge a philandering boyfriend who the girls accuse of acting suspiciously. He arouses suspicion by answering his girlfriend's phone calls in the sort of neutral monotone better suited to a chat with a bank manager than a lover. Asked to say her name there and then to prove there's not another woman in his bed, he falters – and it could be another heartbreak moment in the making.

'Stay', one of the album's few slow jams, depicts a girl who feels neglected by a boyfriend who has more time for his male friends than her. The scenario reflected the frustration of countless teenagers who felt they'd turned into a Playstation widow. These girls were no strangers to being dumped by a partner while he spent hours in the pub or hiding the remote to sidestep an afternoon that would otherwise be invariably devoted to the big match. A little controversially, the lyrics hint at using sex to manipulate a man to stay, asking whether offering more than kisses would coax him into spending more time with her.

Next came 'Sweet 16', recognition of the growing pains suffered by a girl in her mid-teens. The lyrics reference a story all too often told in America – about someone who gets carried away by a fleeting love affair only to find herself barefoot, pregnant and alone. Cautioning that teenage romance rarely lasts, but that the little gifts they can leave behind are a responsibility for life, the girls urge listeners to move slower and be smart. The song ends with the positive affirmation that no matter what mistakes are made, at just 16, it's never too later to start over again.

Ironically, just five years later, Beyoncé's sister Solange would give birth to a son while still a teenager – as the result of an unplanned pregnancy.

The advice about starting again, however, was also meaningful for Kelly, who had already been through a few fresh starts in her life. But even that was put into perspective when the girls read a letter from a troubled fan who had been on the brink of taking her own life but, on hearing 'Sweet 16', had had a change of heart.

"[She] was about to commit suicide," Kelly revealed to *Cosmo Girl*. "Right as she was about to kill herself, she heard the words to 'Sweet 16'. She got this sense of empowerment and she felt that she could be OK."

That was a profound moment all round. It was the first time Kelly realised that the music she made wasn't just giving people pleasure on a superficial level, but it was changing their lives too. It put a whole new slant on being an entertainer.

The next track, 'She Can't Love You', sees a girl vent about the indignity of her boyfriend disappearing into the arms of an inferior woman. Unable to bear her love rival's smug smiles and little triumphant glances, she speculates incredulously on what her ex could see in the new girl when she can't love or touch him like she did. In the end, she finds herself fantasising that when he's with his new lover, he pretends it's her.

Finally, the album drew to a close with a rendition of 'Amazing Grace', their second dedication to their dearly departed ex-manager Andretta.

While the group was locked away in the studio, their third single, 'Get On The Bus', was hitting the charts. It had originally been written for the movie *Why Do Fools Fall In Love?* starring Halle Berry. The film follows the true life story of the late child star Frankie Lymon whose life ended just seven years after his biggest hit, the 1956 song which gave the film its name. The track was aptly named given that, following his death, three women tried to stake a claim on his fortune in the courtroom. One's testimony even claimed she had prostituted herself to pay for his rehab fees after a long prevailing addiction to heroin. Despite its dark subject matter, the movie was a victory for black audiences, who often felt under-represented in popular culture – and particularly at the movies. It later won several awards celebrating ethnic achievement.

'Get On The Bus', a Timbaland production, was released on February 23, 1999 and – following Mel B's 'I Want You Back' – was the second song to be released from the soundtrack. Lyrically, it blasts an ungracious lover, threatening to lock him out of the house and coldly advising him to catch the next bus out of town. A Europe-only release, it would achieve moderate chart success, but the real excitement was when it came time to promote the new album, starting with lead single 'Bills Bills Bills'.

Released on June 22, 1999, the accompanying video acted as a dedication to Tina Knowles, featuring the group in a hair salon. As Beyoncé obligingly teases and tweaks a customer's hair, her fictional 'scrub' of a boyfriend walks in and demands to use her car. Begrudgingly handing over the keys, she then moves straight into the lyrics, providing sympathetic head-shakes of horror from the salon's other clients.

Meanwhile, the blink-and-you'll-miss-it band member Farrah Franklin, who would join Destiny's Child for a few months the following year, had a minor role in the video as a client.

The track was extremely successful, becoming the group's first number one single in the US, but – like many musical success stories – it wasn't without controversy. In fact, complaints about the audacity of the girls made the letters pages of national newspapers.

There was a simple explanation. Many listeners, hearing the chorus but not paying attention to the verses, had denounced Destiny's Child as gold-diggers. They had mistakenly interpreted the words as expressing the band's point of view when, in fact, it parodied what good-for-nothing scroungers might say to them. Outraged men believed the girls were giving the men in their lives ultimatums: either pay their bills and maintain their luxury lifestyles or risk being kicked to the kerb.

They postulated that the girls were prostitutes masquerading as nuns, using a so-called love of God to gloss them over with a thin veneer of respectability. They were also portrayed as snobs – pampered princesses who cared little for the charms of a down-to-earth loving guy and instead craved obscenely wealthy footballers or high-flying businessmen. The girls were also linked to a new wave of feminism, one driven by man-haters who saw the opposite sex as little more than sperm donors or walking cashpoints at best.

Beyoncé, the group's defence minister on the matter, hit back: "Why would we ask a guy to pay our bills? Only if he runs them up!" She added, "We wrote the verses about him taking advantage of us, even though nobody paid attention to that part. People took it the wrong way."

However, as the girls would later point out, there was nothing like a good scandal to garner publicity. In fact, amid all the controversy, 'Bills Bills Bills' made the record books by tipping the *Billboard* charts for nine weeks in a row – longer than any other artist that year.

However, every rose had its thorn – and the boyfriend-less group couldn't help worrying that all the bad publicity might have ruined their chances of finding a man – or even any male fans – at all. After all, they'd now been publicly branded gold-diggers around the world.

"We don't want to be known as a women's rights band," Beyoncé later agonised to *The Sun*. "We are strong women but we don't hate men – that's not what it's about... Guys are scared and think 'I ain't approaching no independent woman.' We like our music to appeal to everyone and we sure don't want to scare any guys away."

Kelly added, "We'd all love to be in a relationship, but it's difficult... We're lonely sometimes... A lot of guys don't understand when they approach us, we are just normal girls."

Nice, normal girls next door – albeit with MTV on speed-dial and a number one single topping the charts. It would be hard to blame the men for feeling a little intimidated. The album, which followed on July 27, made its chart debut at number six and would go on to quadruple the success of its self-titled predecessor by selling over 12 million copies. In fact, it wouldn't leave the top 200 on the US charts for almost two years. The album was a hit in the rest of the western world too, earning double-platinum status in Canada and triple-platinum status in the UK, New Zealand and Australia.

Destiny's Child were successful, but all four members claimed they were lonely. Continuing on the independent women theme, subsequent single 'Bug A Boo' didn't do much to improve their chances of finding love, either.

The video saw the band desperate to escape the affections of over-attentive men. While trying to lose some persistent admirers in a nearby car, the girls accidentally break into a men's locker room, which is teeming with nearly naked sportsmen preparing for a game. Actors in the scene included the basketball star Kobe Bryant. Another scene saw the girls cheerleading with the UCLA marching band being led by Wyclef Jean.

While it sold reasonably well, the single would become one of the two lowest-performing Destiny's Child songs of all time, missing out on the Top 10 altogether, and prompting speculation that the group was already losing its grip on the R&B world. And there was worse news to come.

A few months later, on December 14, 1999, Beyoncé and Kelly would find themselves faced with a real-life bug-a-boo – in the shape of their two bandmates. That day, a letter arrived at the Knowles household disaffirming their management contract – just two weeks before the group was scheduled to film the 'Say My Name' video. It wasn't the best Christmas present Destiny's Child could have hoped for.

"As of this moment, please do not transact any further business on my behalf, individually or as a member of Destiny's Child," the letter read. "You do not have any authority to do so."

Just a few months before the letter landed on Mathew's doorstep, LeToya had affirmed the group's love for one another, claiming: "I think the difference between us and other groups is the fact that we love each other. We're more than just a singing group. It's like a sisterhood and even if we couldn't sing with each other, we'd still be together."

Yet according to Kelly, nothing could have been further from the truth. She would later confess: "We stopped getting along almost two years before the break-up and in interviews we couldn't say we were unhappy because we didn't want to let our fans down, because they're our number one priority, So we agreed to act like everything was OK, even though it wasn't. It all felt like one big lie."

Tina Knowles would go a step further, dating the tension back to the days when Destiny's Child didn't yet have a record deal. "From the time LeToya got in the group [at age 11] there was always drama, always jealousy, always madness," she had claimed.

LeToya and LaTavia were seeking outside management as they felt Mathew was too biased towards his daughter's interests and wasn't in a position to be impartial. According to them, life under an increasingly controlling Mathew's rule had gone from a harmonious sisterhood to a living nightmare. They claimed he had exerted control over everything from what they ate and who they dated to how they spent their time and had even tried to poach the girls from their parents by asking them to sign legal documents that made him their official guardian.

Mathew ultimately saw them as disposable, later insisting that their absence was insignificant as they barely sang anyway.

Yet this was precisely what concerned LeToya and LaTavia. Speaking to *Vibe* of their ever-demanding role, LeToya revealed, "Everything was like 'This is my group, my daughter is going to sing lead, deal with it.' He would say things like, 'If you don't like it, then you need to get another career. This is my group. I made it.' He believed it so much that it became a reality."

LeToya's grievances seemed to be supported by Mathew's attitude on a subsequent 2011 reality TV show, *Breaking From Above*, which followed his attempts to put together a new girl group. Live on air, he did little to counter his reputation as a control freak, making statements such as "This is my world, I'll pick my damn group how I want to!", "[band member] Shae thinks her vocals are irreplaceable, but that group will do just fine without her", "if you want to quit now, there's the door... It'll save me the time", and "In the end, I decide who takes to the stage!"

However, LeToya and LaTavia would claim that Mathew's influence extended far further than merely the stage or the studio – he would even deny them access to their parents.

On one tour with Columbia label mates Jagged Edge, LeToya suffered from a series of debilitating asthma attacks, but alleged she was denied the comfort of having her mother by her side. Pamela Luckett was ordered off the bus while LeToya gasped for breath, which Mathew would later claim was necessary as the group's insurance didn't cover her to join them in the vehicle. What was more, he insisted that the other girls didn't want her around.

"We were just so disgusted," Jagged Edge member Brian Casey raged afterwards. "Not for one moment did Beyoncé and Kelly put themselves in LeToya's shoes."

Mathew was also keen to protect the Destiny's Child brand – and that meant no sex scandals. However, LeToya and LaTavia had recently broken free of the "no boyfriend" curse afflicting the group and had started to date the twin brothers of Jagged Edge, Brian and Brandon Casey. On hearing of the relationship, a furious Mathew – who wanted to portray all four girls as innocent and untouched – intervened.

"He was all up in my personal business, telling me who I can and can't date," LaTavia recalled indignantly. "He told me if I wasn't a virgin, I'd have to resign from the group. He told me I made the rest of the girls look like sluts. He was totally controlling."

Yet for Mathew, image meant everything – and he was terrified that one wrong move could destroy Destiny's Child's painstakingly constructed public reputation for good.

"I think he feared anyone he couldn't control," a source revealed to the author. "In the inner circle there'd be jokes about how, because the Casey brothers were twins, they could partner-swap and neither of the girls would know the difference. I guess he was terrified it would go beyond a joke and end up a news headline. But these were modern girls from liberal families – and they objected to being marketed like nuns."

"Their vision of Destiny's Child was different from mine and Kelly's," Beyoncé would later reveal to *The Times* solemnly. "They wanted us to be more street and less Christian."

It wasn't just sex that was objected to either – it was the amount of time LeToya and LaTavia devoted to their relationships. "They lost focus," Beyoncé claimed to *Vibe*. "They didn't want to do interviews, rehearse or take voice lessons. Anybody that met us could see that me and Kelly were one group and they were another. It was obvious."

In contrast, Mathew had instructed the girls not to be distracted by the inevitable temptations of the opposite sex and to make music the first love of their lives. Was his attitude a step too far, or was it a stroke of genius, teaching the girls a type of discipline that was perhaps a prerequisite for success in an increasingly competitive field? Either way, Mathew was resolute, asking Beyoncé to report back to him if she spotted the slightest mistake in rehearsals.

"She was forever telling her father that LeToya and LaTavia refused to concentrate," a source disclosed to the author. "She thought they tired too easily and, if they didn't get the dance steps right, she would let him know. There were slaps exchanged between the girls on more than one occasion, with the exception of Kelly. She was very submissive back then and I don't recall that she ever raised a hand to anyone. She just looked on while the drama unfolded. If it came down to fight or flight, she'd rather walk away."

However, that wasn't an option. The moment the cameras stopped rolling, the girls seemed to be at each other's throats. Yet the biggest bugbear of all for them was money. Despite having a string of successful singles in the charts, LaTavia and LeToya had earnt less than £30,000 each. From LaTavia's perspective in particular, who'd been there from the start, it wasn't much to show for a decade of hard work and intensive training.

The aptly named 'Bills Bills Bills' should have put Destiny's Child in a whole new tax bracket. Yet while LaTavia and LeToya still drove bottom-of-the-range cars, Beyoncé and Kelly had upgraded from Ford Explorers to Jaguars. Beyoncé had even splashed out on some diamond jewellery.

Plus, while Kelly was living with the Knowles family and was part of the inner circle, the other two girls began to feel increasingly out of the loop and excluded. They didn't want to move in with their bandmates, but they didn't want to see themselves penalised for not doing so, either.

Even worse, they began to have sneaking suspicions that Mathew may have been misappropriating the group's funds. Confessing that, as young teenagers, they hadn't yet mastered the finer subtleties of good negotiation, LeToya and LaTavia didn't schedule a meeting with Mathew to voice their complaints. "If they had, we could have sorted something out," a plaintive Kelly would claim later. Instead, the girls sought legal action – and there was no going back. They learned that, as their contracts had been signed while they were still minors, they had the right to free themselves immediately. "We got a paper written up to disaffirm our personal management contract," LaTavia recalled to MTV. "The papers said that we are not by any means quitting the group. We were ready, willing and able to fulfil our duties to Destiny's Child."

However, that decision may have been taken out of their hands. At first, both parties went willingly into legal negotiations, speaking via their lawyers almost every day – and for a moment it looked as though the girls might be given the outside management they craved.

Then one day, LeToya's phone rang – and the caller had news that would divide Destiny's Child straight down the middle. "The group just shot a 'Say My Name' video," the voice on the other end of the line intoned, "and we just came from it. Where were you?"

Chapter 6

The Cut-Throat World Of Showbiz

When Kelly and Beyoncé received LeToya and LaTavia's letter, they did what they always did in times of trouble – they prayed. However, the writing was already on the wall for this group – and it spelled out a future without their former sisters.

Mathew had felt the girls weren't committed to a future in music, and perhaps he was right. According to a candid interview with *The Times*, LeToya would often rather have been at school than in the studio. "Just as I thought I was going to get to stay in school for a while, they would suddenly say, 'You guys got to go over to LA to record' and we would start home-schooling again," she revealed. "I wanted to be a cheerleader, I wanted to be part of the school band... but they would always take us out of school."

Meanwhile Mathew had no time for someone who craved an ordinary childhood. He wanted hard-working girls who weren't prepared to stop until they hit the big time. Plus, in his eyes, he hadn't given up a high-flying career for nothing – just as he had boasted of being Xerox's number-one salesman, he was intent on managing America's number-one girl group, too. For him, nothing less than number one was good enough.

However, that type of work ethic meant sacrifice from everyone involved. By now, life in Destiny's Child might have seemed like an episode of *I'm A Celebrity, Get Me Out Of Here!*, where terrified contestants took on fearsome challenges to guarantee their group's survival.

Yet while Kelly was willing to roll with the punches, even insisting, "You need people who can tell you off," LeToya and LaTavia had no wish to toe the line.

According to music historian Patricia Romanowski, that was why they hadn't made it. "You're either with the team or you're not," she claimed. "The groups that succeed are less forgiving. They get rid of the problem. It's very Darwinian, survival of the fittest."

Beyoncé and Kelly fired off their own emotional letters to their former bandmates to try to clear the air. "I never complained when you didn't sing one note on numerous songs on the album," Beyoncé's read. "I've never complained that when I was working my butt off in the studio, that the two of you were both either sleeping or on your phones approximately 80% of the time. I never complained when the two of you were lip-syncing to my vocals on some of the videos and on stage. In fact, I only helped make our contributions appear to be equal to the public." She signed off by saying she didn't deserve any more "drama".

Kelly's letter was a little less heated, but equally pained. "I think it's so funny how every time there is something good going on with Destiny's Child, one of you will spring something on us," she wrote. "Before, I've tried to forgive and forget and move on, but I refuse to be run over and receive punches from y'all. Y'all have taught me not to take crap from anyone and to always watch your own back."

Once the pair had pressed send, they knew there was no turning back. That was when the trauma kicked in. Devastated by what they saw as a personal betrayal, the pair withdrew, locking themselves in the bedroom they shared for two weeks straight. "There was a point where we did not eat," Kelly revealed to *Vibe*. "We went into a huge depression." In fact Beyoncé would even report that they had been "on the verge of a nervous breakdown".

Not only had the group as they knew it changed forever, but the pair had also lost two of their best friends – and they were inconsolable. While the pair cried and agonised over the future, Mathew was desperately searching for two new girls to fill the gaps. The group was already behind on schedule to shoot the 'Say My Name' video – and if they were going to find replacements, it was now or never.

For their part, Kelly and Beyoncé prayed. "We said, 'God, we are not trying to put a time limit on you, but we are asking you what to do,'" Beyoncé recalled to *Ebony*. "'If you send new members to us, then that is what we will do. If not, then we know that you want Kelly and me to just finish out the album [alone].'"

Within days, Farrah Franklin – who'd first appeared as an extra in 'Bills Bills Bills' was on their team. Then Destiny's Child's choreographer Junella Segura recommended young hopeful Michelle Williams, who already had an impressive showbiz CV. She had trained to become a forensic psychologist, but had left college at 19 to promote a career as R&B songstress Brandy's backing singer.

When it came time to audition her, Kelly and Beyoncé weren't asking for much. They needed a girl who was beautiful yet not overly sexy, someone who was confident in her abilities but humble too. Their ideal girl would need to have a huge voice but a minuscule ego – she would have to be willing to take a back seat when necessary and not to overshadow Beyoncé. She had to be collaborative, not competitive – and on team Destiny's Child, not team Michelle. They were looking for someone who had ideas and could offer input but who knew her place as a newcomer and wouldn't try to call the shots. Above all, she'd have to be a Christian.

In spite of their high expectations, the girls loved her instantly. "When Michelle walked in, she was perfect," Beyoncé recalled. "She was beautiful, she went to church and she could sing."

However, it wasn't over yet: the biggest test for the newcomers was yet to come. They'd appear in the 'Say My Name' video on a trial basis as dancers, but if they didn't make the grade there, they wouldn't be taken any further.

Initially it didn't bode well for them. This was an audition like no other – the tape was going to be watched not by a couple of music moguls but by millions of music fans all over the world. What was more, they would quickly expose their flaws. Despite originally being an awkward dancer, Kelly's years of practice had paid off and she and Beyoncé were head and shoulders above their new bandmates. In fact, the complex choreography the girls had planned had to be scrapped as, unlike their predecessors, the new recruits couldn't dance in four-inch stiletto heels.

They also had a lot to learn before they could measure up to Destiny's Child standards of high-octane glamour. While Michelle was gorgeous, she was far from glamorous – and before she joined the group, she had never worn make-up in her life.

What was more, she was also shy and conservative – she shunned miniskirts and at the time saw flashing her midriff as tantamount to a public sex session. The Knowles family was faced with the daunting task of reassuring her concerned mother that they were Christians too and wouldn't be corrupting her beloved daughter or turning her into a 'tramp'.

That said, both girls were in for an emergency image overhaul – and for Michelle, that included the painful process of facial hair removal.

Meanwhile, Tina was adamant that there should be a redhead in the group – and that was Farrah. While Farrah had a light caramel complexion, Tina was intent on moulding her into a carbon copy of the darker-skinned LaTavia – and ordered her to tan. All of this before they had even officially earned a place in the group,

If Michelle resented being manufactured into another girl's image and potentially stifling her own identity in the process, she didn't show it. Destiny's Child was one of the hottest girl groups around and being invited to join was the chance of a lifetime.

Even when her real name, Tenetria, was adapted to make her relatable to mainstream, white audiences and changed to the stage name of Michelle, she was malleable. "I wouldn't dare make that an issue," she exclaimed to *Vibe*. "You're travelling every day, flying first class, staying in the best hotels and you're tripping about a hair colour and your name?!"

It was this attitude that would later see Beyoncé and Kelly describe her as everything LeToya and LaTavia were not. But for Farrah, who felt she was being unjustly painted over, the tension was beginning to build. She didn't want to be LaTavia Mark Two – she wanted to be herself.

However, there was little time for last-minute jitters – the girls were now embarking on a fast-track course to learn in two weeks the skills that Beyoncé and Kelly had been perfecting for 10 years. Each day brought 12-hour rehearsals, until finally, when the two weeks was up, an announcement was made that they would be staying in the group.

"It was like, 'All right God, here you go, you answered our prayers and sent us Michelle and Farrah,'" Beyoncé recalled to *Ebony*. "'We said that if you sent them, we would use them.'"

So they did just that – and by February 13, 2000, the new line-up had their first performance together, as part of the NBA All Star weekend.

Meanwhile, 'Say My Name' was hitting the airwaves and, when the video premiered, the music world was in uproar. Michelle and Farrah had deliberately been camouflaged to blend in with the other dancers so that drama about the line-up change wouldn't overshadow the impact of the song. Not that it worked, of course: it was soon the hot topic of conversation of every gossip site around.

To add to the drama, a string of award ceremonies followed, at which the former members were nowhere to be seen. Back home in Houston, they were in emotional agony. The most wounding part of all for them was catching snippets of 'Say My Name' on music channels and seeing two strangers lip-syncing to their vocals.

Michelle and Farrah had also been showing up at public events in their place. While LeToya and LaTavia had privately arranged their own tickets for the Grammys, they missed prestigious ceremonies such as the Soul Train Awards altogether. According to their accounts, they hadn't even been told they were nominated. 'Bills Bills Bills' was up for an award that night, but two of the girls at the ceremony hadn't contributed a single word towards the song.

Michelle and Farrah felt equally uncomfortable taking the credit. After all, they were riding the wave of public applause for 'Say My

Name', another song which they hadn't even contributed to. "I was comparing myself to the other members," Michelle later confessed. "[I was] battling insecurity."

Meanwhile, for LeToya and LaTavia, seeing their replacements claim the Sammy Davis Junior Entertainer of the Year Award was one insult too many. By the time Destiny's Child hit the number one spot in early March, the divide between them and their former bandmates was vast. LeToya and LaTavia launched a lawsuit implicating Mathew and all four members of the group, claiming that their contract had been breached. A war of words instantly broke out in the press, with Kelly and Beyoncé claiming that their rivals were "tone deaf", "lazy" and hadn't deserved to be in the group.

Kelly delivered one of the most painful putdowns of all, later claiming, "They weren't able to do leads by themselves. We went to voice lessons because we wanted strong vocals. They wouldn't do that. They'd just show up when it was time to make money."

Their former vocal coach, David Lee Brewer, was so outraged by the "slurs" that he joined the debate, insisting, "Neither of the girls are tone deaf... [The group was] completely out of line saying that." He added, "I'm very disappointed. It's not what they were taught."

In a desperate bid for damage limitation, the girls released a statement promising that their innocence would be revealed in court. "Destiny's Child has always been about honesty, respect and being positive," it read. "Along with good music, friendship was at the heart of this group. We all wanted the same thing. When two people decide they want something that's against the philosophy of the group, that will ultimately cause problems. This lawsuit makes false accusations and we're confident the truth will come out soon, either in court or in mediation."

And with that, the group hit the road for an extended tour of the USA and Europe. At first, the mood was unavoidably dark. Kelly had been terrified that the line-up change and talk of legal action would reduce the group they had worked so hard to create into a laughing stock.

However, the shame-faced girls quickly found that the spat hadn't damaged their popularity – in fact, if anything, sales were increasing.

"We never would have sold as many records if these member changes did not happen," Beyoncé would later assert in Destiny's Child's 2002 autobiography, *Soul Survivors*. "Up until that point, we were squeaky clean nice girls who grew up in Texas. We had all been together for years – lifelong friends since childhood. We couldn't get on the covers of any magazines. I guess the media felt our story was too boring. Then two members were gone and soon all eyes were on us… It must be a part of human nature to love drama."

How right she was. In the year 2000 alone, their album sold nearly four million copies, while the group won 16 awards. 'Say My Name' had become an international breakthrough as well. With the single, Destiny's Child reached Asian shores for the first time ever, hitting the number one spot in the Philippines for seven weeks running. In fact, they were the first girl group to retain the top position for so long. They also introduced Australia to R&B music, when they became the second group of their genre ever to make it to number one there, beaten to the privilege only by TLC with 'No Scrubs'. Destiny's Child seemed to have done what they did best – turned a negative into a positive.

What was more, the group's next single, 'Jumpin' Jumpin'', was just as successful. Its video depicted the group departing from their good-girl style and transforming into slightly sexier performers. One scene from the video showed Beyoncé and Kelly, primed for a night out, drive fast enough to leave skid marks. Their destination? The nearest nightclub. Clad in hotpants and bras, the girls dance suggestively on a podium while a group of men look on admiringly, drinks in hand. With this imagery, Destiny's Child were no longer the angelic girls that the media ignored. While they still held Christian values close to their hearts, they were now a little edgier, a little more street.

'Jumpin' Jumpin'' would become one of 2000's biggest radio hits. It now seemed like Destiny's Child finally had some stability. Beyoncé even jubilantly revealed, "This line-up is here to stay!" but, as it turned out, she'd spoken too soon. 'Jumpin' Jumpin'' would be the last video Farrah would ever appear in.

She was becoming increasingly dissatisfied with her role within the group – partly for trivial reasons and partly due to more serious issues.

Things had got off to a bad start when she'd been asked to dye her hair red. "I hated it," she declared to *Sister 2 Sister*, a black entertainment magazine. "It kind of upset me because I thought they were trying to make me look like or be LaTavia and I wanted to have my own identity."

She became even more frustrated when the constant colouring of her hair with abrasive chemicals caused it to break off in clumps – something she blamed on Beyoncé's mother. "Pretty much everything was going crazy because my hair was breaking," she continued. "I actually stopped letting her mom do my hair."

As the only person in the group who didn't rely on hairpieces or a weave, her natural locks were important to her. However, it quickly caused tension when, in interviews, the other girls would praise Tina's styling and Farrah would counter that she had her hair done separately from the others, back home in LA.

That wasn't the only image-related problem – she resented wearing hand-me-downs that had belonged to the group's former members and at times felt guilty for taking their places. In fact, when she was faced with what she saw as favouritism, she started to wonder whether she had more in common with them than she had realised.

"It was scary because a lot of the stuff they were talking about that was being done to them was being done to us," she claimed. "Regardless of how much anyone wants to say there's no favouritism, there is going to be favouritism when your whole family is running the show... There was no way that group would ever have been equal."

Farrah had interpreted a seemingly innocent request for her to tan as one example of that favouritism. She believed that she, like Kelly and Michelle, was expected to be darker to create more of a contrast with the paler-skinned Beyoncé so that she could stand out. "Every time I looked at a picture, she stood out more because she was the brighter one," Farrah insisted. "Not because she was the prettiest, but because she was lighter."

She rarely socialised with the other girls and became quiet and withdrawn. She claimed that she was almost always forbidden from singing live. "I didn't join the group to lip-sync," she raged. "I was pretty much an overpaid background dancer." She added, "I didn't feel like I was being accepted. I felt like I was just being used. I was being used to finish the album and after that, I felt like Beyoncé was going to do her solo album and we were going to be kicked to the kerb."

The other girls later contested that Farrah was simply unable to cope with the pressures of fame and the constant travelling and touring. They claimed she made no effort to bond with her new bandmates, refusing to join them on evenings out, or – even worse – appearing at events by herself that she hadn't invited them to. While Farrah claimed she felt marginalised, Beyoncé and Kelly countered that she had been solitary by choice. Either way, she simply didn't fit in – neither on a professional level nor on a friendship level.

Things finally came to a head in July at a festival in Belgium. Thousands of miles from home, Farrah started to vomit uncontrollably. The following day, taking advantage of a little time off, she flew home to LA, where she made a visit to the emergency room of her local hospital. There, she was diagnosed with dehydration and gastric flu.

"Five minutes after I was finished seeing my doctor, I got a call from Mathew," Farrah told *Sister 2 Sister,* "saying I needed to get my ass on the airplane or I could just stay in LA because they don't need me anyway. And he was yelling."

An MTV special was about to be recorded, and an entire production crew was gathered in Houston waiting to film the group. Farrah saw Mathew's threats that she wasn't needed as intimidation, a means of controlling her by targeting her fears that she would be ousted from Destiny's Child.

On the other hand, Mathew believed success was impossible without sacrifice and that, if there was a major TV appearance at stake, a true professional would make it happen, no matter what.

"It took us nine years to get on MTV," Beyoncé concurred. "It showed how she'd only been in this for five months. That's what happens when you give somebody that kind of success in two weeks and they don't have to work for it."

In the end, Farrah made the appearance, but she was crying hysterically. The following morning, she could hardly bear to speak to

Beyoncé's father. When the other girls noticed the tension, they asked what was wrong, only for Farrah to snap back, "I didn't speak to him for a reason." Beyoncé replied, "Well, if you don't want to speak to him, you don't gotta speak to me either."

Had it merely been a schoolgirl spat, it could have been dismissed as insignificant – but when it involved one of the USA's biggest girl groups, it was going to have serious repercussions.

That day, MTV would continue to film them as they journeyed to Seattle. On arrival in the city, there was a 15-minute break in their schedule to allow them time to check into their hotel room. MTV's All Access show was the first programme exclusively dedicated to Destiny's Child and the girls were concerned about making a good impression. Yet the moment the cameras stopped rolling, unbeknown to producers, there was an emotional behind-the-scenes meeting.

"They were like, 'How can you come to my house and not speak to my father?" Farrah recalled, "I said, 'Well, how can your father speak to me in such a manner? I've never been spoken to like that in my life and I'm not going to let it start now.' I said, 'I don't know how he talks to you or anyone else, but I know how he's not going to talk to me.'"

The group began to put forward their concerns – she was quiet and withdrawn, she hadn't made friendships within the group, she flew home every time she had a day off and she had raised queries about how Mathew was distributing the money.

Farrah had alleged that Beyoncé's sister, Solange, was travelling with them and that their airline tickets and accommodation was sponsored with money that came directly out of the group's cheques. "She was supposed to be a dancer," Farrah raged, "but she never danced for us until I left the group. So when I was asked why we were paying her [per diem and through flights and accommodation], my manager was like 'Why do you care about where $300 is going when you're getting paid this?' And I'm like, I don't care if I'm getting paid $1 million – if I want to know where five of my dollars are going, there shouldn't be a problem with me asking."

A lively debate ensued, which ended with Farrah storming out. Beyoncé, Kelly and Michelle were desperately trying to maintain an illusion of normality – after all, they had an MTV crew on standby for one of the biggest promotional events of their lives – and they didn't know how to explain Farrah's disappearance.

She was a no-show at a radio appearance in Seattle and a subsequent filming at a seafood restaurant. The others felt compelled to explain her absence by apologising that she was "sick". In reality, she had fled on the next available flight back to LA.

Soon afterwards, the rest of the group arrived in LA themselves en route to Sydney – they were visiting Australia for the first time ever for a series of appearances. There was still a residual flicker of hope in everyone's minds that they could persuade Farrah to resolve her differences with them and rejoin the tour. Beyoncé called her from the airport, insisting that she still had time to catch the flight or that, if necessary, all four of them could book a later one. However, Farrah was resolute – she wouldn't be seeing them until they got back.

"We had five performances," Beyoncé later told *Teen* magazine, "and Farrah decided she wasn't going to come to them. She said she needed some time off, but she wasn't sick. No-one had died in her family. Nothing had happened – so what Farrah did was unacceptable."

Finally, they gave her an ultimatum – if she wanted to remain in the group, she would have to fulfil her contractual commitments in Australia. If she didn't show up, they would have to consider letting her go. However, she resisted their pleas and – when their plane touched down in Sydney – she was unreachable.

The others felt that she left because she couldn't cope with the pressure. "We tried to help Farrah," Kelly told *The Mail On Sunday*, "But I guess the business was too much for her." Michelle concurred, "She should have just said, 'I'm sorry, but I can't handle all the pressure and change. I thought I could, but I was wrong.'"

Farrah, on the other hand, rejected their stance. "I never complained a day in my life," she insisted. "Handling it was not a problem… They didn't understand what I was handling because I never made it an issue."

Either way, in Kelly's eyes, she had broken one of the golden rules of showbiz – professionalism. "She was disloyal to our fans because she stood them up," she commented, "and that's something Destiny's Child does not do. If you have a regular job and you don't come to work, your boss will want to know why. If you don't turn up, you basically quit and that's the way we looked at it."

The girls were yet to make a final decision about how to handle Farrah and, despite a few frantic international phone calls, they couldn't brainstorm much with Mathew while there was an ocean between them. Instead they concentrated on making the trip as a trio.

As it turned out, surviving a crisis together would only strengthen their bond. Kelly, the group's animal lover, had wanted to see kangaroos and koalas, so they made a trip to the city's pet sanctuary. They also ate in a combination of the finest restaurants and the most down-to-earth burger joints. They experienced Australia as tourists and had a great time – but the magic really began when they took to the stage for the first time as a three-piece.

According to Kelly, it instantly felt right. "I remember how intimidated I felt [previously] when the others were around," she recalled. "I felt insecure around them, like I wasn't talented when really I was… I felt uneasy [and] shy and… I was letting that hold me back." Anticipating another argument, she constantly remained in the background – the only place where she felt safe. In fact, she couldn't remember a time since Destiny's Child signed its first record deal when there hadn't been an undertone of tension. With Farrah especially, the threat of animosity had been ever-present. "Whenever I would finally try to come out of my shell, something would happen, a fight or a look," she added, "and I would crawl right back in." Her awkwardness had even extended to the stage.

Without Farrah, however, Kelly would have to overcompensate, come out of her comfort zone and sing for the two of them. It was liberating. "Australia was the first time I did not have to hold back one bit," she concluded, "because I knew there were two people on either side of me who loved me and they would always be there for me."

With the departures of three band members in less than a year, the idea that the other two would always be there might have seemed like a rash assumption – but it was how she felt. On their return to Houston, a group decision was made not to seek a replacement – Destiny's Child would now be a three-piece forever.

Kelly would later describe the previous line-ups as "like being in a bad marriage" and, indeed, statistically two out of every three marriages ended in divorce. Perhaps it was the same with girl groups. Could this line-up be third time lucky?

Not if the initial public reaction was anything to go by. Many journalists and fans queried just how bad life as a member of Destiny's Child had to be if Farrah, the third to leave, had caved in after just five months. It brought a whole new meaning to the term 'musical chairs'.

The public had also noticed striking similarities between the reasons that had driven each band member away. Sympathy for Destiny's Child seemed to have reached an all-time low.

What was more, Mathew would add fuel to the fire after he claimed that Farrah was never a strong singer and that her sole purpose in the group had been for 'imaging'.

He then suggested that all three members of the group were disposable. "Destiny's Child is bigger than its members for the same reason that it doesn't matter who runs Coca-Cola," Mathew claimed to *Vibe*. "It's a trademark. It allows you to be able to change members. As long as you get a hit song, there will always be a Destiny's Child. The day there's not a hit song, it doesn't matter if Beyoncé's singing. If you ain't got no hit songs, it don't matter if Beyoncé's singing. If you ain't got no hit songs, it's gone."

Some listeners objected to having their tastes described in a clinical, calculated and ultimately business-savvy way. Yet there was more. "Don't ever get too hung up on what the girls' names are," he advised. "We can still perform with four, three, two or one members."

For some fans, it conjured up visions that no matter what the line-up, the group would always be Destiny's Child, provided that some kind of sinister, manipulative puppet master was backstage, manufacturing the hits and pulling the strings. It suggested to them that members' identities were artificially created and contrived to the point that they became interchangeable. For many, music was all about emotion – as well as identifying with the people who sang the hits. Hearing Mathew somewhat crudely describe their favourite girl group in terms of profit, imaging and branding wasn't exactly a turn-on for them.

As the inevitable backlash took stage, Kelly began to take stock of her own career. Years or even months earlier, hearing Mathew say the group could function as Destiny's Child with just one member might have made her blood run cold. After all, there was one indisputable leader – and, by all accounts, that was Beyoncé. The comments of her vocal coach might have rung hauntingly in her ears, repeating that her voice was "as thin as air" and that her surrogate sister was the natural talent of the group. However, with just two members to compete with, an increasingly confident Kelly was beginning to find her own voice and – equally importantly – her own value.

"As a trio, the group is stronger," she insisted, "because all of us can really sing. We now have the potential to have three lead singers. We can do things with our vocals that we were never able to do before."

"[People are] so shocked at our vocal ability now," Beyoncé concurred. "[Before] we weren't able to do a lot of the arrangements that Kelly and I had ideas for because everybody wasn't strong."

That year, she even found the courage to record a song with Beyoncé as a two-piece. The track, 'Have Your Way', would go unnoticed by some fans due to its quiet release on the modestly charting soundtrack for low budget film *His Woman His Wife*, but it was still an achievement for Kelly.

The song, like the movie itself, tackles the grief and guilt of a devout Christian woman co-habiting with a partner despite it contradicting her religious beliefs. Her interfering mother doesn't ease her conscience much when she repeatedly points out adverts for engagement rings - and the assurances from her partner that they'll formalise their relationship soon are starting to sound hollow. Kelly and Beyoncé ask why the wedding ring he promised months earlier never materialised. They speak of their shame and ask for God's forgiveness for living wrong.

The moral codes in the song matched Kelly's own and mirrored the dilemma she and Beyoncé may have felt when, as women of God, they suspected their early bandmates LeToya and LaTavia were indulging in premarital sex.

That year, Kelly also collaborated with R&B singer Avant on a remix of his song 'Separated', which fleetingly made it to number one on the *Billboard* R&B chart.

However, Kelly's solo voice finally got a chance to shine when she was invited to contribute a song to the soundtrack for comedian Chris Rock's satirical feature film *Down To Earth*. In it, Chris plays Lance, a struggling version of himself who, despite his best efforts, is always getting booed off stage.

One night on his way home from a meeting with his agent, while leering at a distractingly voluptuous young woman on the street, his bike is hit by a truck and he is instantly killed. The marginalised black comedian manages to convince the angels he meets in heaven that he's died before his time and that his destiny is to return to earth to make it on the stage. The only way to bring him back to life, however, is to resuscitate an obscenely wealthy white businessman who has just drowned in his bathtub and place Lance's soul into his body.

That isn't without its problems either – the businessman, Charles, undergoes a total personality transplant from selfish, snobby billionaire to kind and charitable philanthropist. He also develops a sudden taste for black music such as hip-hop.

A light-hearted look at racism and capitalism, tackling important issues while still raising a smile, *Down To Earth* would earn over $20 million on its later release in February 2001. The soundtrack would see Kelly share the limelight with artists such as Snoop Dogg ('Gin And Juice'), Monica ('Just Another Girl') and Lauryn Hill ('Everything Is Everything'.)

There's also a fitting collaboration between white rapper Eminem and his darker-skinned counterpart Sticky Fingaz. The latter postulates that if he had skin the same colour as cocaine, police would be asking for his autograph instead of finger-printing him. He wouldn't be subject to constant scrutiny and suspicion such as requiring collateral when buying property or being followed by security on the city streets.

Kelly's track, 'Angel', was a little less controversial, instead giving thanks to the angels who rescued Chris for loving someone unconditionally when they didn't even love themselves.

Kelly would also return to her comfort zone when she resumed play with the other two girls. That summer, the deluxe two-CD edition of *The Writing's On The Wall* was released – which would sell over 16 million copies in total around the world – and, meanwhile, Destiny's Child was working on a follow-up album.

The pressure was on, because to continue their domination of the charts on their return, they had to be ready to prove themselves. However, it couldn't have been a better time for Destiny's Child to strike. In the UK, the Spice Girls had just released their farewell album and the UK would be on the lookout for a replacement – perhaps from across the Atlantic. Meanwhile, back in America, TLC – their main competition in the genre – had gone quiet. The following year would bring the passing of R&B star Aaliyah too, leaving a gaping wound for the music scene to fill. Was Destiny's Child up to the challenge?

Kelly liked to think so – and, perhaps due to her success on songs away from the group, she had been promised more of a voice on the third album. "I'm making sure Kelly and Michelle sing lead on some songs," Beyoncé told the *Daily Mail*. "They are both incredible singers and they deserve respect. In the past, I sang lead because that was the decision of the studio or the record company, but I've had vocal injuries from all that singing!"

She was now about to pass down that privilege to her bandmates. However, what wasn't planned was Beyoncé's almost total control in the studio, albeit from behind the scenes. "I actually wrote, produced and arranged the album," she later told *The Mail On Sunday*. "Every song on there."

So much for the others having a say. "She can't help herself," Kelly told VH1. "She just writes hits." Beyoncé concurred, "The label kept saying, 'Do another song, do another song, do another song! It wasn't planned. It wasn't like I said, 'OK, I'm going to take charge.'"

Yet, increasingly, as rumours circulated that Beyoncé was on the verge of signing a solo deal with Columbia Records, Destiny's Child was becoming Beyoncé's child – and Kelly again had to take a back seat.

Having little involvement in the behind-the-scenes work didn't concern Kelly much as she saw herself as a performer, not a producer – but it did underline Beyoncé's position of authority and perhaps even superiority in the group – something which she saw as a bitter pill to swallow.

In spite of that, she was looking forward to recording sessions starting again. The group worked on track after track, but one in particular stood out. For some time, they had been looking for an answer to the public's criticism of 'Bills Bills Bills'. For a multi-million selling girl group splashed across just about every newspaper in town, it didn't seem like it needed much explanation – but Beyoncé wanted to promote that they were breadwinners and paid their own bills. They even resorted to throwing dollar bills into the crowd at gigs, just as Lady Gaga would do on her own tour some 10 years later, roaring "I don't want your money, I want your souls!"

Try as they might, the trio hadn't been able to quell the media headlines that marketed them as gold-diggers. Chart rival Meja would sing on her track 'All 'Bout The Money', that it was all about the money and she didn't find it funny – and that was exactly how Destiny's Child felt.

Then an argument with childhood friend and sometime boyfriend Lyndell Locke prompted Beyoncé to start thinking solo – and she had the brainwave she needed for an explosive new track that addressed these issues.

'Independent Women (Part 1)' said everything Beyoncé wouldn't have dared to tell Lyndell on the phone – and the privacy of the recording studio let her true emotions out. She didn't want her man to blow up her phone – she would call him. What was more, she would call him only when she was lonely and, when an implied sex act was over, the onus was on him to get up and leave. Beyoncé was busy with her own life, looking after number one.

She also advised her fellow women to stop pandering to their men and to take control of their own lives. She told girls to play their men just as, back in the old days, they might have been played.

Coming in stark contrast to the love songs flavour of the rest of the

116

album, it was hard to say whether the lyrics reflected someone who truly valued independence or simply someone who had been hurt so badly that they saw their cold-hearted front as a means of revenge. Either way, the song was rebelliously, stridently, unapologetically, about being out for herself and in control – and the record label loved it.

Seeing its potential but wary of getting the girls' hopes up prematurely, Mathew secretly submitted the song to the producers behind box office hit-in-the-making *Charlie's Angels*. He felt it would be perfect material for the film's soundtrack and, as it turned out, he was right.

The news of the film-makers' interest would come just weeks after Farrah Franklin had departed from the group – and the girls saw the synchronicity as an act of God. "There's three members now and there's three Charlie's Angels!" Kelly would exclaim triumphantly. In their eyes, it was their creator's way of telling them that their reincarnation as a three-piece was meant to be.

They returned to the studio, hearts a little lighter, to make a new version of the song that referenced *Charlie's Angels* – Lucy Liu, Drew Barrymore and Cameron Diaz – a little more obviously. In fact, they ended up with a brand new second song. "The initial idea was just to remix it," co-producer Jean-Claude Olivier, also known as Poke, recalled, "but we ended up remaking the record completely."

In this new version, Beyoncé was even more aggressive, not only stating that anyone attempting to control her would be dismissed – and anyone seeing their handling of the situation with LeToya, LaTavia and Farrah had better believe it – but also claiming that women should depend on no-one else to give them what they need. Giving a shout-out to all women who pay their own way in the world, the group sing out that they buy their own cars, houses, jewellery and diamonds.

On September 14, 2000, 'Independent Women (Part 1)' was released as a single and a tie-in with the film. It was a good introduction for Michelle, whose vocals were appearing on a Destiny's Child track for the first time, as in the UK it instantly debuted at number one. It would go on to hit the top spot in Canada, New Zealand, Ireland

and America – where it topped the *Billboard* chart for 11 consecutive weeks.

The video reinforced the band's image as tough, self-sufficient money-makers, seeing them train at a dedicated Charlie's Angels boot camp. Beyoncé and Kelly had been through enough boot camps in their time courtesy of Mathew to be a little complacent – and they were expecting this one to be child's play.

In reality, the video took several days to film and not only saw them train in agility (dancing), racing (motor-biking) and combat (martial arts fighting) but it also saw them tackle altitude – by sky-diving.

It wasn't just vertigo-inducing but painful. "We were strapped into harnesses and we had bruises when we took them off," shuddered Kelly to *The Daily Record*. All the talk of independence and combat was starting to toughen Kelly up, however – in the same interview, she had such a presence that the newspaper mistakenly defined her as the group's lead singer.

All three were happy with the video and its message, in spite of the difficulties making it. The group might have been wearing Versace outfits, but they had paid for them by themselves. The bruises of the harnesses became a fitting metaphor for the notion of 'no pain, no gain', matching Beyoncé's lyrics that being truly independent involved hard work and sacrifice on a level that wouldn't be easy.

These values – "being able to provide for yourself" and "not constantly depending on other people to do things for you" – didn't go unnoticed by the public. In fact, they even made their mark in the notoriously patriarchal Japan, where age-old gender roles defined women as home-makers and child-carers and men as the breadwinners who provided for them.

'Independent Women (Part 1)' was about to spark a change. "[It] made a huge cultural impact in Japan," Beyoncé recalled. "Until that song became a hit the young girls and teenagers there thought it wasn't cool to buy their own stuff. The thing to do was to get a boyfriend and let him buy everything. Then, after 'Independent Women' came out, all these girls were like, 'You know what? I'm going to pay my own bills and I'm going to get my own phone. I'm going to buy my own jewellery.' The youth culture changed – for the better, I think – all because of one song."

Even back in America, the girls felt they'd started a musical trend. It made a change from the candy-coated, saccharine-sweet love songs that filled the charts at that time, as well as reflecting the priorities of a new generation of working women,

It was a defining moment for the group – they were no longer just entertainers but part of the cultural landscape. They would make the *Guinness Book Of Records* for having the longest-running number one of the year. Destiny's Child were strong, uncompromising women in their money-making prime, just as they portrayed themselves in the song. Or were they?

According to one source, while the song might have dubbed the girls as independent women, the irony was that in reality they were anything but.

"Kelly had absolutely no say in Destiny's Child," the source told the author. "These girls were singing about being independent when in fact they had no choices in their lives and were totally under Mathew's control. If he ordered them to rehearse when they were ill, they had to do it. If they said or did something in their personal lives he didn't like – even if it had nothing to do with him and no impact on the group – they were out of Destiny's Child. He ruled with an iron fist and controlled the girls by fear that they'd lose their celebrity status and their careers. He had the power to make or break Kelly, so she wasn't independent – she had to dance to the beat of his drum. She and the others were going against everything they were singing about."

Kelly was singing that her peers should answer to no-one and should dismiss anyone who tried to control them, when it seemed she didn't have the same luxury herself. The song had inspired women around the globe to demand tougher standards from the men in their lives, while Kelly was still struggling to live out her own words.

Whether Mathew was actually abusive towards the girls or merely a strict but well-meaning disciplinarian was debatable but, by all accounts

– including Mathew's himself – he was a dominant force that presided over Destiny's Child. Why had Kelly accepted this?

Interestingly, when asked why she'd left the group, Farrah had recalled: "Mathew is a controlling person and everything was under his control… I'm too smart to let anyone treat me any kind of way. I'm a strong person and I know that because anyone that didn't have a strong mind would not have left a group like that."

Perhaps then, at heart, Kelly had never identified with the strong women she sang about. These had been Beyoncé's lyrics. Her personality type back then, on the other hand, was shy, sensitive, cooperative, obliging and – above all – indicative of someone willing to toe the line. Not only did this attitude help to keep her place secure in the group, while more headstrong candidates seemed to have quickly been shown the door, there was also a father–daughter relationship between Mathew and Kelly – a love and loyalty that seemed to go both ways. Perhaps having someone to lay down the law made Kelly feel safe, secure and wanted, as she had never had a male figure who cared enough to set boundaries in her life before.

According to popular psychology regarding relationship patterning, women often have a tendency to be attracted to men who are just like their fathers and to make similar mistakes that they saw their mother making when they were growing up.

Kelly had described her own father as controlling, abusive, a bully and someone who was verbally aggressive to her mother – and these were exactly the complaints that previous band members had laid at Mathew's door. As one source suggested, "Her role model of what a father should be was a bully boy." Perhaps Mathew's description was normal to Kelly because she had never seen a collaborative relationship between a man and a woman when she was growing up – only an abusive one.

"That was fine for Kelly back when she was young and shy – being ruled by someone else who knew what they were talking about and made all the tough decisions suited her just fine," the source added. "She hadn't been ready to branch out but, ultimately, there would come a time when she wanted to spread her own wings."

As 'Independent Women (Part 1)' claimed the number one spot all over the western world, that was when the first seeds were sown in Kelly's mind for a solo career – and, while it would take two years to materialise, she was slowly starting to realise that freedom was her real destiny.

Chapter 7

Surviving Solo

The aptly named *Survivor* promised to be the biggest album of Destiny's Child's career – and indeed, after its release on May 1, 2001, it débuted at number one in nine countries. However, in psychological terms, it suffered from multiple personality disorder – the musical equivalent of a bump to the head.

In 'Independent Women (Part 2)', the lyrics advise against getting carried away with romance and salute a woman for not falling in love, while – in stark contrast – 'Dangerously In Love' says that the girls were created in this world purely for that purpose – falling in love.

Similarly, 'Independent Women (Part 1)' credits a girl for keeping her eye on the prize and not allowing herself to be seduced. Yet 'Perfect Man' talks of someone spending their time doing exactly that – lusting after a seductive love interest while urging other women not to let the chance of finding the one pass them by. Logically, the writer of the former would accuse the woman depicted in the latter of wasting her time – yet both songs co-exist on the same album.

Meanwhile 'Bootylicious' depicts the girls scantily clad, moving provocatively and celebrating their curves, while 'Nasty Girl' berates other body-confident women, calling them cheap for appearing to do the same thing.

The video for 'Survivor', the first single, depicts the girls in bikinis, while 'Nasty Girl', where they sneer at under-dressed peers, is notable for being the only video in Destiny's Child history where the girls are covered up.

While some songs state that men are at the bottom of the priority list, others – such as 'My Heart Still Beats' – reveal passionate lost-my-head-style declarations of love where Beyoncé sings she doesn't want to live another day if her man can't be beside her.

'Survivor' claims that the girls refuse to compromise their Christianity by bad-mouthing wrongdoers, while 'Fancy' does just that, denouncing someone who is dishonest.

Then 'Gospel Medley', incorporating traditional hymns such as 'Jesus Loves Me', is a demonstrative expression of religious faith, while 'Sexy Daddy' is a distinctly unholy account of going out in search of premarital sex. Likewise 'Dance With Me' hints at a penchant for one-night-stands.

Songs about independence and opposition to romance share the same album as love song after love song, while the group promote chastity yet sing in colourfully explicit terms about sex.

Listeners could be forgiven for feeling a little confused. And just a couple of years earlier, Beyoncé had assured *Touch* magazine: "We wouldn't do explicit lyrics or show off our bodies too much… there's a certain level that you go to and we're not going to go overboard to sell records."

However, in some people's eyes, she had done exactly that. *The Evening Standard* commented on the album's many contradictions when it remarked: "It is difficult to ascertain whether Destiny's Child are seriously sweet, God-fearing girls or simply incredibly slick media machines."

Were they, as the cynics claimed, factory-produced pop tarts with a built-in sex appeal on-demand button and, incongruently, a God-praising mode? If the album's identity crisis was a marketing strategy, then it had succeeded in several ways.

Perhaps realising that sex sells, the girls had mastered the 'I'm hot and I know it' brand of sexuality. Open cleavages, skimpy stage costumes and suggestive dance moves abounded, all with the tease that – despite their sexual vigour – these girls were unavailable and giving up nothing until marriage.

Even the notoriously explicit Missy Elliot, co-producer of 'Bootylicious', had said she found the girls 'naughty'. There was a Lil' Kim-style mischief about their demeanour, along with an incongruently wholesome edge.

The group also seemed to have kept abreast of trends. Tellingly for an album that centred around love songs, Beyoncé had made the chance remark in an interview that "love never goes out of style".

Plus, at the time of recording, none of the girls were in official relationships and all three would claim they had never been in love, which made the heartfelt sentiments expressed in half a dozen of the songs that bit more surprising – or, in cynics' eyes, suspicious.

Some critics saw the girls as remote-control dolls at the mercy of Mathew and his musical empire, while others saw the girls as fully in collusion with a plan to manufacture themselves for maximum profit, pointing out Beyoncé's goal for them to be "the biggest-selling female group ever".

Whether Destiny's Child was speaking from the heart or not, whether they were their own women or not, most fans agreed on one thing – the material was superb.

Aside from the two versions of 'Independent Women', there were the love songs. 'Sexy Daddy' addresses a man picked out at a club whom the girls prophetically describe as the father of their child. 'Apple Pie A La Mode' describes a man so handsome he has the girls' bodies consumed by lust. Then the intensity steps up a notch with 'My Heart Still Beats', a solo performance by Beyoncé where she gushes that her lover's face resembles the sun, his kiss touches her soul and – as long as he never lets go of her – her heart still beats.

In the same passionate vein, 'Dangerously In Love' was one Beyoncé liked so much she would later adapt it to re-use for her first solo album. 'Perfect Man' and 'Brown Eyes' are idealistic dedications to finding "the one", while the last love song is 'Emotion', originally penned by the Bee Gees in the Seventies for Samantha Sang.

It was one of the group's few ballads and was significant in that Kelly sang lead vocals on the first verse and bridge. She had been terrified of not living up to the song's original glory, telling VH1: "You're always scared to do cover songs because the artists, they're legends. The Bee Gees are legends and we just wanted to do it right."

Beyoncé concurred, "If [cover songs] are not as good, then you shouldn't even waste your time… instead of trying to compete, we did it differently and added our Destiny's Child flavour to it. Vocally, it's the strongest song on our album." In fact, when Bee Gees member Maurice Gibb heard it, he reached out by saying he loved the version – not a wasted effort after all.

Meanwhile 'The Story Of Beauty' featured a girl the group once received a letter from and retells her hate-filled confessions of being molested by her stepfather as a child. No-one believed that she had been abused, instead thinking that she was trying to avenge her tormentor for replacing her father and becoming competition for her mother's affections. Not having a confidante increased the girl's isolation and, touchingly for the group, led her to seek sanctuary in Destiny's Child songs. In adult life, she fell in love with an equally abusive man who mirrored the cruelty of her stepfather and her self-esteem plummeted as she felt that all she had to offer was her body.

The song sweeps away her shame by assuring her she wasn't to blame and giving her a promise that – through prayer and the fortitude it brings – she can survive the inner torment and come out smiling. "[The letter said] hearing our songs kept her going," Beyoncé recalled proudly to *The Times*. "That inspired me. Young girls look up to us and we feel a responsibility to them. We are saying that, whatever happens, you should hold your head up and be proud."

Other songs on a survival theme included 'Happy Face', which reminded the girls of their blessings on the days that they felt down. The group resolve to see the world through a child's eyes, getting excited about the little things that they normally take for granted. The song also realises the golden rule of showbiz – that everyone in the public eye, no matter how many million fans they have, will always encounter haters. To survive this, the group remind themselves that for every person that dislikes them or scorns them in the media, there's another one who genuinely cares, which makes it all worthwhile.

The song was particularly relevant following the line-up changes in the group and the media scandal that surrounded them. "You read something [in the press], you hear something crazy and you get sad and depressed," Beyoncé confided to VH1. "If someone didn't like me, it killed me. My whole thing was to wonder why and to fix it. When someone makes up something, it really hurts and I'm very sensitive. That's why I went through a depression after the line-up changes... [Then] one day I woke up and it was a beautiful day outside and I was like, 'You know, I can feel God. I'm happy and I'm blessed,'"

As for Kelly, she would later remark that jealousy was impossible to fix and that the happiest face she had ever worn was while performing. In honour of that, the group donned customised denim shorts and boob tubes with the words "happy face" emblazoned across them for part of their 2001 tour.

Another song that discreetly seems to refer to the group's line-up changes is 'Fancy'. The lyrics talk of a girl who tries to steal the group's shine – someone who competes rather than collaborates and favours rivalry over friendship. The reference to a girl who wastes her time flirting with boys could have been directed at LeToya and LaTavia while the reference to someone who's lying could have been about the legal drama that the pair had started. In media interviews, the group talked of previous members in terms of their "competitive instinct" and attempts to "take advantage" – both themes which appear in the song.

Combining deeply emotive love songs with ruthless feminist anthems, *Survivor* was undoubtedly an album of contrasts and extremes – but which songs showcased the real Destiny's Child? Perhaps the most authentic and personal was the title track, directly reflecting what the group had been through in the months leading up to the album's release.

There had been regular taunts about the constantly rotating musical chairs effect of the group's line-up. Then, Beyoncé heard a radio DJ joke, "Why is Destiny's Child like the *Survivor* TV show? Because you never know which member will get voted off the island next." She was inspired by her anger.

"It was creative, it was clever," Beyoncé claimed to *The Birmingham Post*. "But I was like, 'If I hear one more joke, I'm happy that that mean radio station said that little funky comment, because it inspired a song. Got anything else to say?"

That DJ may well have been eating his words when Destiny's Child hit the world's TV screens on location from a remote island in the South Pacific. They weren't exactly the most obvious victims either – instead of looking hungry, dishevelled and exhausted, they were dancing jubilantly in the ocean. Plus there were no signs of having been stranded or near starvation – unless looking trim and toned in their swimwear counted.

Kelly switched from a bright red salsa outfit to khaki military wear and danced in front of a Mayan temple before surviving through a lightning storm to reach the shore. All three were precariously piled into an inflatable rubber ring but, as they flagged down a plane overhead and rushed to safety, there was barely a hair out of place. The message was clear – no matter how many line-up changes or moments of adversity life could throw at them, the girls were promising to come through it unscathed.

"Even if we had to go through 20 line-up changes, we would do it!" Kelly declared defiantly, "because it would be what [God] wants. We don't control our careers. He does!"

Two people who didn't feel the same were LeToya and LaTavia. They had dropped their earlier lawsuit under the condition that neither party would speak negatively of each other. However, they interpreted the lyrics of 'Survivor' as a breach of that agreement.

Former vocal coach David Lee Brewer agreed, telling *Sister 2 Sister*, "I don't think it's fair that people would say negative things about them in trying to destroy their chances of having a career." Ominously, he added, "I was there from the beginning and I know who I am dealing with."

However, Beyoncé vigorously denied that the lyrics were directed at their former bandmates, claiming that they were a general war cry against adversity. "'Survivor' is about our whole struggle and where we've got to now," Beyoncé told *The Birmingham Post*. "We were so young when we were trying to get a record deal and we couldn't. Then when we did get our first record deal, we were dropped and had to start all over again. There have been a lot of people in our lives that thought we were crazy to try and make it in such a tough business. They really put us down and pretty much told us to give up. Basically, everybody has things they have to survive."

Kelly, on the other hand, confessed that – while exiled singers weren't number one on her hit list – they were included. "'Survivor' is a message to everybody," she announced to MTV. "Right from the record label who dropped us when we were young to the people who made fun of us having big dreams when we were in the fifth grade – and to the group members who let us down. All the haters have contributed to our success."

They'd certainly been successful. 'Survivor' had made it to number one in several countries, including the UK and Japan. Was LeToya and LaTavia's lawsuit based on a legitimate concern that they had been slandered, or was it a case of sour grapes that the group had only become more successful since they had left?

Intriguingly, the pair announced within days of filing their lawsuit that they had formed a new girl band called Anjel. Cynics might have argued that the two had a well-timed publicity campaign in mind – but if that was the intention, it failed. Anjel received very few record sales and little media attention and disbanded soon afterwards.

Even more controversially for Destiny's Child, the following year they would be hit by another lawsuit relating to 'Survivor'. Beyoncé had insisted she wrote the song herself "in five minutes" in an attempt to "write us out of all the negativity" – but little-known producer Terrence "T-Robb" Robinson begged to differ.

According to him, it was strikingly similar both lyrically and melodically to a song he submitted to Mathew while the group was making the album, but he had been neither credited nor paid for what he claimed was unauthorised use of his work. Embarrassingly for Beyoncé, it wouldn't be the last time she was accused of copyright infringement or theft.

However, either way, the two longest-reigning members of the group had conquered adversity time and time again – and Kelly had proved that on a personal level by returning to the stage after breaking two of her toes.

In October 2000, while the group was supporting Christina Aguilera, Kelly found herself racing backstage to change her clothes in total darkness. As she desperately tried to follow the sound of her soul sisters' footsteps, she ran into something with a sickening thud. "Our costume-changing booth was so far away from the stage, it was hazardous," Beyoncé sympathised to *Teen*. "Kelly was running full speed and it was dark and she ran into a ramp right in the middle of our performance. We heard her screaming and crying and we were like, 'Oh my God, she really hurt herself!'"

Beyoncé looked on in horror as Kelly, who had sunk to the floor in agony, tried to squeeze her swollen toes – which by now were bruised bright purple – back into her four-inch stiletto heels. It was impossible.

As much as she wanted to get back out there for the encore – her favourite part of the show – she was rushed to hospital instead, where the bad news was confirmed. For the remainder of the tour, Kelly would pass over the more strenuous dance routines to Beyoncé's sister, Solange. Some might say that Kelly's keenness to get back on the stage was a message to LeToya, LaTavia and Farrah about what really constituted being 'sick'.

By the time 'Bootylicious', the group's third single from *Survivor*, was filmed, Kelly was well and truly back on her feet. It was just as well, because the video featured the girls doing the distinctive 'booty dance' that would become synonymous with Beyoncé's name. A slim-line Kelly struggled to master it as she wasn't quite as curvaceous as the other two – she often complained about her flat bottom and the "tiny nuggets" she had for breasts – but the message was that anyone could do it.

To prove that, the video featured a variety of women, including plus-size girls, strutting their stuff – indicating that sexuality came from within and was as much to do with inner confidence as it was with attaining the 'perfect' body type.

Soon after the single debuted on May 20, it seemed that Destiny's Child had sparked a trend. Women in nightclubs everywhere, from the US to the dance's spiritual home, Africa, were trying to perfect the simultaneous hip-swivel and jelly-jiggle they had seen on TV.

"That dance is in our souls," Beyoncé joked to *The Sunday Times*, "but for some reason when I did it, it became a Beyoncé booty dance!"

Not only that, but the term "bootylicious" then earnt its place in the Oxford English Dictionary, with a definition of "very sexually attractive". Technically, Destiny's Child hadn't created the term – it had first been used to describe someone's "rhymes" in a Snoop Dogg rap on the 1992 Dr Dre single 'Fuck Wit Dre Day'. However, it was Destiny's Child who had made it fashionable.

On June 19, 2001, Destiny's Child opened the first ever BET Awards – created to celebrate the best in black entertainment – with the track, which prompted Michael Jackson of all people to start singing along. According to the group, who met him afterwards, "He definitely knew what bootylicious meant!"

Meanwhile the video had paid homage to many of his dance moves, most notably from his 'Billie Jean' video. It also featured a brief cameo from Stevie Nicks, the performer whose guitar riff had been used, and Beyoncé's sister, Solange. That wouldn't be the only version of the video either – a bootleg combining 'Bootylicious' with the music from Nirvana's 'Smells Like Teen Spirit' would also hit the airwaves afterwards.

There was plenty of praise in store for the song – which many believed promoted body confidence and rearranged not just dictionaries but also people's understanding of what it meant to look and feel desirable. However, it also sparked criticism. For example, many felt it was an inappropriately demonstrative display of sexuality from a group of girls who marketed themselves as modest Christians and as teenage role-models.

However, Beyoncé had an answer to that. "I'm so proud," she told the *Daily Mail*. "We showed that we could carry ourselves as powerful women. Some people thought 'Bootylicious' was about being sexy, but it was more about having confidence in your own skin."

There was one criticism, however, that would prove more difficult to shake off: another drama about who'd written the song. Beyoncé had told VH1 she wrote it after having a brainwave on a plane, claiming: "We were bored on this long flight to London and I started listening to this Stevie Nicks track, 'Edge Of Seventeen', and I'm like, 'This is hot!' The word bootylicious just popped in my head. I was ashamed to tell Kelly and Michelle because I didn't know what they were going to think."

Co-producer Rob Fusari was upset when he heard her seemingly take credit for the song, telling *Billboard* that he had had the idea for the track, written it and later replaced the original guitar riff he had intended to use with the Stevie Nicks one. According to him, when he complained to Mathew, he'd been told, "People don't want to hear about Rob Fusari, producer from Livingstone, New Jersey... That's not what sells records."

The next single, 'Emotion' – released on November 13, 2001 – was the group's first ballad single and revealed a softer side to the girls. Instead of being cold-hearted independent women, survivors on the warpath who saved themselves with military precision or bootylicious sex sirens with formidable confidence, they're wrapped up in sorrow and begging a partner to come back to them. The video ends with all three embracing each other. In fact, the song became an anthem for victims and survivors of the September 11 terrorist attacks that year, due to its emphasis on love and unity.

On a happier note, 'Emotion' was shortly followed by a holiday album, *8 Days Of Christmas*. Its title track – adapted from the carol *The Twelve Days Of Christmas*, is a festive song with a difference. Instead of the traditional gifts of the original rhyme such as a partridge in a pear tree, the girls' true loves are offering up marriages, designer clothes and diamonds.

While a bemused shopkeeper looks on, the video sees Destiny's Child storm a department store dressed in Santa outfits, loading their trolleys with festive goodies. Light-hearted and materialistic, it didn't exactly market the true, more spiritual meaning of Christmas, but it was just what shell-shocked Americans needed after the terrorist attacks of the late summer.

The group's fifth album, *This Is The Remix*, came just months later in March 2002 and reached number 29 in the US charts, an almost unheard of achievement for a CD compiled entirely of remixes.

The following month, the group's fifth and final single from *Survivor* was released – 'Nasty Girl'. Featuring a stomping beat based on glimpses of Salt 'N' Pepa's 'Push It' and Baltimore's 'Tarzan Boy', it was another successful chart hit – Destiny's Child had brought two Eighties tracks right into the 21st century. However, any track even faintly associated with Salt 'N' Pepa wasn't exactly going to be squeaky clean.

Like 'Bootylicious' before it, the song sparked its fair share of controversy. *The Evening Standard*, for example, quizzed: "Surely [condemning women who wear tarty clothes] is outrageously hypocritical, coming from a girl group who wear thigh-skimming micro-minis and bra tops in every video?"

After a brief but uncomfortable silence, with Michelle sporting a frown, the girls answered. According to Beyoncé, the song was "about a tramp" and there was a big difference between "looking sexy and being plain trashy". Kelly chimed in: "I never wear hotpants and stuff unless I'm on stage or in a video. I'd never walk down the street like that."

Some onlookers, however, might argue that this made little difference. Walk down the street in a skimpy outfit and just a few passers-by in your hometown catch a glimpse of the goodies, but do the same thing on the front page of a music magazine or live on MTV and it's public property for the entire nation.

In some people's eyes, dressing demurely in public after being plastered on billboard adverts in just a bikini was akin to closing the stable door after the horse had bolted. Meanwhile those in opposition to the girls' liberal dress sense pointed to other Christian artists such as India Arie who, through her lyrics, prided herself on valuing her voice and mind over her body, and dressed conservatively on screen.

However, the girls contested that their local church's pastor, Rudy Rasmus – the reformed owner of a motel catering to prostitutes – had approved the way they looked. What was more, they argued that – provided they acted like young ladies – what they wore on the outside was immaterial.

"A woman can cover herself from head to toe and still be the biggest slut in town," Kelly asserted. "It's all about the way you carry yourself. Destiny's Child doesn't go over the top. When we're in concert, some people say, 'Oh my God, they have no clothes on!' But sweetie, as long as we're not coming on stage naked, people shouldn't complain."

The closest Kelly ever came to appearing in the nude was an embarrassing onstage moment when a front-to-back zip on her trousers came undone during a dance move and she ended up "showing the band my butt". Bootylicious as charged!

The murmurs about 'Nasty Girl' had only just died down when it was time for another big announcement that would keep Destiny's Child on everyone's lips: the girls, while not splitting up, would be temporarily disbanding to focus on solo projects. It was an opportunity for the trio to introduce themselves as individuals with three distinct musical personalities.

"Being solo I get a chance to try things Beyoncé and Michelle wouldn't have wanted to try," Kelly confessed to *Blues & Soul*. "In Destiny's Child we could only express ourselves one way – as Destiny's Child."

Yet Michelle had a passion for gospel and choir-influenced music – reminiscent of her school days spent singing in church – and Beyoncé was obsessed with mainstream pop. That left Kelly, who – confounding everyone's expectations – wanted to mix the soul rhythms of Sade with alternative music and a touch of hard rock.

It made sense for the girls to go solo to showcase their separate styles before coming back together again as a three-piece afterwards.

Prior to recording her solo début, however, Kelly had already stepped out as an individual in her own right by beginning her career as a TV actress. On April 13, 2002, she appeared on the TV drama *Taina* for one episode, 'Starstruck'. Kelly played a misunderstood actress, Nicole, who attends the same university as Taina – the star of the show. When she arrives, she is shunned by her fellow students who believe the rumours that she's snobby, selfish and mean, without getting to know the real her. When they finally do set aside their preconceptions and spend time with her, they discover she's nothing like they thought.

The plot turned out to be a fitting metaphor for the journey Kelly and Beyoncé were about to embark on. For Beyoncé, the challenge would be proving to the public she was no diva, didn't have a monumentally huge ego and wasn't trying to eclipse the other girls in Destiny's Child. Meanwhile for Kelly the emphasis would be on reversing the perception that she was nothing more than a backing singer for Beyoncé, destined to remain in the background unnoticed.

The following month, she hit the big screen again for the two-part series finale of TV drama *The Hughleys*. Kelly secured the part – again playing a college student – via an invitation from executive producer Chris Rock, whom she worked with on the soundtrack to his movie *Down To Earth*. In reality, while, at 21, Kelly was the perfect age to play a university girl, most of her peers would have only just graduated and might be looking to upgrade their poorly paid part-time jobs in a bar or a restaurant. Few would claim several number one singles and a place in one of the biggest girl groups in musical history. In that sense, portraying an average 21-year-old student would be just that for Kelly – acting.

There was little publicity about her appearance in the shows beforehand, leaving bemused fans to take to the internet, querying, "Was that Kelly Rowland I just saw on my screen?"

Although reviews were for the most part overwhelmingly positive, a fresh scandal would interrupt the start of Kelly's solo career when she found herself part of a very public and deeply embarrassing legal dispute. Mathew Knowles stood accused of stealing $32 million from the estate of the late Andretta Tillman, who had co-managed Destiny's Child from the start until her death in 1997.

The allegations were that the formerly squeaky clean Mathew hadn't just been managing Destiny's Child – but a string of prostitutes too. Andretta's two sons, then aged 18 and 21, were requesting payment and claiming that Mathew squandered the money owed to them on class A drugs and parties with hookers. While he immediately denied the financial charges against him, he did admit previous drug and sex addictions, defiantly insisting to *Star* magazine that he was "not ashamed".

"My wife, Tina, and I had some real problems with our marriage and I was having some affairs at the time," he confessed. "I went to a treatment facility in 1992 and they didn't have a real definition for my marital infidelities. But if you did a little alcohol or drugs it was all lumped together as substance abuse related. In 1998, when I was treated a second time, they had a more defined definition of sex addiction, but sex addiction has such a broad range. My treatment was regarding my continued extra-marital affairs."

According to the lawsuit, his "uncontrollable addictions" to sex and cocaine had impeded his ability to manage the group, but he had kept the extent of his problems a secret from Andretta. The lawsuit also accused him not only of "solicitation and/or marketing of prostitutes" – implying that he was involved with selling their services as well – but also of "arranging sex parties".

Tina dismissed the claims, arguing, "He'd be dead if he spent $32 million on drugs and sex. My husband works 16 hours a day. I don't know when he'd have the time."

Regardless of the truth, the revelations were badly timed at best – because, that very same month Kelly was releasing her debut single, 'Dilemma'. Her two bandmates had already found solo success – Michelle's début album, *Heart To Yours*, had made it to number one on America's gospel charts, while Beyoncé was a hit on the silver screen, starring in box-office smash *Goldmember,* the third of Mike Myers' Austin Powers comedies – and Kelly was expected to follow suit. However, without the safety of the other girls to hide behind, a nervous Kelly had been dragging her feet – until the decision was taken out of her hands.

Rap superstar Nelly had been listening to the music from vintage love song 'I Love, Need And Want You' by Seventies songstress Patti LaBelle, which he intended to sample on his second album, *Nellyville*. However, there was one thing missing – a female vocal.

The song would be a departure from his trademark style in many ways. His usual songs were profanity-laced raps about wealth and women, delivered in his videos with a gold-toothed grin. He was an archetypal player and Nelly's fans bought into his man-about-town reputation. Previous video 'Hot In Herre' had featured a room full of nearly naked women writhing around underneath a shower with him – and it had gone straight to number one. It seemed as though listeners got a voyeuristic thrill out of his tales of living the high life.

However, Nelly was looking to take a risk and change the winning formula with 'Dilemma', a *Romeo And Juliet*-style love story about falling for someone and fighting temptation. The female lead is an attached woman with a husband, a child and enough baggage to singlehandedly occupy Heathrow Airport's workforce. She longs for infidelity with the eye-catching boy from across the street, while Nelly describes himself as a neighbour who is unwilling to break up her happy home – hence the pair's dilemma. Nelly's 'Hot In Herre' alter ego, on the other hand, wouldn't have thought twice.

Not only was Nelly changing his reputation, but the woman who would star alongside him had two different sides too. The obvious choice for collaboration was, of course, Beyoncé, who ranked more highly in the popularity stakes. Up to that moment, unless they had an honours degree in R&B, most music fans would probably have met talk of Ms Rowland with blank stares and the bemused retort, "Which one is Kelly?"

Nelly, however, wanted to do something unexpected and picked the underdog – little did either of them know they were about to record the number one single in America. He and Kelly had moved in the same showbiz circles for a couple of years and chemistry was fast developing between her and one of his closest friends, so he already knew her well.

The pair took to the studio, where Kelly gained a reputation as a perfectionist by repeatedly re-recording her vocal, before sending the finished track to Mathew for his approval. Kelly was on tenterhooks to hear his reaction, but she needn't have worried. "I said immediately, 'This is a number one song'," Mathew explained to MTV. "And Destiny's Child has had seven number ones so I know one when I hear one!"

Mathew was right – it reached the top spot so fast that the pair hadn't even had time to record a video. In fact, it hadn't originally been intended as a single at all, but radio stations had other ideas, seizing on the track after receiving advance copies of Nelly's album – and it soon went viral.

It was an inviting prospect for music fans – Nelly, the hottest rapper to hit the charts that year, abandoning his womanising streak to get with God-fearing girl-next-door Kelly, who stars as the unintentional seductress. It wasn't often that listeners rather than the record label dictated which songs would become singles but, on July 30, 2002, the pair bowed to public demand and officially released the single – by which point Nelly's former effort 'Hot In Herre' hadn't even reached its peak.

A video followed, which was filmed at the back of Universal Studios, sharing its location with the TV series *Desperate Housewives*. It saw Kelly channel the girl-next-door vibe in casual denim jeans and a cropped haircut. The pair's relationship is at first confined to snatching longing glances at each other over the garden fence or wistfully thinking that they see one another in local stores. As time passes, the pair grow closer and night-time dances and declarations of love follow, much to the horror of those in Kelly's life. Basketball star Larry Hughes of the Washington Wizards played Kelly's possessive partner, while Patti LaBelle played the role of her mother, hollering at Kelly to stay away from her illicit love interest and come back into the house.

Patti was a Nelly fan, joking that 'Hot In Herre' matched the hot flushes phase of her menopause – perhaps not what a lustful Nelly had meant when he sang the chorus, urging any nearby women in the vicinity to take off their clothes. Meanwhile Kelly had been terrified that she wouldn't live up to the expectations of the original song's owner; but, as it turned out, Patti also instantly loved Kelly. "I was so happy to hear them use my song, I jumped for joy," she confessed to MTV, before adding: "I recorded that song before either of them were born and Kelly is such a sweet person that I would welcome her into my heart and my home. Actually if I ever had a daughter, I would envision Kelly."

The affection was mutual. "I started crying," Kelly exclaimed, "because there's nothing like hearing that the artist who originally did the song likes your version."

It wasn't just Patti who liked it either – in less than two months, it knocked 'Hot In Herre' off the top spot, giving Nelly his second consecutive number one from the album and Kelly her first number one as a solo artist. "Beyoncé had the number one movie, Michelle had the number one gospel album and I had the number one single!" she told MTV. "You couldn't ask for anything more."

What was more, when she made it to the top spot, Beyoncé was the first person to call and congratulate her. However, the unprecedented success of the song brought on a real-life dilemma. Beyoncé was the first child destined to release a solo CD, with her first album due out in the autumn of 2002 and Kelly's scheduled to follow up to a year later.

However, 'Dilemma' – once a last-minute addition, modestly tucked away on a Nelly album, now an international chart topper – had changed everything. Now that Kelly's name was on everyone's lips, it made sense to strike while the iron was hot, capitalise on the hype and bring forward her own solo album.

Mathew decided that the two girls should switch places. If this caused flickers of irritation for Beyoncé, that was nothing compared to how Kelly would feel when she was forced to record her debut album on her own in a matter of weeks. She was accustomed to peeking out from behind Beyoncé's shadow or watching from the sidelines as she scaled greater heights – in fact, she enjoyed having someone to hide behind who could cushion her from the blows of showbiz.

Kelly was shy and didn't see herself as a leader, so – as long as she was fulfilling her passion for singing – the arrangement suited her. However, circumstances dictated that it was now her turn to take the reins – and she was terrified.

"I was the first one from the group to have that level of success outside the group – that bugged me out," Kelly told *Blues & Soul*. "I wasn't ready... They gave me 90 days to do an entire record."

While the media speculated that she and her bandmates would be fighting like cats and dogs for the number one spot and musical supremacy, all sisterly bonds forgotten, in reality Kelly was turning to her girls for support. "I remember calling and telling them that I missed them," she confessed to *Jet*. "When I was in the studio, I remember times I couldn't get through the sessions without being frustrated. The girls would calm me down every time a situation like that would occur and tell me everything is going to be OK. They would pray with me and give me words of encouragement and I got through because of them. This time I had to depend on myself."

Kelly also felt the pressure of branching out into a new musical genre. Now that all eyes were on her and she was standing alone, the onus was on her to show listeners her individual personality – and that meant taking a risk with a tinge of rock. "I'm sure most of my fans didn't realise how much I have always loved rock," Kelly confessed to *Jet*. "What I am doing has a little bit of edge to it. I call it R&B with an edge."

She added, "I put all of my influences on the album – R&B to hip-hop to rock to Sade. I put Sade in a category all of her own. I remember talking to the producers and telling them what I wanted and they must have looked at me as if I was crazy, because I gave them four different sounds and they said, 'How are you going to put four different sounds in a song?' And honestly, about halfway through the recording process, even I was wondering if you could mix those influences together."

Fortunately, she had some of the best producers in the business to guide her through the process, including Mathew, who was the album's executive producer.

One of the more unusual writers on the album was Beyoncé's 16-year-old sister, Solange. Amid a team of experienced producers with a string of number one hits under their belts, Kelly was a little dubious about working with someone she saw as her little sister. What did Solange know about love, loss and heartbreak? Despite being several years older, even Kelly had never written before – so could Solange really fit the bill?

Once they started, she was pleasantly surprised, describing her as very similar to Beyoncé, but more mature and intense than she had been at her age. "Solange is an incredible writer," Kelly told MTV. "It's so hard to think she's 16 years old. To write about love and so many things I'm talking about on the album, it blew me away. I'm like, 'What are you thinking? I can't even think that way.'" It might have been a sore point for Kelly – because, as yet, she had never experienced falling in love.

Perhaps the reason her heart remained closed was down to the early loss of her father, something which the pair tackled in the first track they worked on together, 'Beyond Imagination'. "I talk about growing up without a father and me and my mother struggling," Kelly revealed. "I told [Solange] exactly what I wanted it to be like. I wanted people to feel the pain that I felt living in a broken home. You can hear it in the vocals. We were all crying in the studio session, it was really emotional."

The track starts out like a traditional R&B ballad – albeit a downtempo one – with nods to En Vogue, but it soon becomes clear this could never be a Destiny's Child song. After the second chorus, Kelly abandons her inhibitions and lets the pain come pouring out, unleashing both her anger at her father's absence and the secret rock side her fans knew nothing about.

Her newly mature vocals gave a nod to Alanis Morissette, Kelly Clarkson and early Avril Lavigne. However, as Kelly grew up on a diet of super-size soul songs by the likes of Whitney Houston, the result is an interesting marriage of R&B and soul and soft-rock influences.

Lyrically the song has similar sentiments to Massive Attack's 'Unfinished Symphony', where the singer laments that she's in a body without a heart and is missing every part – Kelly, on the other hand, feels incomplete without the love of both parents.

Her father's absence not only left a void, but it was also a recipe for a childhood where she constantly felt her classmates were pointing and laughing. Kelly felt conspicuous when she had to announce to a crowd of curious – and sometimes knowingly cruel – children that she didn't know why her father hadn't made it to the school sports day or the parents' evening – or even where he was.

Kelly became the object of ridicule, the school joke – not only was she virtually the only black girl, but she was the only girl whose father wasn't, at the very least, on the other end of a phone line. All the way up to adulthood, she had kept the pain in, as she hadn't wanted to trouble her mother by broaching the subject.

"I had so many questions about my dad that I wanted to ask my mom – like, for starters, 'Mama, why did he leave?'" Kelly clarified, "but I didn't. When I was younger, I never wanted to ask her because I didn't want to upset her."

This song was her way of exorcising the pain of those unanswered questions. As the words suggest, a younger Kelly had felt obliged to be her own comforter and psychiatrist, but then singing became a healing tool, something that took her to a place where she could be free of the pain.

As the main lyricist, Solange acted as the therapist, interpreting Kelly's angst and putting it into words for her. That was what made her solo material different from performing with Destiny's Child. Previously she had sung tracks other people had written and had been the soundtrack to someone else's life story, her only contribution a beautiful voice. Now, however, the words she was singing were a window to her soul – and, with 'Beyond Imagination', she was giving her fans an access-all-areas pass into her heart.

Solange also co-wrote 'Obsession', a production-heavy track about an intoxicating, all-consuming love affair from the point of view of someone inexperienced who knew only too well the effects of a school-girl crush, but had never actually been obsessed – until now.

Finally, Solange also co-wrote the title track, 'Simply Deep', a gentle ballad about a lover's heart. Solange not only contributed lyrics, but she also joined Kelly on vocals, where the pair's harmonies on the chorus had strong elements of a Seal single.

With Solange on vocals, Mathew on production duties and a team of writers including those who loomed large on Destiny's Child's albums, on paper Kelly's project seemed to have all the ingredients for a CD that was merely Destiny's Child Mark 2. But anyone expecting the album to be predictable was in for a big surprise.

Sound wise, it was an obvious departure from the group. While 'Haven't Told You' was a slow, intense, confessional song about leaving her heart in someone's hands, 'Can't Nobody' confounded listeners' expectations that the album would be full of slow jams by countering them with a throbbing bass-line and a club classic beat.

Although Kelly's message is a shamelessly immodest warning to a partner that she's irreplaceable and that no other woman he meets will be capable of filling her shoes, it could just as easily have been a metaphor for her new album, telling fans that no-one else hits the same spots musically, that the solo project is sure to be unique.

In proof of that, 'Love/Hate' sees Kelly become a trendsetter. Before then, there had been very few tracks in the charts that captured the frustration of being desperately in love with someone, but at the same time hating them too – the "can't-live-with-or-without-you" syndrome. But 'Love/Hate' would be followed by both Amerie's 2007 track 'Hate To Love You', and Rihanna's collaboration with Ne-Yo, 'Hate That I Love You'. Who would have thought the "quiet one" from Destiny's Child would turn out to be so influential?

Kelly puts her aim to go where no-one has gone before into words on 'Train On A Track', where her talk of exploring previously uncharted territory acts as a metaphor for branching out on her own as a solo artist. The melding of multiple influences on the album sees her dare to be different and try to breathe underwater. For a petrified Kelly, the musical roles she was taking were akin to diving without oxygen or bungee jumping without a harness, but it seemed to have paid off.

Conveniently placed towards the end of the album, 'Train On A Track' leaves listeners wondering where Kelly's fast-moving musical train will take her next.

The slow jam 'Coincidence' is a love song pairing metaphors of crashed cars with similarly self-destructive emotional symptoms, while 'Every Time You Walk Out That Door' is a ballad of sadness and longing about someone irreplaceable who is long since gone, leaving just an empty chair behind to remind her of him.

The song shares its theme of love, loss and heartbreak with the Bill Withers track 'Ain't No Sunshine' – one of the songs Kelly had performed when she first auditioned for Columbia Records as part of Destiny's Child.

Poignantly, the lyrics – which saw Kelly lament that, although she could live without her mystery man, he can turn darkness into light and winter into summer and make her life much better – could just as easily have referred to her fractured family situation of growing up without a father.

However, now all of the tracks truly represented Kelly. 'Past 12', for example – which was a nod to 'Jumpin' Jumpin'', spoke about bottles getting popped and a party getting 'crunk', even though in reality Kelly was teetotal. That said, Kelly redressed the balance and found her own voice in the three songs that she co-wrote.

At first, her fear of failure had been so intense that she found herself "too scared to even try" writing. However, this was her chance to step away from her reputation as merely a cute girl who could sing and show her fans that she was a competent songwriter as well. The desire to do that helped her break through the fear barrier.

"Beyoncé really encouraged me and told me I could do it," Kelly recalled to MTV. "I was nervous, but when I was working on my album, I collaborated with the other writers and they really gave me the courage and tools to put my thoughts on paper."

One such track, '[Love Lives In] Strange Places', is a tale of a woman who's always been unlucky in love but then finds romance in unexpected ways. Initially dismissing one love interest as not her type, she plays it cool, until he eventually finds the love within her she had tried to suppress. This mirrored Kelly's own attitude to love: despite being one of the music world's highest earners, she was down to earth enough even to date a plumber.

"If I meet a plumber that makes me feel incredible in the way that everybody talks about in a song then hey, that's what happens," she told *The Daily Record*. "I don't think people should just like somebody for what they do. That don't matter to me, because if they can love you the way you feel you want to be loved, then that's all that counts."

Kelly might not expect a nation of workmen on meagre wages to surround her doorstep, simultaneously wolf-whistling and praying that one of them was 'the one' for her. However, Kelly was in no hurry. As she said in the song, she couldn't control fate and would leave finding love down to her faith – and that reflected her real-life opinions, too. "I'm leaving romance to God," she'd insisted. "He'll find a man for me when the time is right."

Meanwhile '[Love Lives In] Strange Places' also bore a striking resemblance to a later Destiny's Child track, 'Girl' – which was rumoured to have been an unused leftover from *Simply Deep* that made its way onto the subsequent Destiny's Child album, *Destiny Fulfilled*. If so, that indicated that Kelly was no longer just being dictated to by Beyoncé or Mathew, but that she too had an influence on the group.

She also co-wrote 'Make You Wanna Stay', which featured guest vocals from rapper Joe Budden and saw Kelly play a fantasy role. No longer the shy and retiring southern belle she seemed to be in her own life – the one who insisted she would never dare approach a man – she was playing a straight-talking seductress who demands an instant meeting with a man on the phone. Taking the lead, she reveals she wants to take their flirtation much further and make him hers.

Finally, she co-wrote 'Heaven' – a blast from the past as it was co-produced by Alonzo Jackson, who'd worked with Destiny's Child in the Girl's Tyme days. However, Kelly was about to show just why, as a grown woman, she was so different to how she had been all those years before.

For a start, after all the talking, she had finally fallen in love. Other album tracks had been a challenge for her, because – as a love virgin – she hadn't been able to relate to emotions that even 16-year-old Solange knew all about. Aside from archetypal schoolgirl crushes, the concept of true infatuation was still alien to Kelly – something even she had been incredulous about when she agonised, "I feel I have accomplished so much – I just want love!"

Indeed, she was ahead of most of her peers in everything else – so love seemed to be the only thing she hadn't accomplished. In fact, she'd even admitted to *The Daily Record* that her songs were "based on what I picture love to be like", rather than from genuine experience.

Yet, as the album sessions drew to a close, things were changing and Kelly's relationship with a mystery friend of Nelly's was deepening. Ironically, the world's gossip columnists were speculating that she was getting it on with Nelly, little imagining that she was dating not him but one of his friends.

Kelly had already warned that love lives in strange places – and 'Heaven' was dedicated to her new man. "I'd never been in love and then I met someone and he made me feel like heaven," she explained. "This song is an expression of those feelings."

Recording her solo album saw Kelly achieve two of her greatest ambitions. Firstly, she learned what love felt like. Secondly, she had found a voice outside of the group. "I wanted people to be able to see me as me," she revealed, "not just as that girl from Destiny's Child."

While parts of *Simply Deep* acknowledged her roots in the group – for example, 'Make You Wanna Stay' was a musical nod to 'With Me' – she also had slow and sultry soul diva moments to rival Sade and some shouty vocals to accompany guitars playing rock chords. She was about to showcase all of the reasons why she had more strings to her bow than a mere R&B sideliner – and the BBC agreed.

Its review claimed: "[The album] highlights she is more than a mere backing vocalist for Beyoncé Knowles." Kelly's mission was accomplished – and it had made all the strife worthwhile.

"I remember how happy I was when we finished *The Writing's On The Wall* and *Survivor*," she told *Jet*. "I wanted to recapture that feeling when I made my own record and when I sat back and listened to the finished album, I felt so blessed. I thought, 'Gosh, God is good!' because I was allowed to see my vision through and it all worked out so well. Yes, I'm very happy."

Chapter 8

Cinderella Dreams

Kelly was soon back to work, but it wasn't quite business as usual – instead, she was letting out a blood-curdling scream that made unfortunate onlookers grimace and cover their ears in horror. It wasn't just a particularly bad studio session, nor did fans need to worry that her vocal chords had been replaced by those of a strangled cat. On the contrary, Kelly was crossing one of the last hurdles that stood between her and Beyoncé, by starring in her very first feature film.

She was determined not to fall prey to comparisons either. "I don't know why [people] would compare me to Beyoncé, because we're different," she defended to the *Daily Mail*. "The only thing that we will be doing is going from a singing career to an acting career and people do that every day. Jennifer Lopez has gone from an acting career to a singing career and Cher did it before her. Everybody does it, not just Beyoncé."

What was more, the pair's roles couldn't have been more different. Beyoncé had recently played the glamorous Foxy Cleopatra in *Goldmember*. But, while some might say acting 'shagadelic' wasn't a huge departure from Beyoncé's day job, Kelly had a slightly bigger challenge at hand.

She would be starring in the horror movie *Freddie vs Jason*. Brutal and bloodthirsty, the film sees innocent victims slashed to death with machetes or beheaded as two monsters return from hell – although older viewers might better remember them as characters in the *A Nightmare On Elm Street* and *Friday The 13th* series – to create a hell on earth and engage in the ultimate battle.

The two monsters, Freddy and Jason – played by Robert Englund and Ken Kirzinger respectively – are in competition to see who can kill the most victims and Freddy doesn't take kindly to his rival intruding on his territory.

Kelly played Kia, one of an innocent group of teenagers stalked by the pair in their dreams. Kia's role was to try to save her friends from Freddy's clutches, until she gets killed in the process.

At first it might have seemed that Kelly was a mismatch for the role – after all, she claimed to be a "scaredy-cat" who was too frightened even to watch Michael Jackson's 'Thriller' video, let alone a horror movie. "I have some serious psychological issues," she confessed to *The Daily Record*. "I used to peek from behind my door and close my eyes when the terrifying scenes [from a film] came on screen."

Her brother would torment her by re-enacting scenes from the movies, but he didn't have to try very hard – even so much as singing the theme tune to *Halloween* had her breaking out in a sweat. Not only that, but this wouldn't be Kelly's first encounter with Freddy: she had reluctantly watched all seven *A Nightmare on Elm Street* movies as a child. "When I used to go to bed at night, I'd think I could see Freddy above my head!" she recalled.

Her phobia meant she struggled even to research her part – when it came to watching the previous movies in the series again, she only managed one before switching it off halfway through in terror. It wasn't just the unlikely prospect of coming face to face with a machete-wielding monster that scared her either. She was faced with a terror greater than anything a fictional horror movie monster could induce – the very real fear of failure.

Faced with the pressure of being judged by strangers, Kelly was out of her comfort zone, so – on the first day of filming – she called Beyoncé and Michelle and burst into tears.

"We were on three-way," she recalled. "I was like, 'I'm terrified. I'm standing outside the door right now and I don't want to go in.' I was so scared because you've got Robert Englund, you've got all these people who have acted before and producers and directors and I'm thinking they're going to judge me. Beyoncé said, 'Breathe, pray and just go in there and do your thing. If they didn't want you, then you wouldn't have gotten the part, so just chill out!'"

Kelly obliged on one level by showing up on set, but chilling out was never going to happen. However, whilst being a self-confessed 'cry baby' might have made her a laughing stock in her schooldays – seeing her classmates sneer at her for dodging the more gory movies – on a horror-movie film set, being able to turn on the tears or portray wide-eyed fear on command was an advantage. "The director was like, 'Act scared, Kelly!'" she joked to *The Western Mail,* "and I was like, 'You don't have to worry. I'm already scared!'"

Yet while the terror was genuine, playing the rough, straight-talking Kia – a teenager with a "mean streak" – wasn't quite so easy. Just as the God-fearing Beyoncé had struggled to channel a manipulative seductress with passionate kissing scenes in the MTV-screened show *Carmen: A Hip Hopera,* even asking producers to tone her character down, Kelly's Christianity made it difficult for her to let loose the profanities.

Not only that, but she was face to face with Freddy, the man she had been petrified of for years. "It was kind of hard because I am talking to my childhood fear," Kelly explained. "Robert Englund really helped me through that scene. I was like, 'I don't know how to do it. I never cuss people out!' And he says, 'Cuss me out. Tell me I'm a punk. Tell me I'm stupid.' So it was fun."

Before too long, Kelly had even started channelling Kia in real life. "I hurt this lady's feelings," she continued. "This lady in a store, I think she told me something smart like, 'That skirt doesn't look right' and I said, 'And it would look better on you?' That was a Kia moment!"

The only part of the role Kelly stayed away from was the screaming. Her multi-million-dollar voice was the primary money-maker – and, for fear of damaging it, she only delivered her scream of terror once, leaving the producers to dub it for subsequent use. "I did one good scream, at least!" she joked.

Once filming was over, it was time to release her debut solo single, 'Stole' – a tale of opportunities thwarted and lives cut short. If Kelly's goal was to feature a deeper, more pensive side of herself than previously seen, she had succeeded. The velvety-voiced ballad, which contained hints of Sade and saw Kelly blinking back tears in the official video clip, seemed unusually intense for someone who just a year earlier had been on the world's TV screens boasting about her bootylicious body.

To some music fans, it was about as surprising as the time party-loving socialite Paris Hilton left jail pledging to give up alcohol and nightclubs for an extended visit to Africa on a charity mission. In reality, she was seen in a nightclub two weeks later, dirty dancing with a drink in her hand – and it wasn't long before she confessed she thought Africa was not a continent, but a country.

Kelly's transformation, on the other hand, came across to many of the public as more genuine, as though she was exposing a secret side of herself – perhaps one that being a Destiny's Child girl didn't allow scope for.

The video for 'Stole' portrays three separate tragedies. The first centres around the archetypal school geek – someone so unpopular that he sometimes isn't even deemed worthy of teasing. Quiet and socially isolated, he usually shrugs off his unpopularity by burying his head in a science book – until one day the fury of being rejected reaches fever pitch. To top things off, that morning at breakfast, he sees his mother crying at the kitchen table, a victim of domestic violence.

Unable to take any more, he slips off to school with his father's gun, intent on wreaking havoc on his tormentors at school before ending it all. He is determined that, no matter what, he won't die anonymous. With his story splashed all over primetime news, the geek gets his wish not to be invisible any more – but the cost of that much longed-for attention is his life.

His story echoes the Columbine shootings, where two Colorado schoolboys went on a killing spree, gunning down teachers and pupils alike before finally committing suicide. While the video doesn't show any direct violence, it does picture the boy ending his life in a bathroom, where a girl named Mary – who is clutching a pregnancy test in her hand – hears the gunshot and goes in to discover his body.

An aspiring actress, her dreams are cut short when she discovers she is carrying a baby. The camera zooms in on the Christian cross around her neck as if to remind viewers of the consequences of falling pregnant as an unmarried teenager from a religious family. The lyrics talk of putting her fingers in the imprints at Mann's Chinese Theatre Show – a reference to Grauman's Chinese Theatre in Hollywood. The hand-prints of celebrities are preserved there in cement, with Marilyn Monroe adding her imprints in 1953.

By singing that Mary had the same size hands, Kelly is using the metaphor that she could have slotted perfectly into the Hollywood scene and that her talent was substantial enough to fill the shoes – or, in this case, hand-prints – of the greats. Because of her unplanned pregnancy, however, it was not to be – according to Kelly, her life was stolen.

Finally, another wasted talent is revealed in the shape of Greg. A basketball player with dreams of competing professionally, he is shot dead by another student before he could make that a reality. A tearful Kelly looks on as Mary visits a memorial for the two dead students.

While the song highlighted the frustrating loss of potential, as onlookers would never know what the three could have achieved, it was a little controversial to suggest that a teenage mother's life might be over due to the birth of her baby.

Nevertheless, it was a thought-provoking video and – although 'Dilemma' hadn't shifted from the number one spot by the time it was released – the public soon warmed to it, and it peaked at number 12. As the album had been rushed out to capitalise on the success of 'Dilemma', 'Stole' hadn't been produced specifically for the album, but had instead been unearthed from a pile of demo-tapes at the Sony Music offices.

However the instinctive choice had clearly been a good one and, despite lacking input into the song's lyrics and meaning, Kelly had made it her own when she wore a T-shirt to the video shoot emblazoned with the faces of Notorious B.I.G and Tupac Shakur. Both were successful rappers who had become entangled in a world of gangsta warfare and both were shot dead, leaving chart-topping albums behind them. The T-shirt was Kelly's way of paying tribute to the lives cut short. "I loved the song when I heard the lyrics and I hoped it would touch young people and inspire," she concluded to CNN.

Now that Kelly had a single to promote, she was back on the road to take part in interviews and a tour. She'd done it all before with Destiny's Child, but this time the difference was that she was alone. "I didn't know that stepping on the stage yourself would be so frightening," she revealed to *The Evening Times*. "The first time I performed alone, I hate to say I cried… That's how I get it out."

It wasn't just the spotlight that Kelly shrank away from – it was also the prospect of doing long, arduous journeys without her sisters around. "I [missed] the companionship of travelling with the girls," she explained to *Blues & Soul*. "We always had the best times travelling together, cracking jokes and everything, but when you do go off on your own, it pushes you to grow a little bit more."

Besides, any fear Kelly had felt about going it alone was silenced when, in February 2003, her duet with Nelly landed her a Grammy – the first one she had earned without Destiny's Child. The same month, her second single, 'Can't Nobody', was released to the public. Its uptempo beat and modern bravado and swagger made it the polar opposite of 'Stole', warning critics that they couldn't pigeonhole her musical style.

The diversity of the material sparked curiosity about what the rest of the album might sound like and, right on cue, Kelly released the international edition of *Simply Deep* on February 15. It sailed straight to number one in the UK, where it sold more than 100,000 copies in its first week and it also excelled in foreign territories such as Asia.

Meanwhile 'Can't Nobody' also emphasised Kelly's appeal across the Atlantic, peaking in the Top 5 in the UK. Of course, it helped that Rich Harrison had been on board – someone *The New York Times* had crowned "one of R&B's most exciting producers". He lived up to the billing, going on to produce 'Crazy In Love', 'Freakum Dress' and 'Suga Mama' for Beyoncé.

As her solo success continued to rise, a thrilled Kelly announced to *The Evening Times*: "My record went gold here in the States. It's platinum in Australia. In Britain it's double platinum!" However, she soon had a contender for all the attention when, in June 2003, Beyoncé released a much-awaited solo album of her own, *Dangerously In Love*.

The same month, Kelly's one-off collaboration with the French rapper Stormy Bugsy, 'Une Femme En Prison', was released, but it only charted in France, where it achieved a paltry number 62 ranking.

Meanwhile, as the rave reviews for her soul sister's album came pouring in, it seemed as though she was slipping behind Beyoncé yet again. She'd thought succeeding without the others had been difficult, but the biggest pressure of all turned out to be maintaining that success. As the lyrics to 'Une Femme En Prison' had warned, without dreaming, freedom had no meaning – so, to make the most of her time in the spotlight, Kelly would have to dream bigger.

She stepped up her game by making a brief appearance in the American sitcom *Eve*, starring the rapper of the same name, and also earned a singing role on the comedy drama *American Dreams*, performing a rendition of the Martha and the Vandellas track 'Nowhere To Run'.

That year also saw the release of *Freddy Vs Jason*, a nerve-racking moment for someone with a fear of failure. Kelly had agonised, "I didn't want people to say, 'She sucked in her first movie!'" However, the film was loved by the public, breaking even in its first weekend and making an overall total of almost $115 million.

Then, in August 2003, Kelly released the final single from *Simply Deep*, 'Train On A Track', which also made it onto the soundtrack for the movie *Maid In Manhattan*. The film is a modern-day Cinderella story, featuring Jennifer Lopez as an overworked and underpaid chamber maid in New York hotel The Waldorf-Astoria (renamed The Beresford Hotel for the movie) who meets and falls for a wealthy businessman.

The use of Kelly's track on the film was apt, chronicling her rise from an under-privileged backing singer to a star in her own right. However, it was the following year, 2004, that would prove just how accurate the analogy was to be.

At that year's Grammy Awards, Beyoncé earned five trophies in one night and duetted with her idol, Prince, indisputably repositioning her ahead of Kelly in the popularity stakes. Plus, while Beyoncé was singing tracks like 'Purple Rain' and her own song 'Crazy In Love' live on stage with a veteran performer, Kelly's achievements paled in comparison. In the flurry of number one hits that Beyoncé had achieved, it seemed as though her own high point, 'Dilemma', had been forgotten altogether.

While many artists might have been content with that level of success, Kelly didn't want to be complacent – with Beyoncé as one of her peers, she had a lot to live up to.

In the classic fairytale, Cinderella had enjoyed one fleeting night of freedom from her duties as a household maid, but when the clock struck midnight, she had to flee the ball or risk being turned into a pumpin. Was Kelly's time already up?

To make matters worse for Kelly's ego, Beyoncé was far from an ugly sister – by now, she was a fully-fledged beauty icon, cinema sex siren and acclaimed songstress, and most of the critics were saying she deserved every accolade that came her way. Was Kelly's moment in the spotlight already over, or – like Jennifer Lopez in *Maid In Manhattan* – could she too hope for a happy ending?

It was something that had certainly eluded her in the love department. Beyoncé wasn't just ahead of her musically – she also had a more promising love life. Her new partner, Jay-Z, was a male Cinderella who had risen from being a poverty-stricken hustler in inner-city New York, where everyday gang warfare forced him to stare the possibility of death in the face, to a hugely successful rap artist and entrepreneur with a net worth of more than $450 million.

While Beyoncé had combined business with pleasure by recording a track with him that name-checked herself and her new beau as the modern-day Bonnie and Clyde, Kelly had broken up with the mystery friend of rapper Nelly with whom she had her secret relationship. Since then, she had been waiting for a handsome prince to happen upon her glass slipper.

As a traditional southern girl, Kelly wouldn't settle for anything less than a fairytale romance. The pairing of Beyoncé and Jay-Z had raised some eyebrows both due to their different backgrounds and Jay's reputation as a womaniser and seasoned misogynist. His reputation was certainly of great concern to Beyoncé's father, who snapped in one 2004 interview that he didn't "care for him at all".

Yet while Beyoncé was arguably enthralled by Jay-Z's down 'n' dirty ghetto image – a life so different from her own sheltered upbringing – Kelly was resolute about what she wanted. She was looking for a gentleman, not a bad boy, and her high expectations were making it tough to find a partner at all. "There's no such thing as a gentleman in the music business," one of her friends would later chuckle.

Nevertheless, nothing would stop Kelly trying. "My mum has always told me to make sure a guy respects you," she revealed. "Every woman should be treated like a queen – if you're on a date and the man doesn't open the door for you, honey, that's your cue to leave."

Meanwhile, as Kelly saw her body as a "temple" and sought to be squeaky clean, she was looking for a man who was teetotal. A heavy drinker would bring back memories of a painful childhood at the mercy of her father's addiction and she didn't want history to repeat itself should she have her own child. "My father was an alcoholic and I remember him being drunk, so I don't like alcohol," she confirmed resolutely to the *Daily Mirror*. While finding a man who wasn't an alcoholic would be easy, finding someone who abstained completely was another story altogether. In fact, in the boozy world of showbiz, it seemed almost an impossibility.

Kelly was also wary of men who were attracted not to her, but to her fame, claiming she could sniff out such types in "the first five minutes". "They'll start talking about Destiny's Child, but they should ask you more about your intellect and actually get to know you," she told *The Daily Record*. "That's how you can tell."

Magazine reporters picked up the news that Kelly was still single incredulously, but in spite of her fame and fortune – or perhaps even because of it – maybe it was harder for Kelly than the average woman to find love. From the start, she was dodging fame-hunters and freeloaders as well as those who had heard Destiny's Child described as "R&B porn queens" in the press and were expecting her to be nothing more than an easy lay.

Yet the fact that she was emblazoned across magazine covers and constantly in the charts made it all too easy for prospective dates to form preconceived ideas about her. After all, she had publicly declared herself an independent woman – something that might intimidate men and encourage them to label her as a man-hater. That was as if approaching a member of one of America's biggest-selling girl groups wasn't nerve-racking enough already. In reality, Kelly saw herself as much more down to earth than her media persona might suggest.

Despite her bulging bank balance, she claimed to be shocked at the idea of spending a million dollars on a home. Kelly was impressed by the type of gestures that would turn off a gold-digger straight away so, whilst many men might have felt obliged to use their wallets to impress, show-offs and big spenders weren't for her. "Someone's intellect and sense of humour are what's important," she insisted, "not the material things."

Perhaps her caution stemmed from her tough upbringing, when she and her mother had anxiously counted every penny. For them, even having a roof over their heads had been a blessing. "I remember the first time we toured, I was like, 'Wow, where did all these lights and the backdrop come from?'" Kelly had recalled to *Stylist*. "I was told, 'Well, they come from your pocket. You're paying for all of this!' So I started asking, 'How many people are part of the tour crew? How many people do this or that? Do we actually need this?' I want to be smart. I've had a lot of money and I've had a little. I know what that feels like." A man of means, then, was of little consequence to Kelly.

Looks didn't matter much to her either. In fact, Kelly believed that she was far from an oil painting herself. "I'm no sex symbol!" she contradicted in an interview with *The Mirror*. "You must be confusing me with Jennifer Lopez or someone. Me sexy? No way." That was another reason why a man just couldn't second-guess Kelly: the real her seemed to be a million miles away from the sexually charged girl who danced in the 'Bootylicious' video.

So, Kelly wasn't asking for much – her ideal man could easily be a down-to-earth, financially challenged plumber with average looks who didn't have to keep her in Louboutins – but it was imperative that he was a Christian. "I was watching the video tape of the *Billboard* awards and when he won, the lead singer of Creed [Scott Stapp] was like, 'First I would like to give thanks and praise to God,' and I was like, 'Yes!'" Kelly explained to *Cosmo Girl*. "I think it's so beautiful when a man can be proud of God and talk about it."

She added to her list of requests in an interview with *The Daily Record*, when she revealed: "I'm looking for a Christian man with family values and some respect for himself. He should not be insecure, should be a good communicator and be affectionate to me. I want a man who isn't afraid to hold my hand in public."

However, the men she met were either "on an ego trip" or found her more frightening than watching *Freddy Vs Jason*. Even worse, a false story had broken in Germany that she and Nelly were engaged – and before long, the whole world believed that she was already taken.

By this point not so much unlucky in love as a leper in love, Kelly was beginning to give up on ever finding her other half. "The truth is," she told *The Mirror*, "I just can't find the right kind of guy who treats me as I should be treated. He has to know how to treat me well, make me feel like a queen and make me feel appreciated… Men just don't know how to treat a girl most of the time… One day I will find the right guy, but I'm not holding my breath for it to happen at the minute."

When love finally did come her way, it was at a time when she hadn't expected it. In February 2004 – the same month that Beyoncé was outshining her at the Grammy Awards – Kelly was working hard on the romantic comedy *The Seat Filler*. Its plot was like *Maid In Manhattan* reversed.

Kelly played a wealthy, successful pop superstar named Jhnelle, while actor Duane Martin played Derrick, a penniless law student who catches her eye. Desperate to pay his way through university, Derrick gets a job as a seat filler at award shows, filling in gaps in the audience to appease the vanity of big shots in Hollywood. His contract forbids him from talking to the celebrities that surround him, but – when it comes to Jhnelle – he makes an exception.

What's more, when she mistakes him for a high-profile player in showbiz, he isn't about to argue. By the time the pair grow closer and fall for each other romantically, Derrick is desperate to come clean, but he fears in doing so that he will lose her altogether – exactly the dilemma Jennifer Lopez faced in *Maid In Manhattan* the previous year.

The movie would also see Kelly work alongside Mel B of the Spice Girls, who plays her best friend and assistant, Sandie, while Will Smith and his wife, Jada, were executive producers. Kelly contributed to five songs to the film – 'Train On A Track', which was making its second movie appearance, 'Bad Habit', which was co-written by Kelly and Solange Knowles and later appeared on the next Destiny's Child album as Kelly's solo song, and three tracks written specifically for the film – 'Heartbreak', 'Follow Your Destiny' and the aptly named 'I Need A Love'. If the latter was a hint to God, the one she expected to solve her dating dilemmas, her prayers were answered during filming.

Kelly had said she didn't need a handsome or wealthy man, but by most people's estimations, American footballer Roy Williams was both. When the pair met socially by chance, he fell for her so fast that he contacted *The Seat Filler's* producers offering to invest in the movie.

"He was absolutely besotted with her," an anonymous insider revealed to the author. "He loved the fact that she was independent – it wasn't that she needed a man but that she wanted one. She wasn't needy but she knew how to give affection, so she had the balance right. She loved spending time with him, but she had her own life as well."

Roy also found that Kelly was every bit as deep as her album title suggested – with probing questions and sensitive conversation, she wanted to get to know him on more than just a superficial level. Perhaps that set her apart from the gold-diggers who frequently targeted him both in and outside of showbiz. "You'd be surprised how many cute singers there are in showbiz that are all the same," the insider added. "Any guy in the street would do anything to get with a girl like that, but a footballer's seen it all before. He has girls throwing themselves at him every day, so when he actually falls in love with one, you know that person is pretty special."

The insider also distinguished Kelly from her friendly rival Beyoncé. "What Roy loved about her was how comfortable she was inside her skin," she continued. "For Roy, the sexiest thing about a woman is confidence – and by now she had that. Sure, she ate healthy but she wasn't starving herself. She didn't get caught up in the silly stuff like being sexy, because she knew that beauty comes and goes. Instead she put all the emphasis on improving herself as a person and as an artist. To be honest, he couldn't have imagined someone like Beyoncé acting that way."

Roy echoed her words himself, telling *Vixen*: "I got to know Kelly when she wasn't in the group. You could see her true colours – a very humble, inspiring woman with the fire and the desire to succeed, and I love that. I love her soul. It was just so pure, so innocent and sweet. I fell in love with her. Hard."

It hadn't been long since Kelly had recovered emotionally from her previous relationship, but Roy had been persistent, wooing her with flowers and hand-written letters. She would later describe him as the "knight in shining armour" who'd rescued her from her heartbreak. She quickly gained confidence in his intentions. As he was already in the public eye, he wasn't seeking fame through association. He had his own money, so he wouldn't be asking her to pay his bills. Even better, he had had his fair share of experience with the paparazzi, so he knew how to handle them. They started dating and, by May, the pair were already engaged.

That spring also saw Kelly reunite with Beyoncé and Michelle for another Destiny's Child album. Speculation had been rife that the group was about to split up – after all, Michelle had released two successful gospel albums and dabbled in musical theatre with a stint on Broadway as Aida; Kelly had excelled with *Simply Deep;* and, arguably, Beyoncé's success as a solo artist was beginning to overshadow anything she ever did with the group.

More to the point, their solo albums highlighted that all three were moving in different musical directions. However, according to Kelly, getting together again was "a no brainer". "That's where we started," she assured MTV. "That's the mould we grew from and you can't just stray away from that… we wouldn't have done the solo records if it wasn't for Destiny's Child records."

In fact, their individual successes simply meant that the girls would return to the studio on a more equal footing. Now more experienced, they all shared writing credits and stand-out lead vocals on the CD and, for the first time, the three also joined Mathew in the joint role of executive producer.

Now more than ever, the trio's own vision was coming through – and, perhaps because Beyoncé and Kelly were both in love, the album had a more gentle ambience than its predecessors, and it was full of slow jams.

Delighted to be back together again, the first week in the studio had been set aside for girly chats as they filled each other in on the developments in their lives. On the surface, they were like any other group of friends enjoying a gossip – except that this group was recording their chats. They were played back later and formed the basis of the themes on the album, meaning that instead of singing along to mass-produced pop, they would be portraying a genuine reflection of what was going on in their lives.

Not only had the tempo changed, but the themes had too. If the death of feminism had a sound, 'Cater To You' just might have been it. Just by falling in love, the girls had transformed from feisty, independent women more likely to take men on in a fight than date them, to submissive girlfriends who sing that they are willing to serve their men. Now they were spoiling them with the intensity that would put the average girlfriend to shame – running a lover's bath water, combing his hair and giving him massages and manicures.

It wasn't the first time that a Destiny's Child album had shown opposing themes, but nevertheless Beyoncé felt she had some explaining to do. "I know it's going to be very surprising to a lot of people that the independent survivors are being submissive to their men," she emphasised to MTV. "But it's important that people know that, you know, it's fine if your man deserves it and gives that back to you."

Other love songs included 'T-Shirt', a track all about the sensual pleasure of wearing a boyfriend's clothes – which is a theme previously explored by En Vogue in their hit single 'Don't Let Go'.

Then there's the simply titled 'Love', a passionate dedication to a man who restored a partner's faith at a time when she felt ready to give up on romance altogether. His love becomes so much a part of her life that it's her oxygen supply. This is the track that most accurately describes Kelly's romance with Roy.

Of course the girls had also had their fair share of heartbreaks and disappointments in the past – all part of the package when falling in love – and these were reflected in songs like 'Is She The Reason'. Thematically similar to the Etta James classic 'I'd Rather Go Blind (Than See You Walk Away)', it highlights a woman's suspicions that the man in her life has his eye on someone new and sees her mourn the loss to come before he's even gone. The confrontation sees her plaintively question why, if she's not the one, he could ever let their romance go so far.

Meanwhile, 'Girl' is a celebration of sisterhood, a gentle nudge from a woman's friends to break free of her love-related depression and confide in them about what's wrong. With this track, the three were able to distance themselves from the media histrionics that accused them of catfights and bitter rivalry. Here, they are not competition for each other, but dependable friends.

Other slow, sad loss-of-love songs included 'If', 'Free' and 'Through With Love'. The latter is a woman's explosion of anger, challenging a partner for undermining her and expecting her to be a stick-thin model like the pin-ups he sees on TV. After months spent swallowing her pride and deferring her dreams, she realises her lover is holding her back and it's time to leave.

However, the most important such song for Kelly was 'Bad Habit'. It was a song that she had co-written away from the group when filming *The Seat Filler* and it would see her singing solo. The track tells of a toxic love affair about as addictive as any drug. Like Lauryn Hill's 'Ex Factor', both partners are desperate to break the bad habit, but each time they try to end their ill-fated relationship, one of them comes back for more.

elly prepares to party the night away, celebrating gay and lesbian festival Mardi Gras in Australia. Despite her religious obringing, Kelly has always been liberal about alternative sexualities. CAMERON RICHARDSON/NEWSPIX/REX

Nelly, Kelly and songwriter Patti LaBelle take a break from filming 'Dilemma' outside LA's Universal Studios. Kelly bears a striking resemblance to Patti, who also plays her mother on-screen. MARKUS CUFF/CORBIS SYGMA

Kelly takes time out from her role as leading lady in 50 Cent's 2009 video 'Baby By Me' for a candid moment with the singer himself, who would later describe her as "the most under-rated female artist of all time". JARED MILGRIM/CORBIS

ly launches into song for a 2009 charity concert at London's
svenor House to benefit Elton John's AIDS Foundation.
JARD YOUNG/REX FEATURES

Draped with pearls, an elegantly turned out Kelly is pictured
at New York Fashion Week 2009, alongside glamorous socialite
and reality TV star Kim Kardashian.
GREGORY PACE/BEI/REX FEATURES

ice Commander: An Amazonian Kelly with David Guetta,
producer who revitalised her career by introducing her to
ce, at the MTV Los Premios Awards in 2009.
E GIRO/RETNA LTD/CORBIS

Kelly arrives at the VH1 Hip Hop Honours: "The Dirty South"
Show in New York with fellow Southern belle Brandy.
WALIK GOSHORN/RETNA LTD/CORBIS

An elegantly turned out Kelly sports a canary yellow designer dress in her judging role on TV series *The Fashion Show*. She would he
aspiring couture designers fight their way to a career-changing clothes commission. THE KOBAL COLLECTION/BRAVO TV/MCNEAL, KELSEY

Kelly sings her heart out with Michael Buble on the ITV show *Home For Christmas* in December 2011. ITV/REX FEATURES

Like Simon Cowell, Kelly devises her own signature gesture as she prepares for her first stint of auditions as an *X-Factor* judge, in June 2011. SPLASH NEWS/CORBIS

Kelly lives up to the name of her song as she performs 'Down For Whatever' live on the German *X-Factor*, sporting a gold sparkly dress and looking ready for anything that fame might throw at her. ACTION PRESS/REX FEATURES

Staying True To The Sisterhood: Kelly shows there's no bad blood with her former Destiny's Child band-mate Michelle Williams as she steps out with her in a hot pink mini dress for the 2011 *Billboard* Music Awards in Las Vegas. D/KABIK/RETNA DIGITAL

Kelly with rapper Sean 'Diddy' Combs at the Lakewood Mall, California. She was the promotional poster girl for his Empress fragrance – marketed at a "powerful, enchanting, uniquely feminine woman". ALLEN BEREZOVSKY/WIREIMAGE

Record label boss Sylvia Rhone accompanies Kelly to the third annual Black Women in Music reception in LA in 2012. HAEL TRAN/FILMMAGIC

The following day, Kelly attends the film premiere of *Think Like A Man* in Hollywood with her best friend, tennis champion Serena Williams. ERIC CHARBONNEAU/WIREIMAGE

Kelly hits the stage doing what she does best – this time the recipients of her live show are fans at Sydney's 2012 Supafest.
BRENDON THORNE/GETTY IMAGES

Primarily an album of ballads, the CD yielded just two tracks fans might have called "lively" and both of those were singles. The first, which preceded the album on September 21, 2004, was 'Lose My Breath'. It was a feisty return to the pop scene, audaciously spelling out that if a man failed to satisfy in the bedroom, he was dismissed. Learning that a man's sexy words are all talk and bravado, the girls are frustrated to find themselves led out into the deep end by a man who can't deliver.

The song introduced to the public a side of Destiny's Child which was both raunchy and street. But the dust had barely settled on 'Lose My Breath' when 'Soldier' was released, featuring guest raps from both T.I and Lil' Wayne. Like T.I.'s last collaboration ('Live Your Life' with Rihanna), it hinted at a gesture of political support for American soldiers in Iraq.

However, it also referenced a different kind of war – that of streetwise gangstas in the 'hood, the only type of guys likely to catch the girls' eyes. Again, men are given their marching orders if, among other requests, their 'things' aren't big enough – something which the girls later implausibly defended as a reference to pregnancy.

'Soldier' became one of the biggest hits of the year, although not everyone felt the same. Perhaps the strident demands for someone who measured up in the bedroom department touched a raw nerve for one critic, who complained the girls were classlessly panting about the subject like "dogs on heat".

Despite the occasional bad press, the song – released on December 7 – reached the Top Five in both the UK and the US. Likewise, 'Lose My Breath' reached number two in the UK, losing out by a whisker to Eminem's 'Just Lose It'. The girls also claimed the Christmas market that year with an animated version of 'Rudolph The Red-Nosed Reindeer'.

By now, the group's image as risqué sex sirens was established, although, behind the scenes, neither Beyoncé nor Kelly lived up to the myth. Both still claimed that they were virgins and, despite having more than enough reasons to celebrate, they never so much as sipped champagne. Under Mathew's watch, the teetotal girls were unlikely to grow up too fast.

Yet the dichotomy was that their public persona presented them as the total opposite of that exaggerated good-girl image. In spite of his extra-marital affairs, Mathew felt sexually active women who weren't married were 'whores' and, while he condoned selling sex by audacious references to it in music, he didn't want that to translate into real-life lust for his girls.

Michelle, meanwhile, was accused of hypocrisy when she insisted she wanted her body to be a 'mystery', the sight of which was reserved only for her future husband. In contrast to the words, however, she regularly wore cleavage-spilling bikini tops and revealing micro-mini skirts on stage – and Destiny's Child had been lauded in the media as the sexiest girl group of all time.

They tried to emphasise their softer side with 'Girl', which was released on March 16, 2005. However, it quickly became apparent that perhaps it was their sexy side that appealed most to fans, with 'Girl' becoming the lowest-charting single in Destiny's Child history.

The previous month had seen a similar disappointment for Kelly when her appearance as a featured artist on Earth, Wind And Fire's 'This Is How I Feel' had an equally lukewarm reception. The song had been created for the movie *Hitch*, about a 'date doctor' whose courses give hapless men the A–Z on how to seduce beautiful women. In reality, the so-called love expert quickly finds out for himself that his techniques don't work. Despite starring big names such as Will Smith and Eva Mendes, the film under-performed at the box office and Kelly's songs received very little press.

The plot of the film proved apt when, on Valentine's Day – three days after its release – despite repeated calls from fiancé, Roy, she was nowhere to be found. Kelly had desperately wanted a fairytale wedding, but now it seemed she was getting cold feet.

As it turned out, the feeling was mutual. At the same time as their wedding was being promoted to the press, the couple were having secret marital counselling sessions, hinting at troubled waters before they had even set out for sea. While filling in a questionnaire in the therapist's office, Roy realised he couldn't answer a single significant question about Kelly. Feeling they were moving too fast and needed to slow down the pace and simply get to know each other, he asked if they could postpone their engagement. The only problem was that, by this time, Kelly had already posed on the cover of *Modern Bride* – in a wedding dress. "I sat her down on the bed and said, 'Kelly, we don't know each other well enough to get married,'" Roy claimed. "At the time she was cool with it [but then] I started catching a lot of heat just for doing the grown-man thing about it."

Kelly saw things differently: in her eyes, a grown man would never have taken things so far if he hadn't been certain of his feelings. Plus, as a public figure, the prospect of the world knowing her husband-to-be had changed his mind and wasn't ready to commit was humiliating. At a time when she was splashed all over the newspapers, she just wanted to hide her face from the world.

Roy had proposed to her in the archetypal romantic setting, getting down on one knee with candles and rose petals surrounding him, and had 'stolen' her heart. Yet now her dream wedding was not to be. "I didn't even want to get out of the house," Kelly later confessed to *Vixen*. "I was just in great sadness. I really didn't want to put my family in that kind of position as well, to where they have to answer questions that they really don't know the answers to, like, 'When is she getting married?'"

Years later, she conceded to *Cosmopolitan* that – at just 24 – she might not have known what she wanted either. "I was too young for marriage," she explained. "I remember Beyoncé asked me one question. She said, 'Well, you know what you want now, don't you?' and I was like, 'Yes'. It was so hard and embarrassing because everyone knew. I'd posed for the front cover of a magazine in my wedding dress and it was on sale! But sometimes you fall down and you learn from it."

One of the things Kelly learned was that Roy might have been a rebound relationship. While he was perfect on paper – wealthy and handsome, romantic and skilled in the art of respecting a lady – something was wrong with the picture. She had said, "If I had just one wish for the rest of my life, I'd ask for a good man to settle down with and be the father of my babies."

Yet now she realised that – to complicate matters further – she was still in love with her ex. "You know when you're at the end of one relationship and you think you're over it," Kelly explained, "but like deep inside your mind, you're really not. I was in that phase – like, I'm over this and I'm going to move on. I'm going to put the past behind me. Roy was like this knight in shining armour that was oh so sweet – and I fell in love with that."

But the love might have been a mere infatuation. When asked later how many times she had fallen in love, she answered, "Once." Did that include the man she had been engaged to? Kelly blushingly corrected herself, recalculating the figure to twice.

In psychological terms, it also seemed possible that the events reminded Kelly of her father's abandonment and that, as a defence mechanism against being hurt further, she removed herself from the position of vulnerability that could allow Roy to emotionally damage her by walking out of her life. Whatever the reasons for her change of heart, the reality was that she and Roy now had different priorities. He intended not to end the engagement, but to postpone it – but the next thing he knew, Kelly had called off the entire romance and he lost her altogether.

A heartbroken Roy later told *Vixen*, "Sometimes do I wish I was by her side? Yes, I'm not going to sit up here and lie. But what can I do? You can't change somebody's heart. If they want to be with someone else, that's what it's going to be."

For Kelly's part, she told the *Daily Mail*: "I wanted that wedding. I wanted to be married. You can just make wrong decisions in life. That was all part of growing up."

The split was finalised by April, leading to heartbreak on both sides, but a well-timed release saw *The Seat Filler* eventually replace the failed romance in the gossip columns that summer. Posters advertising the film featured the slogan: "She's rich and famous and he's poor and shameless", picturing the two leads sitting together in a movie theatre. Seeing the familiar face of Kelly in such an unfamiliar role prompted curiosity and the film was a Top 20 hit.

Claiming that Kelly was a believable actress who easily persuaded viewers to "emotionally invest" in her character, the respected review website *HomeTheaterInfo.com* said, "She has what it takes to be a romantic comedy success. She is pretty, talented and can be the girl next door or the sought-after star."

Yet for all her success and seemingly abundant strengths, Kelly just couldn't make the one thing she was yet to achieve work – a steady relationship. What was more, there were further endings in store that year – this time for Destiny's Child. There had been a certain finality about the album – from the title, *Destiny Fulfilled*, suggesting that there was little left for the three-piece to achieve, to the ominously worded bonus track, 'Game Over' – but up to that point the girls had always insisted that, as "sisters", their group would be together forever.

That said, the album sleeve itself held another strong hint that there was no future for Destiny's Child. In the Thank You section, the girls stated: "This album speaks of destiny fulfilled. If you listen closely, it tells a story about life and love with all its ups and downs and how, in the end, destiny is fulfilled."

Hence, it came as a shock, but perhaps not a surprise, when, on June 11, at a show in Barcelona, they announced live on stage that all three would be going their own separate ways.

An official statement followed this impromptu announcement, explaining: "We have been working together on Destiny's Child since we were nine and touring together since we were 14. After a lot of discussion and some deep soul-searching, we realised that our current tour has given us the opportunity to leave Destiny's Child on a high note, united in our friendship and filled with an overwhelming gratitude for our music, our fans and each other. After all these wonderful years working together, we realised that now is the time to pursue our personal goals and solo efforts in earnest."

It seemed that the ending might have come at the right time when, despite the media frenzy surrounding the split, the increased publicity didn't translate to greater sales. In America, the group's final single from the album, 'Cater To You', failed even to make a dent in the Top 10. In addition, magazines such as *Rolling Stone* were starting to criticise the "endless string of overwrought R&B ballads" they felt the album provided.

Bowing out now at least allowed them to leave on the high note their statement had spoken of, while the girls still felt they were what Kelly would later describe as "at the top of their game". Interestingly, she also stated that she was glad to leave while all three were "still friends".

Perhaps this hinted that tension was brewing in relation to the group dynamic, and that both she and Michelle had outgrown playing second fiddle to Beyoncé. Plus, now that Kelly had achieved mainstream success as a soloist in her own right, perhaps Beyoncé was struggling to hold on to her formerly indisputable label as "lead singer".

The Guardian and *Entertainment Weekly* had both noticed the shift, describing *Destiny Fulfilled* as "a democratic album" and noting that they all shared the lead vocals much more. Perhaps this was even more reason for each to shine as a solo artist.

Kelly claimed she had rushed into her engagement because she wanted to "lean on somebody". While Roy had provided the support in her love life, Beyoncé and Michelle had been the people she leaned on in her career. But things changed. Just as she claimed: "Now I love the fact that I can just be a single lady, chilling and hanging with my friends and travelling the world – it's a pretty good life," perhaps now she was gathering confidence and prestige to launch herself in the world, and she no longer wanted or needed bandmates to hide behind.

However, the group still had some commitments to fulfil together as Destiny's Child, including the conclusion of their world tour, which earned $70 million in the US alone.

Kelly also found time to strike out on her own. She showed signs of crossing over to a bad-girl image when she collaborated with MC Trina, who was renowned for sexually explicit, straight-talking songs and who had stormed to public attention with lyrically arresting hits like 'No Panties'. That track had featured Tweet of 'Oops (Oh My)' fame, the first chart hit explicitly about female masturbation – guaranteeing an explosive and headline-pulling combination.

However, 'Here We Go', the track that Kelly appeared on, had a slightly different flavour. It was an angry ode to a partner who, for the umpteenth time, had passed off a woman calling at 3.a.m. as merely a friend. Echoing the theme of J-Lo's 'All I Have' – on which she tearfully storms out of the marital home into the snow with a string of Louis Vuitton bags behind her – 'Here We Go' also warns that the protagonist will be gathering up her jewels and furs and leaving for good.

The track, which was released on September 22, made it to the Top 20 in many countries around the world, increasing Kelly's confidence that – in spite of the split with Destiny's Child – she could still make it on her own.

Yet that didn't mean she wasn't up for the occasional collaboration. That year, she got together with Beyoncé again in aid of the Hurricane Katrina disaster, which had caused many Americans in New Orleans and beyond to lose their homes. The pair appeared on the charity album *The Katrina CD* with a track named 'All I'm Looking For' and took things a step further when they teamed up with the rest of Beyoncé's family to set up the Survivor Foundation. The charity would raise funds to provide transitional housing for Houston residents left homeless by the hurricane.

Then, on October 25, the group released their final album – a compilation of their top hits, simply titled *#1s*. Like its namesakes, the album became a number one hit. Finally, the group would come together as Destiny's Child for the very last time on the celebratory single 'Stand Up For Love'.

By that time, the group's middle name might as well have been platinum. In fact, when they earned a star on the prestigious Hollywood Walk Of Fame the following year, the accolade could have seemed less of a humbling coup and more an inevitability that was long overdue.

They had sold over 40 million albums. They had gone down in history for their female empowerment anthems, but had also been unafraid to release tender ballads praising and appreciating their men. They were strong, self-sufficient women, but it didn't make them ice queens: they had romantic streaks too. They combined raunchy sex appeal with traditional values, giving praise both to God and to the naked female body – and they had even put the word bootylicious in the dictionary.

They survived three line-up changes and had emerged triumphantly until the end. Even better, at the 2005 World Music Awards, they were crowned the biggest girl group of all time.

Destiny had indeed been fulfilled and now it was time for Kelly and her sisters to move on to bigger and better things.

Chapter 9

No Future In The Past

Now that Kelly no longer had Destiny's Child as a comfort blanket to fall back on, she was pursuing her solo career in earnest. Over the years, she had grown from a tentative, almost reluctant soloist, who was often reduced to tears at the stress of stepping out alone, to an ambitious young woman who had kept the values of sisterhood close to her heart, but was still striving to keep Beyoncé on her toes. It was just as well: now her greatest friend was also her biggest competition.

"One of my best friends, [tennis player] Serena Williams told me she and Venus love each other," Kelly mused. "She said, 'We're going to be sisters, period [but] when we have to play each other, we're competing and we both want to win.'" The battle cry was clear – and, as she added to *The Scotsman*, "Now I'm not in a team. The only person I can see is me."

Not only that, but Kelly was no longer a teenager: as a confident woman in her mid-20s, it was almost as though she had outgrown Destiny's Child. "'Bug A Boo' annoys me so much now," she later confessed to *Stylist*. "Some of the stuff in that song makes me feel like I'm 17 years old… What terrible lyrics. At the time we were so into it, but now – what on earth were we thinking?"

Kelly also promised an album that was not only more mature, but that also revealed exactly who she was. She was no longer the sweet, demure young girl afraid to make mistakes. "You know what, I think the only thing that holds us back is ourselves," she declared to *Now* magazine, "and I have to admit that on my first record, I was scared."

In 2006, however, Kelly had shaken off the fear – and while she conceded that being referred to as "one third of the biggest-selling female group of all time" was "quite an introduction", she was no longer letting the past define her. The next goal in her sights was to be the biggest-selling solo artist of all time – with no-one to thank for her success but herself.

"When people hear [the next] album, I want them to hear me for me," she told *Urban Bridgez*. "Not Kelly from Destiny's Child, but Kelly Rowland. Don't get me wrong, I love and respect Destiny's Child, but with this album, I want to stand on my own."

First, however, midway into a year of recording her own material, Kelly had some final unfinished business to attend to on behalf of the group. At the MTV Asia Awards on May 6, she picked up the Special Achievement In Popular Music trophy.

The award might have been for Destiny's Child, but the night belonged to Kelly. Not only was she co-hosting the show together with the America-born Taiwanese pop star and actor Leehom Wang – honouring an age-old tradition of combining both eastern and western influences on the show – but she was also premiering her long-awaited new solo single, 'Gotsta Go'.

At the after-show party in Bangkok, Kelly was described as hyperactive, grinning broadly and telling the story of her forthcoming album to anyone who would listen. Beyoncé might have earned starring roles in two film releases that year – *Dreamgirls* and *The Pink Panther* – to Kelly's paltry three episodes in a minor role on the TV sitcom *Girlfriends*, but – in the words of Beyoncé's *Dreamgirls* character Deena herself, "I'm somebody and nobody's going to hold me down!" This described exactly how Kelly felt.

She was in equally high spirits later that month when she was invited to perform at five shows for Vixen Model Search, starting in her favourite American city of Atlanta. The organisation fought specifically for the rights of women of colour to have a public image, a cause which was very close to Kelly's heart. She felt that models in the western world were predominantly Caucasian and had previously remarked, "It's hard for young girls when all they see is white blonde girls on TV."

"It's sad to me, I must say, to not be able to get a cover to a magazine unless I'm either white or fair-skinned," Kelly added to *Clay Cane*. "When a black woman is on the cover of a magazine, it doesn't sell. How sad is that? When they do take a risk at it, it's always that answer, 'See, we took a risk and look what happens, we didn't sell the magazine. We didn't sell as much as we would have,' or whatever it is, which is really sad to me."

Racism, whether it be in music, modelling or movies, was an important issue for Kelly – and she had seen it from both sides. In her childhood, she was bullied by her white peers for being black and by her black peers for having white friends. "My black friends would call me 'white girl' and tell me I was selling out," Kelly told *Cosmo Girl*. "I was like, what's wrong with being a white girl? [But] I'm not downing my race."

Consequently she'd spent her schooldays labelled as a "wigger" – a black girl who others accused of trying to act Caucasian – and had often trodden a no-man's-land between the two.

Later, as part of Destiny's Child, she'd been told she didn't qualify for VIP or priority services in airports because she was part of an R&B group – a category typically associated with ethnic singers.

"Even though we've sold way more records than some artists and we're way more successful, they're treated like more of a priority," Beyoncé recalled at the time. "One airline said they couldn't consider R&B to be VIP, which was very insulting."

To add further insult to injury, all three girls had experienced suspicion from air hostesses while on board flights. "Sometimes the flight attendants will ask to see our boarding passes," Michelle had told *Cosmo Girl*. "I don't know why they're so shocked to see black people flying first class."

Finally, it hadn't failed to escape Kelly's notice that light-skinned black singers seemed sometimes to be treated more favourably than their darker-skinned peers. This reasoning meant that Beyoncé, with her mixed-race descent and caramel-coloured complexion, might have been considered more worthy of music roles or press attention, under the assumption that this was what sold.

There were statistics to back up the favouritism, too. As an example, nearly nine million readers had cast voters for *FHM* USA's 100 Sexiest Women poll. When the results came in, just four women of black origin had made the list. What was more, all of them were mixed race, with much lighter skin than a traditional black woman. Those chosen were Halle Berry, Selita Ebanks, Rihanna and Beyoncé.

One reader raged on web forum *Gossip Rocks*: "There is this huge issue of colourism, where the mixed-race, lighter-skinned women are considered hotter."

Some cynics even believed that the Knowles family had used the controversial colour issue themselves to propel Beyoncé to the front of Destiny's Child. According to ex-member Farrah Franklin, she had been asked to tan with sunbeds so that Beyoncé could stand out as the palest girl in the group.

Regardless of the alleged controversy behind the scenes, however, there were bigger issues at hand, with another forum reader angrily contesting that "99% of the women in the showbiz industry are white".

Although black women remained a minority group in North America compared to those of white origin, the results of the poll nevertheless raised the awkward question of why more black women were not chosen to be singers or actresses and why many of those that did make it were rarely featured in the public eye. To some, women of colour were deliberately marginalised and when they were seen, their appearance seemed to be a mere token gesture. It seemed that even selling more than 40 million records and being appreciated by black, white and mixed-race fans alike didn't make Kelly immune from the injustices of racism. "It's sad that we still live in a time like that," she mused. Consequently, the five-date tour for women of colour would see her become a public campaigner for the issue – and fans had the opportunity to see 'Gotsta Go' live, too.

The single was scheduled for an imminent release, with a full album, *My Story*, following in July. However a shock announcement changed all of that, when fans learned that Kelly was scrapping some of her material and postponing the album until 2007.

To confuse things further, manager Mathew Knowles's explanation wasn't exactly plain English. According to him, it was all about "making sure our marketing strategy is a multi-tiered approach that capitalises on the synergies afforded by her other projects".

Whatever the truth was, it seemed carefully shrouded in seemingly meaningless PR clichés, leaving fans none the wiser. One thing Mathew was clear about was that "everyone is pleased with the record Kelly made". However, as it later emerged, that didn't include Kelly herself.

"I just felt like it wasn't ready," she confessed to *Blues & Soul*. "I thought my last album was rushed so I didn't want to make that mistake again. 'Dilemma' was such a huge success, my label was so excited about putting that out, so I was thrown into the studio to rush an album within two or three weeks. But we learn from our mistakes and I did, so I took my time with this album."

It wasn't just a timing issue though – Kelly had been unhappy with the combination of tracks on *My Story*. As the album title suggested, she had wanted the songs to be personal, meaningful and descriptive of the experiences she had had since her last CD. Unfortunately, that time had been crammed full of heartbreak and endings - and she'd been left with an album of sad, pensive and melancholic slow jams.

"It was basically a list of songs that I put together about the past three years of my life with love and relationships," she told MTV. "And I remember listening to the record and I was just like, 'I don't want this to be deep to where, you know, I lose people.' I still wanna have my party records and I still wanna make people get up and bob their heads and vibe a little bit – and the album was full of mid-tempos and ballads, so I wanted to bring it up a little bit. I mean, I'm 25, I'm young!"

The single 'Gotsta Go' was one of the tracks that Kelly didn't feel reflected her youth. It saw her collaborate with Da Brat, the first female rapper in the world to have a platinum-selling album. She was no stranger to working with Destiny's Child, having already been featured on the remixes for 'Survivor' and 'Jumpin' Jumpin'', and she'd also rapped with Ludacris on the remix of Mariah Carey's number one single 'Loverboy'.

Despite her success as an MC, however, she had a colourful history that was steeped in violence. In 2000, she assaulted a woman by repeatedly beating her over the head with a gun after a dispute over VIP seating and had narrowly avoided a jail sentence. Later, in 2007, she wouldn't be so lucky, serving three years in prison for a second assault.

However, Kelly's concern wasn't her musical playmate's extra-curricular violence, but the song itself. Like most of the others on the scrapped album, the track had given voice to Kelly's sadness and frustration about her break-up with Roy, as well as her unfinished business with her previous ex.

The lyrics were extremely intense, talking of a betrayal so bad that it felt like "a hole in my soul" and hinting at drinking the pain away to forget. "She sounded like a depressive alcoholic," one insider claimed. "People wanted music they could lighten up and dance to and Kelly was convinced they would never go for that."

Kelly concurred when she told *Now*: "For fans who had followed me since Destiny's Child, I would be cheating them if I didn't put at least one uptempo track on there. I wanted to go back in and pump that out."

So it was back to the studio for Kelly – a decision that she insisted was entirely her own – and she was ready to be ruthless. 'Gotsta Go' was relegated to bonus track status, while some of the other tunes were binned altogether. Just five other songs from the original sessions made the cut.

'This Is Love' described the start of an ill-fated romance and the first time she felt love sneak up on her. However, the metaphor of those emotions assaulting her like a soldier when she least expected it signalled that the writing was already on the wall for the relationship and that she had pictured the ending before it had begun.

'Interlude' is a short expression of regret after an ending while 'Flashback' expands on the theme. The latter sees Kelly reliving the ghost of a previous relationship, rewriting history to try to convince herself that the mistakes her lover made weren't as bad as they seemed. She shatters the illusions of her so-called flawless world, revealing that underneath the glitz and glamour she is unbearably sad.

She shares a side of herself that's plaintive and desperate – a depth of emotion that's synonymous with her growing maturity. No longer is she indulging in petty fights with lovers over a pair of shoes, à la 'Bug A Boo' – instead the archetypal teenage "fuck you" attitude to relationships has been replaced by deeper, more enduring feelings. However, because it's no longer puppy love, there's more pain at stake; and, as Kelly's lyrics suggest, she might have the perfect life on the surface complete with all the material things she needs but it doesn't mean she's immune from crumbling like anyone else when love comes to an end.

The context of her angst is spelled out even more clearly on the less than coyly titled 'I'm Still In Love With My Ex'. Here, Kelly makes a public apology to Roy for jilting him, reassuring that while he could have made the perfect husband, ultimately she couldn't shake off the emotional baggage of the past.

Finally, the equally downcast 'Better Without You' is an ode to moving on, a last goodbye before closing the door on an ex-partner for good.

With the tracks, Kelly had gone through every conceivable stage of lost love from the first flashes of euphoria ('This Is Love') to the bitterness when it all goes wrong ('Better Off Without You'), along with regret ('Interlude'), candid confessions (I'm Still In Love With My Ex') and fantasising paired with outright denial ('Flashback').

As far as catharsis was concerned, each number had hit the spot, with Kelly even describing 'I'm Still In Love With My Ex' as "the best writing experience ever", something she had played a key role in creating. The tracks also had an aura of rawness, honesty and vulnerability about them – but uptempo and cheerful they were not. She removed the worst offenders, which – according to Kelly – "would have made people cry", and now it was time to counterbalance the existing melancholy with something "sassy".

Early on, she turned to multi-platinum producer Scott Storch to help reinvigorate the album. He'd been responsible for the hypnotic rhythms of 50 Cent's 'Candy Shop' as well as the high energy, sexually charged 'Naughty Girl' by Beyoncé.

Kelly had expressed a desire to "go back to my roots" and experiment with the commercial, urban-style beats that had propelled Destiny's Child to fame – and it seemed as though Scott had the experience to take her there.

But there was some controversy surrounding him when they began working together: after collaborating with Timbaland on the Justin Timberlake track 'Cry Me A River', there had been a bitter dispute when Scott hadn't received a production credit on the album, but merely an acknowledgement that he had played piano. A tussle followed which Timbaland turned public on his later track 'Give It To Me', when he spat contemptuously that he was the real producer and his rival was just 'a piano man'. However, Kelly was looking forward to working with Scott – and, when she did, he helped to make clubbing a legitimate part of her job description. Purely for work purposes, the pair hit the nightclubs to research which sounds would liven them up on the dancefloor.

"We wanted to have a party record, a record that'd make you get up and dance," Kelly revealed to *Concrete Loop*. "So we literally went out and we went to a club and partied and we got a little inspiration, then went back into the studio and wrote the song in an hour."

That song was 'Work' – and Kelly didn't know it then, but the lightning-fast creation would later become a hit single. *Rewind* magazine would describe it as "a high energy track that will undoubtedly be a future club banger". Mission accomplished!

Then there was 'Like This', a track which came fully loaded with pre-charged R&B swagger. Kelly enlisted the help of established songwriter Sean Garrett, but was sceptical as he had also worked on several tunes for Beyoncé – 'Ring The Alarm', 'Upgrade You', 'Get Me Bodied' and 'Check On It' to name but a few. She was desperate to avoid the risk of replicating another artist's signature sound – and least of all someone she knew she would be compared to anyway. Fortunately, she was assertive enough to make her feelings known. "If you work with the same producer, you're like, 'Look, I want my own sound!'" she told MTV. "You definitely want it to be different from Beyoncé and Michelle and you definitely have to express that."

However, she and Sean clicked because he took everything that made her an individual into account to craft the tune. "One thing I love about Sean is that he takes the time to know the artist and know their personality," Kelly continued. "We'll sit and have conversations forever and he'll just start to write and you're like, 'How did you know that about me?'"

However the backing track – created by Polow Da Don (perhaps best known for his work with artists such as the Pussycat Dolls) left her incredulous. "The track... had a cowbell in it," Kelly gasped to *Singers Room*. "I was like, 'What kind of sound is this?' He was like, 'No, Kelly, you gotta listen! You gotta listen, Ma!' So I said, 'Fine'. I listened some more and then he started singing the words. And I thought he was crazy but I tried it out and it worked!"

That said, there was something missing – and a rapper might just have been the final puzzle piece. Kelly already knew Eve from their work together on her TV series of the same name, so she put in a call to her and Eve arrived the following day. "The stars were aligned and everything came together beautifully," Kelly told *Singers Room*. "Everything happened for a reason and I'm happy that it did because Eve is one of my favourite female MCs... Doing that together was really hot."

The lyrics already portrayed someone who commanded respect and was in control of their own destiny – with sentiments such as kicking a misbehaving man to the kerb or insisting everyone says "Miss" before her name appearing in abundance – but it was Eve who added the swagger.

Her rap was silky, seductive and quietly self-assured, a drawl delivered with the blasé nonchalance of someone already confident that she's the boss. With her input, the track had gained a self-celebratory feel and whilst the bragging didn't quite reach Kanye West proportions, it was packed with bravado nonetheless. The track wasn't just about ghetto glamour either – there was a subtle empowerment message that made it Kelly's solo version of 'Independent Women (Part 1)'.

"It's important to have a sense of self and know who you are and really know yourself," Kelly told *I Like Music* of the message behind the song. "You have to know who you are when you walk down the street as a person, as a kid, as a teenager, you never want anyone to take advantage of who you are."

Another self-celebratory anthem was 'Comeback', about a sex appeal so hot that even the fire brigade couldn't extinguish it, someone so addictive that they should carry a health warning. It was Kelly's triumphant announcement that love might have temporarily taken her down, but now – like any R&B soldier worth their weight in gold – she was back in town and better than ever. "Being a woman is fly," Kelly told *Concrete Loop*. "Whether it's your smile, your walk, the way you look at someone or, you know, the way you kiss someone – whatever it is, I call it the comeback. You make whoever it is come back for more."

Then there was 'Ghetto'. Kelly had been toying with a then-untitled version of the track back in 2006 for *My Story*, but felt a need to revamp the original to take it into feel-good territory. To do so, she drafted in Snoop Dogg – and, according to Kelly, the collaboration was long overdue.

"Ever since he did [his first album] *Doggystyle*, I was like 'I wanna work with Snoop!'" she told *Blues & Soul*. "He's the king of cool, so I was honoured when he said yes to do the record. It was like a dream come true."

Snoop had been a step ahead of Kelly back in the Destiny's Child days too, when, back in the early Nineties, he was the first vocalist ever to use the word "bootylicious" in a song. He had also collaborated with many of the major chart-toppers, including Justin Timberlake and the Pussycat Dolls.

Unsurprisingly for someone who seemed to be ever-present in the charts, he wasn't short on self-confidence either, once claiming that a song was like a cake with no candles until his rap contributions were added. To him, his vocals were the magic formula that made a merely good track great and sent it to number one – but Kelly viewed his peacock-style arrogance as an asset. As endearing to her as Eve's ballsy demeanour, she felt it matched the ghetto theme. "He put his Snoop-a-fied player-isms on the track," Kelly chuckled. "He just gives it that something."

Tank, who produced the song, also appeared as a featured artist on another track, 'The Show'. On it, Kelly invites a partner to take a front-row seat at one of her concerts and watch as she sets the stage "on fire", before taking advantage of an access-all-areas pass to see how she gets down behind the scenes.

Capturing the excitement and fantasy element of a superstar up close and personal, whilst adding a groupie vibe, the song seemed to emulate Beyoncé's 2003 track 'Hip Hop Star', which shared the same theme. Yet, just as Beyoncé had featured Outkast's Big Boi and Sleepy Brown on her song, Kelly had Tank – a little-known athlete turned R&B singer and songwriter. Lauding him as the music world's best-kept secret, she giggled that he was "just too much for me".

Then there was 'Every Thought Is You', a track about an all-consuming infatuation with a man, suggesting Kelly was over her ex and ready to hit the dating scene again. It benefited from production by Rockwilder, who'd also worked with Jay-Z.

Finally, one of the most special tracks for Kelly was 'Love'. It had an intriguing combination of impassioned singing offset by an icy, robotic beat. The vocals had hints of Mary J Blige and Ciara and – no doubt due to Kelly's studio diet of vintage Whitney Houston CDs – a trace of old-school Whitney too. Co-writer Solange Knowles, now a working mother with a toddler named Daniel, contributed to the song's emotional lyrics. "She wrote a beautiful, amazing track," Kelly praised to *Blues & Soul*. "Solange is so independent. I admire her on so many different levels – as a woman, a mother now and as an artist – so I'm extremely proud of her."

So, Kelly finally had her album. Its ice-cold R&B twist made the slow songs sound much like fellow performer Ciara, with a particular nod to her 2006 album *Evolution*. Perhaps that wasn't surprising as, for example, 'Like This' was produced by Jamal Jones (aka Polow Da Don) and Sean Garrett, who also worked with Ciara – on 'Promise' and 'Bang It Up' respectively.

Plus while the slow songs had the right vibe, there was now a fair share of more upbeat tracks to balance them out, with a little help from the *Billboard* chart's hottest repeat offenders. It was looking promising.

To reflect the upbeat vibe, a new name for the album had also been selected – *Ms Kelly*. "I know half of [*My Story*] was great, but I felt that it was dragging just a little bit and missing elements of me on the recording, like the playful and confident side," she told *Contact Music*. "[The new] album title is personal, the Ms adds the sassiness and the sauciness."

'Like This', the first track to be released from the album, was certainly sassy. Hitting the US charts on March 13, 2007, it became her highest-charting single since 'Stole', marking a victorious comeback. However, when the album followed in June, critics were less than generous with their praise. *About.com* delivered the crushing putdown: "This album cements the reasons why Kelly has failed to achieve the same level of stardom as Beyoncé. If there was still lingering doubt as to whether Beyoncé or Kelly is the more talented singer, the mediocre *Ms Kelly* will probably put those doubts to rest."

Meanwhile *The Guardian* warned that while she was a "viable solo star", she had "failed to step out of Beyoncé's shadow commercially". Although Kelly had brushed off comparisons to her Destiny's Child sister as "only natural", the constant references to her as a poor man's Beyoncé had to hurt.

Even worse, Kelly couldn't console herself by passing off the reviews as isolated opinions – 'Beautiful Liar', Beyoncé's collaboration with Shakira, was already storming ahead of her in the charts. The fact that it claimed the top spot in the UK was a sore reminder of her position in the pecking order.

Her association with Beyoncé was both a blessing and a curse. After all, it was Destiny's Child that had first launched Kelly to fame, but the group's multi-million-selling status had also heightened expectations of her. *Ms Kelly's* first-week sales of almost 87,000 would have been satisfying for the majority of chart-aspiring artists, but with Beyoncé as a peer, Kelly had so much more to live up to.

In reviews Stateside, Kelly didn't fare much better. The *Boston Globe* deemed *Ms Kelly* unremarkable, claiming that it "never takes full flight to become something special" and warning that "she is going to have to push a bit harder if she wants to take it to the next level".

Meanwhile it seemed that *AllMusic* was unimpressed with her attempt to liven up the album, something she had taken so seriously that she'd pushed back the release date three times. "*Ms Kelly* sounds like an album where Rowland is mostly sorting through some deeply personal relationship issues with a couple of relatively light-hearted songs thrown in for variety," it claimed. "Unless close attention is paid to the drastic and fleeting shifts in subject matter, the conscious decision to release an album not completely sad/bitter/angry/regretful… isn't completely apparent." The review added that those not going through a break-up themselves might struggle to connect and relate to the darker side of the songs.

The less than favourable media reputation led to fears that the success of 'Stole' might have been a false start. Five years previously, 'Stole' had dominated the charts and radio airplay, hot on the heels of the number one hit 'Dilemma', but – counter-intuitively – subsequent singles from *Simply Deep* had fared much worse. By the time Beyoncé's debut single, 'Crazy In Love' – a far more dancefloor-friendly proposition – was released, Kelly's work seemed to have almost been forgotten. Like a support act drowned out by the crowd's incessant clamours for the headliners, she faded into the background.

In a last-ditch attempt to revive the album, a second single was scheduled for August 7. 'Work' had been intended as the next release but it was scrapped at the last minute due to loud whispers in R&B circles that the song had little commercial potential. Kelly had put her foot down and told the record company she wanted to release 'Ghetto' instead – a decision both parties would regret.

On the set of the video, Kelly had enthused, "It's really fly… I feel like everybody has some sort of element of ghetto in them. Think about it, right? Wouldn't you say so?"

Not if *About.com* had anything to say about it. The website rolled its eyes at the way the lyrics portrayed her as a street, sexually free woman, instead describing her flirtation with ghetto imagery as "contrived" and "out of character". The public might have agreed when 'Ghetto' became Kelly's lowest-charting single ever, whether with the group or individually. While it made the obscure Bubbling Under chart, it didn't register at all on the Top 200 of any mainstream chart. It was officially a commercial failure.

The track also highlighted that Kelly might struggle to shake off the chains that bound her to Beyoncé and to assert her own identity as an artist. What was more, perhaps the problem was partially self-inflicted. After all, Kelly had described 'Ghetto' as a tune about "good girls who dig bad boys" but as much as she sought to avoid comparisons, wasn't the theme a little too similar to Beyoncé's 'Check On It', about good girls who liked to 'get down with the gangstas'? It seemed as though Kelly would have to try a little harder to stand out in her own right. That said, with a stable of producers who already worked with Beyoncé on standby and a shared love of R&B, it might be hard to distance herself totally from her soul sister's sound.

The pressure came to a head one night in Nigeria when – halfway through a show – Kelly fell unconscious. She was in the bustling West African city of Lagos to perform at the annual This Day Summer Music Festival – but, from the beginning, there were signs that she and Nigeria might be a mismatch.

Firstly, she caused a stir among some conservative Christians by appearing on stage in a shimmery sequined gold mini dress. Yet alongside Shakira's fiery Latino hip-swivelling routines and Rihanna's penchant for fetish gear – both were artists on the bill that year – Kelly seemed positively wholesome in comparison. Unfortunately, that made little difference to religious hardliners and Kelly soon found herself damned as a bad influence on the city's youth.

Then there was a demanding crowd to please. Despite the event being just two years old, past performers at the festival were hard acts to follow. The previous year had seen Jay-Z, Beyoncé, Missy Elliot, Busta Rhymes, Snoop Dogg and En Vogue take to the stage to name just a few. Nigerians were expecting value for money, too. The area was blighted by severe poverty and yet, for the country's global music event of the year, locals had shelled out a minimum of £40 and up to £200 to enjoy the show. The pressure was on.

Yet that night on stage, although it was past 9pm, the heat was overpowering. Plus, according to doctors at the local hospital she attended, Kelly hadn't eaten for over 12 hours. It was a recipe for disaster. Halfway through a rendition of 'Say My Name', that disaster came.

She started swaying precariously as she paced the stage, before raising her hands to her face and slumping into unconsciousness. She was rushed to hospital where it took paramedics over half an hour to resuscitate her. Kelly would later explain via her publicist that she had been suffering from extreme dehydration.

However, some wrote it off as an attention-seeking publicity stunt or − even worse − a joke. The video footage of her collapse became YouTube gold − one of the website's most-watched clips of the month − something which Kelly raged was "sick".

"It was a medical condition, I just happened to collapse," Kelly told *Now*. "If this is the joke of the day, then those people are real sickos." While for the most part she was well-received in Nigeria, collapsing in front of thousands was embarrassing and difficult to live down.

Plus there was more bad news in store for her that autumn when she auditioned for a role in the *Sex And The City* movie as Louise, Carrie Bradshaw's assistant. The TV series on which the film was based was a favourite of all the Destiny's Child girls, with Jay-Z even referencing Beyoncé's love of the show in song lyrics, for ''03 Bonnie And Clyde'. Like Beyoncé, Kelly clearly had no shortage of enthusiasm for the role, but in the end she was unsuccessful, losing out to Jennifer Hudson.

Kelly also auditioned to be a judge on US talent show *American Idol*, but had a brutal knockback, an experience she would later describe as "belittling". Despite flying out to Atlanta, she found producers were completely uninterested. "It was horrible," Kelly recalled to *The Houston Chronicle*. "They were all at their computers, they didn't even look at me. Two of them were talking about what they wanted to eat for lunch." Needless to say, she didn't get the part.

However, as Kelly might say, nothing happens without a reason and − ironically − her failed audition for a judging role taught her how not to judge another person. With the experience of rejection from unfeeling producers fresh in her mind, when she finally did become a judge – on the NBC show *Clash Of The Choirs* – she took extra care to be sensitive, kind and sympathetic. After all, some of the singers were in for a very public dismissal.

Clash Of The Choirs was a talent show televised to millions, just like *American Idol* or *The X-Factor*, but with two crucial differences: it wasn't a pop star producers were seeking, but a group of choir singers, and the prize wasn't a recording contract, but a donation to charity. The theme of the show was to find talented people from diverse backgrounds who were willing to work together to find one voice, united both by music and by God.

Broadcast over the Christmas period, the show would see five celebrity judges narrow down a collection of singing talents from their hometown – in Kelly's case, Houston – from 300 hopefuls to just 20.

Gruelling rehearsals would follow, before four nights of live shows in New York, watched by the nation, after which viewers would do a phone or internet vote for their favourite choir. Each night, one of the choirs would be eliminated until one was left – and the winning group would receive a $250,000 donation for a local community-based charity.

Flanked by her six-month-old Rottweiler puppy – fortunately none of Kelly's 20-strong choir were afraid of dogs – she became a musical mentor and instructor. Ever-sensitive, she was keen to ensure that there were no catfights or battles of gargantuan egos and that everyone was made to feel that they belonged. "No egos, that's the first thing I said," a no-nonsense Kelly told *The Houston Chronicle*. "Everyone should respect each other above everything."

The group was working towards winning the donation for Bread For Life, a charity for the homeless and hungry run by St John's United Methodist Church, Kelly's local. "I feel like I have a choir of 20 secret weapons," she boasted with the air of a proud parent. "Everybody has something beautiful and magically delicious about their voice."

Thanks to Kelly's tender pep talks, her group truly did feel like she was a strong, positive mother figure. One of the girls, Patrice Staten, was especially close to Kelly's heart as she had lost her mother to cancer at the age of five. Kelly was no stranger to losing a parent and as her father had left when she was just two years older, she could relate to the gap a missing parent left in their lives. Even though her father was still alive, she could relate to the feeling of bereavement. She resolved to be the mother Patrice had scarcely had – and to be matriarch in the others' lives too. "We have to do what mama says, because we're all brothers and sisters," Patrice explained.

The miniature family was up against rival choirs led by celebrities Michael Bolton, Blake Shelton, Nick Lachey and finally Patti LaBelle, the woman who had written 'Dilemma' and, ironically, who had appeared in the promo video as Kelly's mother.

As the rehearsals gathered heat, Kelly's competitive instinct came into play and she continually urged the group, "Go rehearse your parts – we've got a competition to win!"

On the night, December 17, her choir performed Michael Jackson's 'Man In The Mirror' and George Michael's 'Freedom', along with a traditional Christmas carol – but, to her dismay, they were eliminated in the very first round. Patti LaBelle's group came second in the competition, while the overall winner was Nick Lachey's group, whose songs on the night had included Natasha Bedingfield's 'Unwritten'.

It was another in a long line of disappointments for Kelly, but she hoped that 2008 would bring better fortune. On January 21, 'Work' was tentatively released everywhere but the USA. It immediately received the Beyoncé comparison treatments with the BBC insisting its "jagged vocal and hip-shaking beat" was similar to Destiny's Child hits 'Bug A Boo' and 'Lose My Breath'.

About.com concurred that the track was "an excellent Destiny's Child-type song", going on to claim that the stellar beat disguised Kelly's alleged "vocal shortcomings".

Perhaps the most colourful comparison, however, came from *DotMusic*, which claimed, "'Work' is a clear attempt to encroach on her old bandmate's hypersexual territory, although it's hard to imagine Beyoncé resorting to as crass a single entendre as repeatedly demanding 'Put it in!' like a hooker on crystal meth."

However, this time the reviews didn't match the public reaction, and

'Work' was hugely successful, charting highly throughout Europe. A remix of the track by the Freemasons – a production team Kelly claimed she had been keen to work with after Beyoncé had recommended them – also hit radio.

Their Indian-influenced dancefloor interpretation of the original also became a hit and was very popular on various request lines.

Finally she was getting some recognition. Oddly, however, in spite of the lyrics, she insisted the song had nothing to do with sex. "It's actually very innocent," she told a sceptical journalist at *Now*. "All I'm saying is don't come around if you're not going to live up to all your talk and, as you know, some guys are just full of talk… It's a little aggressive, maybe [but] it's just a woman saying you can't catch me easy and you have to put in the work… That's it, of course."

As if to punctuate her point, Kelly then told *Vibe* magazine that sex was "overrated", subsequently explaining: "I said it because I think it's important when you decide to take that step with your partner that you're both in love." Her backtracking couldn't have been more of a departure from the heat-filled lyrics but, whatever the song truly meant, one thing was indisputable – it was a floor-filler.

That said, there was a reason her label hadn't released it in America, and there were still some grave doubts about the future of the album. The success of tracks like 'Work' emphasised that faster songs were more popular with her audience – and Kelly had received a flurry of letters from fans asking for more of them. It was with a heavy heart that Kelly went back into the studio to work on *Ms Kelly* yet again.

"I got letters from fans saying they wanted more uptempo songs, so I went back and made sure there were more upbeat tracks," she told the *Daily Mail*. "I want my records to be played in clubs [and] I needed everything to be right, from the songs to the packaging."

The main reason for reissuing the album was due to poor sales, something that Kelly initially struggled to accept. "It was difficult at first," she confided to *Singers Room*, "but then I realised that it wasn't my fault. The reason I say it wasn't my fault is that we live in a very different music industry right now. It's tough to sell records without having someone download it [for free]."

In Kelly's eyes, she'd already hit rock bottom with the album and she felt she had little to lose at that stage. Consequently she was unafraid to take chances with the reissue. "A lot of growth took place," she told *Men's Fitness* of the "anxious" experience. "I actually took risks and I wanted to do the things I've never done before, or I was possibly afraid to do. I just did it. I think that Nike said it best when they said, 'Just do it.'"

With several "feel the fear and do it anyway" style mentions in her mind, Kelly bit the bullet and got to work on the songs. She replaced 'Comeback' with a more lively remix by Karmatronic, removed the original version of 'Work' in favour of the Freemasons mix and axed 'The Show', 'Interlude', 'Flashback', 'I'm Still In Love With My Ex' and the poorly charting 'Ghetto' altogether.

This left five slots to fill with brand new songs. One of Kelly's goals this time around was to stand out from Beyoncé and be an innovator, not an imitator. The original version of *Ms Kelly*, on the other hand, suggested that not every producer working with Kelly had internalised that goal. For example, on 'This Is Love', there'd been lyrical similarities to Beyoncé's love note 'Flaws And All', where she thanks a partner for loving her enough to accept and even treasure her imperfections and for turning them into art.

Meanwhile, both girls suggest that they are not always easy to love. That was one charge Kelly didn't want to see levelled against the album – and, keeping the aim of being herself in mind, she got to work. First there were the angry tracks reprimanding a lover for his betrayal.

'Broken' is an admission that she is still angry at the radio for playing songs that remind her of her ex and that – no matter how many pictures, letters or mementoes she throws away – it won't stop her flashbacks because he's left her broken.

Then there's 'No Man No Cry', a clear nod to Bob Marley, but with a very different beat. The lyrics harbour the bitterness of a much more mature woman, someone who's seen a lifetime of false promises – think Dawn Penn on 'You Don't Love Me (No No No)' or Billie Holiday on 'Lady Sings The Blues'. Yet while these two tracks are filled with resignation, Kelly resolves to take back her life and become an independent woman again. She rages that she has invested her time and affection into a failed relationship for too long and that the man involved won't steal her youth and happiness for a moment longer.

Meanwhile, continuing on the broken relationships theme, 'Love Again' gives an insight into the psychological effects of growing up without a father and of subsequently being let down by men in her adult life. She confesses that her experiences have left her fearful of intimacy and afraid to love wholeheartedly. "I've been in relationships where I've been hurt and I don't want to be there any more," Kelly elaborated to the *Daily Mail*. "You're just kind of walking on eggshells, thinking, 'What are you going to do to disappoint me?'"

The lack of consistency in her relationship with her father might have led to an emotional patterning where Kelly was always looking over her shoulder and anticipating a painful, life-changing drama, not to mention visualising the parting before the relationship had properly begun.

In the song, Kelly offers a thinly disguised apology to ex-fiancé Roy for calling off their romance, and also lets slip some home truths she may have been afraid to divulge in person. For example, she explains that she had built up walls of self-protection due to a broken heart, and that the pain from her previous ex's behaviour had left her too raw and vulnerable to let her guard down again so soon.

Having exorcised some of her vitriol in the three songs – which doubled as therapy sessions – 'Unity' was written on a more positive note, offering hope that the sun will, before too long, shine again.

Finally, Kelly fulfilled her promise to add something uptempo with 'Daylight', an unlikely collaboration featuring emo singer Travie McCoy of the indie group Gym Class Heroes. To Kelly, Travis – who had briefly been engaged to Katy Perry – was a "rapper-slash-poet-slash-rocker" who she got with immediately, although to begin with, her label had been far from convinced. "I love the fact that Gym Class Heroes' music and sound is something different and eclectic," Kelly defended to *Blues & Soul*. "I figured me and Travis together would be an unusual type of duo and I'm happy I trusted my instincts because it turned out to be really cool."

For fans, the beauty of 'Daylight' was its simplicity. Against an infectiously catchy groove, the pair confess their love for the nightlife where one night of clubbing regularly turns into three at a time. In his rap, Travis cheekily references clubbing sessions that last as long as Paris Hilton's jail sentence, while Kelly asserts that she gets to sleep when the rest of the world are just waking up.

The track had originally been intended purely for the soundtrack to *Asterix And The Olympic Games*, but Kelly was so attached to it that she decided to include it on the re-release of *Ms Kelly* as well. The video, featuring all the members of Gym Class Heroes, as well as a "hilarious" cameo of Travis "riding a weird modified bicycle in the middle of the bustling city" evidenced the rock-R&B crossover and was just the start of Kelly's genre-defying experimentation.

The counter-intuitive collaboration was a risk to take, but the video had been filmed in New York just a few blocks from the Empire State Building – and, as Alicia Keys and Jay-Z had once sung while standing in front of it, if you can make it in New York, you can make it anywhere.

The deluxe version of *Ms Kelly* hit the shops on March 28, while 'Daylight', posing as its lead single, followed on May 5. The song made the top 20 in the UK, outperforming her ranking in the US and – capitalising on her success on the other side of the Atlantic – she started touring in Europe during the summer.

However, the turbulent British weather conditions took some getting used to, with Kelly claiming excessive rain and wind were the only things she didn't like about being on UK shores.

In one amusing moment at T4's On The Beach Festival in July, she attached paper plates to the soles of her five-inch stiletto heels not to help her look fashionable, but to avoid sinking in the sand.

Europe also brought out a new side to Kelly – and it was time for her to start living out the message of 'Daylight'. She thrust herself into a lifestyle of sex, drugs and rock 'n' roll – or at the very least all-hours partying, as she spent the summer stopping by at the hottest dance clubs on the continent. "I spent nights dancing in the south of France from 12.45 a.m. to eight in the morning," she confessed.

One such night was the St Tropez Takeover, an all-night party she was hosting at Nice-based nightclub Amika on August 8. According to reports by *The Mirror*, she had £70,000 worth of alcohol specially flown in for the event. Hearing that a young celebrity had spent long nights partying lavishly would be almost yawn-worthy in most cases because of the prevalence of such gossip, but it hadn't previously been good-girl Kelly's scene.

Living with Mathew Knowles could have been akin to a jail sentence for the average feisty young woman, as conventional pop-star-style misdemeanours had been banned and there were no nights out clubbing under his roof.

Sensational stories might have heightened the popularity of some stars, enhancing their headline potential, but a "crunk" image wasn't what Mathew had in mind – he was intent on cultivating someone with a bleached-clean reputation.

Yet now Kelly was growing up – she had her own ocean-front condo in Miami and there was no possessive father figure to answer to there.

She was quickly growing apart from both Mathew and all that he represented. Her transition was highlighted by a confession she made to MTV, finally admitting that 'Work' wasn't as wholesome as she'd originally claimed. "OK, yes, it means exactly what you think it means," she conceded. "I give up... The lyrics are very sexy. They were out of the box for me. Destiny's Child was so 'hush hush' about sexuality, but [now] I've grown into my sexuality and I'm very comfortable with it."

Letting the interviewer into a secret about how she and the producer had plotted to throw listeners off the scent, she joked: "I remember when the writer was writing it and he was like, 'Put it in, put it in!' and I said, 'This is a nasty record!' He said we could completely throw people off with it and 'put it in' could be about putting work in to get somebody." The public wasn't easily fooled though and, one might suspect, neither was Mathew.

By January 2009, Kelly had made it her New Year's resolution to part ways with Mathew for good. A statement that her former manager released to the media suggested that his love for her was as strong as a father's for his daughter and that – despite putting an end to a 14-year working relationship – the decision to do so had been a friendly one.

"After a very positive meeting between Kelly Rowland and myself, we have amicably decided to end our professional relationship," he announced. "My company, Music World, will continue to manage Destiny's Child as a group. As an artist, Kelly has incredible talent and I only wish her the best. We will always be family first and foremost and as a dad, I can only have love for Kelly."

But why the sudden decision to part company? Perhaps Kelly, who regarded Mathew as close as a blood connection, had found it hard to mix business with pleasure and felt it wiser to separate the two for the sake of their personal relationship. On the other hand, perhaps there was more to it.

Could it be that Kelly wanted to distance herself from the dubious reputation Mathew had gained over the years? The dramas had begun as early as 2001, when he had been accused of squandering money belonging to the late Andretta Tillman's estate to support an addiction to drugs and hookers. Two years later there had been a $200 million lawsuit launched against Mathew and all three members of Destiny's Child for stealing the song 'Survivor'. Not only had it been an embarrassment but the bad press around it had also coincided with the worst charting song of Kelly's career to date. She might have felt that the scandals about Mathew were responsible for the dip in her career.

'Cater 2 U' and the 'Independent Women' tracks came under similar legal scrutiny, but even after Kelly had left Destiny's Child, she was still plagued by the constant string of lawsuits directed towards Mathew and Beyoncé. The legal action had become so prolific that it grew to be an in-joke among journalists that Beyoncé's only destiny these days was in the courtroom. She had been sued for copyright infringement on 'Baby Boy' and 'Kissing You' and was also accused of dishonesty by Ne-Yo, who went on live radio to insist he'd co-written 'Irreplaceable' but that she'd taken all the credit when talking about the song. Then 'Crazy In Love' producer Rich Harrison appeared on MTV to complain that she had publicly taken credit both for writing the song and finding the musical sample, when he had written it and had kept the sample in his collection for years.

The constant complaints made Beyoncé's talent seem fraudulent and based on trickery – and Kelly might have feared being tarred with the same brush.

Perhaps the last straw for a shamefaced Kelly had come in 2007 when the website *Aishamusic.com* announced plans to sue the Knowles family for hacking into company computers and stealing the songs 'Worldwide Woman', 'Amor Gitmo' and 'Welcome To Hollywood', as well as copying scenes for Beyoncé's videos 'Beautiful Liar', 'Suga Mama', 'Flaws And All' and 'Greenlight'. The website claimed Beyoncé had commissioned hackers to illegally access copyrighted files and that she had even been tracked as a visitor to the website where the files were held herself.

"My copyright catalogue [of songs], valued at billions, was illegally copied," a post from the website owner raged, before accusing, "Beyoncé, who couldn't direct traffic, took credit as the director for the music video treatments she stole. She is not a director."

It added: "The Knowles clan claim to be Christians, but they are not... [They are] crooks and criminals. They believe in stealing money and assets from people to enrich themselves. They are terrible people with no sense of decency as their legal history clearly illustrates." The website went on to publicly denounce Beyoncé as a "fraud", a "fully fledged felon" and "a criminal thief".

Whether Mathew and Beyoncé were innocent or guilty was almost beside the point, as such claims would be a blemish on their records that could take years to fade – and by association, it could also have a devastating impact on Kelly. Over the years, she had plucked up the courage to dabble in songwriting herself – and one day she might decide she wanted to write for other artists.

However, *Aishamusic.com* had claimed: "You will never sell Beyoncé as a songwriter [because] she has stolen from so many people." Kelly didn't want to face the same problem, that people were reluctant to employ her as they feared she would be using stolen goods. Even if Kelly never utilised her writing skills for another artist, the allegations about Beyoncé had destroyed working relationships for her left, right and centre.

Rich Harrison had also worked with Kelly. Yet Mathew was now seen by some producers as less trustworthy. Perhaps Kelly felt distancing herself both from the Beyoncé brand and the Knowles family name would reduce the risk of being seen the same way. After all, she had wanted to go down in history as a legendary performer, not a legendary thief.

Yet the benefits to leaving Beyoncé's family behind went beyond the criminal issue. Perhaps her departure would also encourage people to think of her as an individual and to stop comparing her music to Beyoncé's. Moreover, a new manager might have the insight into how to carve out a new niche for herself.

The comparisons had been frustrating for Kelly to the point that, in one interview, she resorted to some straight-talking. "I said, 'You know, if you guys would be a little more intelligent and ask me about myself [instead of Beyoncé], we'd have a much better interview," she recalled to *Vibe*. "You can't want a story from me and keep asking me about the past."

Then there was Kelly's increasingly liberated image, which was at odds with Mathew's vision. Her songs had more sexual content and partying had become a more prominent part of her life. In other words, she'd grown up – and perhaps Mathew couldn't handle that.

Part of growing up also meant making her own decisions and rumour had it that Mathew was incensed to hear she rekindled a casual friendship with ex-band member LeToya Luckett. The two had been pictured together at social events and, while LeToya had told Kelly she loved the *Destiny Fulfilled* album, Kelly had reciprocated the praise by commenting on LeToya's recent solo work. Mathew might have seen her attempt to make amends and her public forgiveness of a woman who had sued him twice as disloyal.

Yet Kelly had to live her life independently now and, however much even a biological daughter might love her father, eventually the time would come for her to flee the nest. Perhaps seeking alternative management now was symbolic of that divide. Finally, Kelly might simply have wanted to start afresh. She had become a millionaire under Mathew's wing, but she didn't want a debt of gratitude to allow him to control her every business move.

With an impartial manager, someone with whom she had no history and no ties, she wouldn't feel obliged to be obedient or loyal – she would be able to make her own decisions. As one song collaboration she did would claim, there was no future in the past. When she was young and inexperienced as a singer, having someone to guide her career had acted as a comfort blanket, but the album title *Ms Kelly* was her way of asserting her new-found adulthood – and, as it would soon emerge, as a grown-up there was no place in her life for Mathew.

"It was just a feeling of growing and wanting to call my own shots," Kelly confirmed. "I thank Mathew for everything he's done for me. He made me a millionaire at 18 years old. Then I felt like, 'Well, I'm an adult now and I want to do things this way.' It was more difficult [because I'd lived with him since childhood] but I needed to be selfish for a minute. I had to reclaim my power."

Many people's New Year's resolutions might last a couple of weeks, but Kelly's was more permanent. There was relief, but there was also a sense of bereavement and sorrow.

"I did feel an exhale moment," she confessed to *Vibe,* "but I also felt like, 'Oh my God, what have I done?!' I stayed in the house for two days. I was sad – it was like a funeral. I had to deaden that situation in order to start afresh."

Chapter 10

When Dance Takes Over

The year 2009 was one of change for Kelly. Beyoncé was now officially the first lady of pop, having sung at Barack Obama's presidential inauguration ball in January, and Kelly was determined not to be left behind. She replaced Mathew Knowles with new manager Jeff Rabhan and was working ferociously on a new strategy, when some life-changing news came: she had been dropped from Columbia Records.

Despite the fanfare surrounding her album's reissue, 'Daylight' had barely existed to American ears. It had fared better in the UK, but had still charted lower than 'Work' or 'Like This' – and record-label bosses were allegedly at the end of their tethers.

Beyoncé was also on Columbia Records, but her solo successes, from a financial standpoint, seemed far more worthy of investment. She had been on stage with Prince and Tina Turner and had collaborated with big names across the rap-soul-reggae-R&B spectrum such as Jay-Z, Alicia Keys, Outkast's Big Boi, Luther Vandross, Sean Paul and Shakira.

Kelly's collaborations, on the other hand, had mainly been restricted to pairings with obscure international artists unknown outside of their home countries. For example, her song with French R&B songstress Nadiya, aptly named 'No Future In The Past', had been released in September 2008 but had only charted in France, outside of the Top 40.

Despite a striking single cover – featuring Kelly and Nadiya posing back to back and appearing to emulate Shakira and Beyoncé in 'Beautiful Liar' – and sensitive lyrics about dancing to break free from the past and finding the strength to move mountains of ice and snow, it just didn't catch on.

Then there was 'Breathe Gentle', a duet with Italian singer Tiziano Ferro. It had made the number one spot on the Italian airplay charts and even scored a Top 10 ranking in Holland, but outside of these territories, the single failed to ignite.

A cross between a James Bond movie and an Italian mafia-inspired adventure, the video portrayed Tiziano and Kelly as lovers and thieves who are on the run from police. Shot at Lake Garda, it was the Italian version of Jay-Z and Beyoncé's ''03 Bonnie And Clyde', playfully romanticising the gangster's-moll scenario – but it had a much lower chart rating. Kelly just wasn't pulling in audiences. She was slowly but surely building up a dedicated fanbase in Europe, but that wasn't enough for Columbia, as the label expected equal success Stateside. Destiny's Child had now sold enough albums to top the 50 million mark, whereas Kelly had only sold four million CDs as a solo artist. It was hardly a failure, but for a heavily promoted artist in whom Columbia had invested considerable amounts of time and money, it just wasn't good enough.

It was a double blow for Kelly as the figures also implied she couldn't be successful without Beyoncé. Over a seven-year solo career, Kelly had still sold less than a twelfth of the albums that the group had sold, and the *Survivor* album alone had dwarfed Kelly's three solo albums put together.

The writing was on the wall for Kelly's future with Columbia, and – even more hurtfully – rumours had surfaced in the press that she was dumped for no longer being "commercially viable".

Label boss Rob Stringer quickly came forward to counter that the decision had been "agreed upon mutually", although this might have been merely a polite formality to allow a once-loved artist to leave with dignity. Either way, it didn't stop the rumour mill from turning. One well-placed source even claimed that Mathew had influenced the label to drop Kelly. "When she left his management, it was not on good grounds and, as you may know, Mathew also got Kelly dropped from Columbia," the source wrote. "He thought he was teaching her a lesson and she would be 'nothing' without him."

Intriguingly, Kelly didn't deny these rumours. When *Vibe* questioned her on whether she felt her split from Mathew was connected to being dropped from Columbia two months later, she simply said, "I can't speak on what I don't know."

Would Columbia really have been swayed simply on Mathew's say-so? After all, he'd once joked to MTV: "I wish I had the [amount of] influence people [attribute] to me!" On the other hand, he was the father and manager of one of the label's top earners, so pulling some strings might not have been impossible.

Either way, Kelly was about to have the last laugh. It had been speculated that she and her label had suffered differences when she became desperate to change direction and branch out into new musical genres but Columbia remained hesitant. To the label, stepping away from the formula that had made her a multi-millionaire was a monumental risk and one that wasn't worth taking. The label had already been badly stung by the flop of *Ms Kelly*: perhaps in its eyes, she had simply run her course as an artist?

Kelly was out of favour and out of fashion. But, within just three weeks, she rose from the musical dead with 'Love Takes Over'. Now the nation's DJs could think of nothing else.

It had all begun the previous summer, which Kelly had spent touring and clubbing in Europe. "That influenced my music in so many ways," she revealed to *Frontiers LA* of her globe-trotting. "More so above everything, it was just going out and getting a chance to party. My whole vision changed."

The most memorable part of the summer, however, had been a trip to the south of France. As well as co-hosting a night at legendary Nice nightclub Amika, she had also performed live in concert in Cannes to a celebrity-studded crowd that included Brad Pitt, George Clooney, P Diddy, Jay-Z and Beyoncé. She'd extensively explored the club scene and the truth was that – for a newly liberated Kelly who had just come out of her shell – that was the best part of all. "[It] meant so much in the sense that I didn't care what time it was," she said. "I didn't care what I had on, I didn't care what drink I had – it was just about the music."

However, one night stood out in particular for her: catching one of French producer David Guetta's DJ sets. She lost herself in the beat and realised that – in contrast to her R&B roots – this type of music wasn't about the clothes, the jewels, the eye candy on someone's arm or the ostentatious glamour. It was all about simply letting your hair down and having fun. "That's what an experience with music should be about," she told *The Scotsman* defiantly. "When people want to stand on each other's shoulders and they go crazy and they're sweating and they're having a good time, that's all that counts. You feel so much love in the crowd! It's such a good feeling and that's what I want my music to do."

For a moment in her mind Kelly left the image-conscious world of R&B behind and started "dancing all night long" to release her from her inhibitions. David played song after song, including 'Love Is Gone', featuring Chris Willis, which became a personal favourite for Kelly. Then he decided to try a new song out on the crowd – the instrumental backing track for what would eventually become 'When Love Takes Over'.

When she heard its combination of "uplifting" piano and percussion, Kelly was left "overcome with emotion". She burst into tears right there on the dancefloor, before running up to the turntables to get David's attention. "I lost my mind so much I cried," she recalled. "I had to sing on that track. He was still DJing and I was like, 'I need to talk to you, I need that track!' I couldn't wait!"

David and Kelly's musical styles couldn't have been more different, but they met at the right time. Kelly was growing tired of her usual sound and wanted something that would set her apart from the others on the scene. "I was kinda bored with where R&B music was and I wanted something different that I would actually stand out with!" Kelly revealed to *Blues & Soul*. "Coming from a team – Destiny's Child – where I felt each one of us had something so special that we brought to the group, I wanted to make sure I also brought something on my *own* that was special and that I could grow with."

Meanwhile, David was actively looking to build a crossover album that combined his dance roots with the influence of R&B and hip-hop stars. He was an experienced DJ and producer who had run his own club nights since the late Eighties and, to dance enthusiasts in the know, he was a musical genius. Yet while he had released several albums and had been winning awards for his DJing for years, he had yet to reach international acclaim. He was hoping for a change with his new album – and so was Kelly.

"I had never thought about recording a dance track myself [but] hearing David's song made me consider taking on this whole new style," she mused. And while she was taking a tentative step into the European dance camp, her musical partner was opening his eyes to the sounds Stateside. "The track with Kelly has made me experiment with a more American urban influence," David admitted to *Dance Music*. "It's opened a new world for me."

Kelly had initially been nervous about going into uncharted territory with the track, but recording 'Work' in 2007 had given her an early taste of the genre. "It opened my eyes more to dance music," she explained to *Frontiers LA*. "I wasn't as afraid of it any more."

Then, when David obliged and gave her a copy of the then unnamed track to experiment with, the pieces of the puzzle began to fall into place. Back at a hotel in London, Kelly temporarily put a stop to the wild nights out and instead put her energy into teaming up with female production duo the Nervo Twins to write the melody and lyrics for the song.

As it turned out, the twins were the right people to bring the song to life. "The Nervo Twins have wonderful energy," Kelly told *Planet Notion*. "If I could sell their energy then I would, because it's just the greatest high that you are on. They have great love and excitement for music."

She bonded with the track instantly too, leading her to believe it was meant to be. "It was easy to do it," she told *The Scotsman*. "It was almost like it happened before me in spirit and I walked right into it."

For her, the track evoked the magic of someone falling deeply in love and losing their mind with emotion, so the lyrics reflected that. Within a day, it was complete and it was sent to David for his approval – to a deafening silence.

After months of the song languishing on his hard drive, it eventually resurfaced when he was about to start working in earnest on his album, *One Love*. He was certain about one thing from the outset – he wanted 'When Love Takes Over' to be the lead single. Instead of looking down their noses at each other because they didn't share the same sound, he and Kelly had widened their musical vocabulary and been able to learn from each other – and that transformation was something David wanted to share with the world.

Kelly felt the same. "David was so gracious to me to open me up to this beautiful culture," she revealed, "a world where people just love the music." To her, the dance genre was a very exclusive, invitation-only private member's club that she felt honoured to have joined, so she returned the favour by introducing David to more urban artists that he could work with. She had promoted him to the Black Eyed Peas, a meeting of minds that led to the smash hit 'I Gotta Feeling', and she also pointed him in the direction of Akon. "First of all, let me just say *I did it first!*" Kelly crowed to *Blues & Soul* triumphantly of her crossover attempts. "Will.i.am, for example, met David right after I did, and then after he and I had done 'When Love Takes Over', I actually remember seeing Akon at Radio 1's Big Weekend. He was like, 'I heard you did a record with David Guetta!' So I said, 'Yeah, and it's amazing! I can't wait till you hear it!' So I there and then re-introduced Akon and David, who'd actually met before. David let him hear 'When Love Takes Over', and straightaway Akon was like, 'Oh my God, David – we gotta get in the studio!' And that's how their track, 'Sexy Chick', came about!"

The first of David's tracks to reach the public, however, was the collaboration with Kelly. It was released on April 21 in Europe and the USA and would see both artists experience greater success than ever before. In America, the song reached number one on the Hot Dance Airplay and Hot Dance Club Songs charts and it was also a number one in Belgium, Hungary, Italy, Ireland, the Czech Republic, Slovakia and Switzerland, territories that Kelly had never conquered solo before.

In the UK, a June release date was intended to coincide with the summer festival season, but it had to be brought forward to May 9 when an "inferior" cover version was released by unknown artist Airi L. Despite concerns that the cover would cannibalise sales for the original version, these fears were proved wrong when it made to number one in the UK too.

The video, which was filmed at Venice Beach, California, was a visual metaphor for how two musical styles had come together. Kelly starts off walking separately, while David is seen pushing his DJ equipment towards the beach. Eventually the two discover each other and unite for a musical party that transcends the boundaries of their separate sounds. "You see Kelly doing her thing and then me on the other side doing mine," David explained. "Eventually we come together just like how we recorded the song. It's all about sharing the love from this record and making a big party."

Yet according to *Hitfix,* Kelly was the true star of the show. "Guetta, who is relegated to a supporting role in his own video, shows up pushing his gear in a cart," the website sneered, "looking basically like any other homeless guy hanging out in Venice." Capital FM expanded on the theme when they compared his appearance to that of "a bin man".

Some of the comments straddled the fine line between satire and sourness, but David had the last laugh when the track gave him the international breakthrough he had been longing for. It also gave him his highest-charting US single to date, despite over two decades in the music business.

As for Kelly, the track put her firmly back on the radar in America. She had become a trend-setter, daring to break away from the musical style that had made her famous. By incorporating dance into the mainstream, she also encouraged followers of her urban sound, who might never have sought out a purely dance track otherwise, to take a listen.

"In the States what I tend to see is that, if someone tries something that may not be what they usually do, there is a tendency for it to be looked *down* upon," Kelly revealed to *Blues & Soul.* "You know, in the States it's more like, 'You did urban, you came out of urban, you should *stay* urban,' and I don't *like* that! I think artists should just be allowed to be *artists* and to try new things sometimes, because that's why they're called artists. You know, we paint our own pictures and I think the sky's the limit to what we can do as people. If it works, great. If not, try something else! And for me, experimenting with dance music has definitely worked!"

So, to some Americans, switching genres might have been like breaking a major taboo – and about as counter-intuitive as the ultra-religious Katy Perry kissing a girl and liking it. However, not only did the crossover work for Kelly, but it also sparked various other successful genre-defying songs in the charts too. "[The trend] just moved itself over to the States," she commented to *Planet Notion*. "Even FloRida, who's a rapper, doing songs like ['You Spin Me Round'] shows everyone's just able to do everything right now. Usher comes from R&B, urban roots and he's sold the most R&B records and now he is selling a load of records doing dance music. So it's just a different time in music where people can try and do whatever they want and it's beautiful."

Kelly's other big venture out of her comfort zone that year was her role as judge on the first series of US TV programme *The Fashion Show*. Televised on Bravo, it would pit 15 wannabe fashion designers against each other for a chance to win $125,000 and have their creations stocked in retail outlets. Veteran designer Isaac Mizrahi and Fern Mallis, senior vice president of IMG Fashion, would be joining Kelly as judges. Yet while they offered feedback and guidance to the hopefuls, in the end the decision would be out of their hands and it would be up to the studio audience to vote.

Some style snobbery came into play when columnists questioned what qualified Kelly to judge budding fashionistas. Their argument was that she only ever graced the catwalk once, modelling for a heart-disease charity at New York Fashion Week, and had no plans to design a range of her own. They also claimed that while she had taken a front-row seat at many a couture show, she was a mere observer and had no practical credentials in the industry.

Yet Kelly had her own unique part to play. While fashion boss Fern brought marketing expertise and business acumen to the table and designer Isaac brought a seasoned eye for cuts, colours and fabrics,

Kelly's role was no less important – she was a mirror for the fashion-buying public. "I wanted my role to be representing the consumer," she confirmed to *Really*. "All I knew was what looked good!"

Plus, despite now having enough cash to afford the top labels, Kelly's childhood background of living on the poverty line at times meant she was also in touch with the practical concerns of possibly cash-strapped high-street buyers. "If something had a weird fit, I wanted to know why, but I also wanted to know how the fabric felt and if it was going to last me a long time," she claimed.

That wasn't enough for one disgruntled critic at *BuddyTV* however, who name-checked the team at rival show *Project Runway*, which included model Heidi Klum, as superior. He insisted that while Heidi and co were "likable" and "knowledgeable", Kelly, as a fashion novice, would have a lot to live up to. That said, Kelly's fans might retaliate that models were merely clothes horses for their brands and didn't necessarily know that much about the art of fashion themselves.

One fan responded to the damning report on *BuddyTV* with the comeback: "I think Kelly is great and knows just as much about fashion as any model." Again, the critics could say what they liked, but ultimately it was the public who would decide if Kelly's residency on the show was to be a success.

Plus celebrity endorsements were widely considered important in the industry, with many fashion houses recruiting musical personalities such as Lily Allen and Amy Winehouse to be the face of their new lines. Even voluptuous Beth Ditto from the Gossip, a size 22, pioneered a plus-size line. Statistics showed that, almost invariably, the music-buying public was influenced by the tastes of their idols and were helping to make their ranges successful.

Most importantly of all, designers and fashion houses would surely be nothing if they weren't attuned to the tastes and preferences of the public who were buying into their products, as only they, finding power in their masses, could make or break an item.

As it turned out, even the experienced designers weren't always perfect at predicting trends. "I learned a great deal from what the public had to say about clothes," Mizrahi admitted. "Sometimes we would say,

'OK, this is going to be in the top two' and then we'd be shocked when it wasn't." Kelly, as a fashion fan, was offering that buyer's viewpoint – and, what was more, held the influence of a celebrity.

In a conference about the show, she defended her right to belong on the judging panel, insisting: "I think what makes *The Fashion Show* so unique is that it's the public's decision and not only that, it's a real show for real people. This is coming from the consumer's point of view – what they like, how it fits, how creative it is."

Fern concurred, "The real truth is that no matter how fabulous any fashion show is, it doesn't matter if people don't wear or buy the clothes."

There was no doubt Kelly was a fashion enthusiast, perhaps making her well-placed to comment. "I just *love* clothes!" she squealed to MTV. "I'm a girl who loves clothes, accessories, shoes, bags and jewellery... Between my stylists, and my hair and make-up team, we just sit there and go through magazines – because we're just fiends for magazines. We'll sit there and just look at things all day and we'll have our little magazine parties."

Her passion had even extended to making conversation with the contents of her beloved, overflowing, shoe closet. "I actually talk to my shoes," Kelly told a shocked *Daily Mail* journalist. "I love shoes and when I get a new pair, I introduce one lady to the rest of the ladies!"

BuddyTV had sneered that Kelly hadn't exactly been a saluted fashion icon in Destiny's Child, and probably they were right – she had relied on the expertise of Tina Knowles to hand-sew the group's matching outfits, a fashionista who later started the clothing label House of Dereon. The critics might have claimed that next to ever-immaculate Beyoncé, who was usually the centre-piece of photo shoots, Kelly didn't stand a chance of being noticed for herself.

Plus Tina had indisputably been in control of their image, even producing a book about style in 2002: Kelly would only speak up on the outfits she chose if they were breathtakingly tight or exceedingly revealing of her figure.

Yet now that she was the independent woman she had once sung about, she was taking control of her own image and – as the magazine parties with stylists showed – it was now more a collaborative effort. Prior to appearing on the show, Kelly's favourite designers had included Ralph Lauren, D Squared, Rick Owens, Donna Karan, D&G, Roberto Cavalli and BCBG. However, the judging slot allowed her to experiment with styles and brands even more than normal, mixing high fashion with high street.

She stepped out in various labels on each episode, for example wearing a bright orange knee-length Zara dress one week and a black lace creation by Chanel the next. Other outfits she paraded included a cream-coloured D&G buckle dress – which could have passed for a bondage outfit if it hadn't been so ladylike – a purple satin Henri Bendel dress, a black Dior dress also worn by Cheryl Cole on the UK version of *The X-Factor,* and perhaps most notably of all, a skin-tight magenta Herve Leger bandage dress.

Kelly's job was not only to look fabulous, but to offer advice to the team of designers. Admittedly she didn't win many points in the popularity stakes, with controversial and outspoken comments like: "60% of the audience thinks your dress looks like the inside of a wig" and the metaphorical, "You're still in the competition but you're hanging by a thread." However, she later explained that she regarded honesty as the best policy.

That said, Kelly was no Simon Cowell. Rather than becoming the Cruella of the fashion world, her aim was to dole out helpful feedback that would help her contestants to learn from their mistakes. "I think we all need constructive criticism when we're trying to become successful," Kelly told the *Daily Mail,* "but I was never there to bring them down. I want to see them grow as designers."

The first series was a success, with ratings proving so high that a decision was made to broadcast the next series in Britain too. However Kelly wasn't able to come back for a second time and, due to a hectic schedule, she was replaced by supermodel Iman, the wife of David Bowie. Yet she had already made her point: against the instincts of her critics, she had taken a risk and had had the pleasure of seeing it pay off. Why shouldn't she add fashionista to her list of achievements?

In fact, the show gave Kelly such a confidence boost that, despite the fact she was without a record label for the first time in 14 years, she returned to the studio with a vengeance, ready to make album number three.

One morning, while rehearsing an early version of 'Commander' with David Guetta, Kelly had discovered she wasn't alone. Sylvia Rhone – now president of the record label Universal Motown – was also in the building. The last time they had crossed paths, Kelly had been a terrified 14-year-old member of Girl's Tyme, shaking with fear as she auditioned for a deal with Elektra Records. Painfully shy, she had cowered behind Beyoncé and her father, barely saying a word, while the 'adults' had discussed the group's future.

Fast-forward a decade and a half and the confident woman now in front of Rhone had finally stepped out on her own. Even without the comfort of a management or record label to represent her, Kelly had seemed to know exactly who she was and where she was going.

Like many of David Guetta's other hits, 'Commander' was all about pounding dance beats with a European flavour. Yet when they heard she had one foot in the dance camp, some producers who pencilled in studio sessions with Kelly backed away open-mouthed. After all, she was the queen of urban hits and Whitney Houston-edged soul ballads – hadn't her flirtation with David Guetta just been a vacation before returning to what she did best?

That was an assumption she loathed. While she didn't want to turn her back on R&B altogether, she refused to be pigeonholed. "Everyone was like, 'Are you going to do a full dance album, or are you going to do an urban album?'" she groaned to the *Daily Mail*. "I won't allow anyone to put me in a box. I've got to find my [own] voice... and I finally have the faith to do that."

What was more, unlike the play-it-safe R&B producers who'd turned their noses up at her ambition to try dance, Sylvia Rhone was different. "She was like, 'Is this the style you're going for?'" Kelly recalled. "I was like, 'Yeah, I love dance music and I love the fact that we're mixing it with the urban.' Once she'd heard me record, she asked me if I was signed. I said no, and next thing I know, I'm having a meeting with her in New York and signing a new deal with Motown!"

A management contract followed with Jeff Rabhan and it seemed the pieces had finally fallen into place. Kelly would claim her new team "truly put their artists first", but most importantly of all, they respected her change in musical direction. Dance was now Kelly's unique selling point – the one thing that divided her from her past in Destiny's Child.

The group had gone down in history as the best girl band of all time on an international level – how could she top that? It was time to separate herself from the Beyoncé comparisons that had haunted her while promoting her first two albums and take her sound beyond the limits of generic pop and R&B. Yet starting afresh gave rise to mixed feelings in Kelly. Beyoncé was the sister she had loved and grown up with – her mother had given her sanctuary in tough times, while her father had made her a teenage millionaire. Yet she was also a rival, someone who continually beat her to the top spot. Beyoncé was the nation's sweetheart. How could any ambitious woman not be fazed by that?

Even hit TV teen musical *Glee* highlighted the problem, featuring a humiliating dig at Kelly's perceived inferiority. "I'm Beyoncé!" the character Mercedes had announced to peals of laughter. "I ain't no Kelly Rowland!"

The message was clear. If she ever wanted to step out of the shadows and become more than Beyoncé's unremarkable backing singer, it was time to move on and produce a definitive solo sound of her own. Releasing another R&B-infused CD would only add fuel to the fire.

"They're going to forever compare me to Beyoncé because we have been in the group together so long [but now] our paths are two different paths – they can't continue to do that," Kelly told celebrity blogger Clay Cane. Dismissing the comparisons as a lack of intelligence, she delivered another unusually aggressive war cry – "I'll give people a reason not to compare us with this record."

That was exactly her mindset while recording the feisty 'Commander'. With Guetta as producer, it featured the same throbbing dance beats as many of his other efforts such as Akon's 'Sexy Chick' and the Black Eyed Peas' 'Boom Boom Pow'. Yet Kelly felt that she could take credit for starting the movement, having introduced Guetta to Akon at Radio 1's Big Weekend, and also pairing him up with Will.i.am.

However, she took a much less domineering role when it came to writing 'Commander'. In fact she hadn't been present at all. "[Songwriter] Rico Love kicked my ass out of the studio, literally!" Kelly joked. "He invited me back when everything was done and I heard this amazing record."

She played a more active role on 'Work It Man', a track featuring Lil Playy for which she earned a co-writing credit. Along with tracks such as 'Keep It Between Us', it dealt with finding – and then keeping – the perfect man. However, the majority of the new tracks were no longer about candlelit dinners and gentle flirtations – Kelly was about to turn the temperature up and remind the world of exactly why she was now a "grown ass woman".

As a blast from the past, 'All Of The Night' featured Rodney Jerkins as producer, but this was no 'Say My Name'. Kelly was no longer the passive partner, pleading with a suspected player to say her name to prove he wasn't with another woman – now she'd taken hold of her own sexuality.

The track references suggestive metaphors and urges a lover to turn her up like his favourite song. Whilst in her rival's track 'Hip Hop Star', a ballsy Beyoncé sneers at a love interest that he might find her irresistible but she has no time to waste with him, Kelly turns the fantasy around – she transforms from a manically busy international superstar with a schedule that bursts at the seams to a besotted lover with enough time to be in the bedroom the whole day through.

Meanwhile, 'Lay It On Me' is a continuation of that sexual theme, with acclaimed guest rapper Big Sean – whose debut album had featured Kanye West and Pharrell – spitting some explicit lyrics about spanking Kelly and turning her into his schoolgirl.

Blending a hypnotic African beat with a contrastingly modern European flavour, the track has hints of the 50 Cent and Jeremih collaboration 'Put It Down On Me'. Not only did the two songs sound similar, but both featured the shamelessly lustful lyrics of a one-track-mind.

Yet if Kelly had been inspired by 50 Cent, the admiration was mutual. She appeared in his video for 'Baby By Me' that summer, a song which called upon a mercenary woman's materialistic urges by promising that a union with him will make her a millionaire.

Convinced that Kelly was his leading lady, 50 Cent had cornered her at the last minute on the way to an airport and persuaded her to delay her flight by one more day. After she agreed to take part, he reciprocated her generosity by dubbing her "the most under-rated performer out there".

That status was set to change with future number one 'Motivation'. The brief from Kelly was "something really sexy... as simple as that" – and her producers didn't disappoint. What was more, one of them – Jim Jonsin – was renowned for creating tracks which blended both dance and urban sounds together.

His musical marriages were already audible on work with artists like Usher, Kanye West and the Cuban rapper Pitbull. However, to add an extra twist, rapper Lil' Wayne was recruited for a verse promising to turn Kelly's lady garden into a rainforest.

The song had all the ingredients for a hit – a catchy club beat, a rap element and demonstrative, abundant sex appeal. Yet Kelly wasn't nearly finished – and the raciest track on the album was yet to come.

In 'Feeling Me Right Now', Kelly's been looking for a hot date at the club, but has found one special person who outshines all the others there – and that's herself. She doesn't need to take anyone's number – she can find it by calling her own phone. After dancing all night with the pretty girl in the mirror, she thinks she's fallen in love. Like Tweet's masturbation-in-the-mirror-themed song 'Oops (Oh My)', 'Feeling Me Right Now' was unmistakably an anthem for self-love.

Another track that showcased Kelly's playful sense of arrogance was 'I'm Dat Chick'. Possibly an answer to the David Guetta-produced 'Who's Dat Chick?', performed by Rihanna, it was Kelly's way of defining herself as a sex symbol. The track was like a hybrid of Beyoncé's 'Ego' and Fergie's 'Fergalicious', with enough diva credentials to rival both put together.

Beyoncé sings of a monstrously large ego too obscenely voluptuous to fit through the door, while Fergie labels herself irresistible in a tone few would dare to argue with, talking of men lining up around the block for a glimpse of her, before suggestively adding they get their pleasures from her photos. The theme was of a woman who knew the power of her own sex appeal, was comfortable with the effects and wasn't afraid to use it.

'I'm Dat Chick' was Kelly's turn to unleash her inner diva and tell the world how much she loves herself. Modesty wasn't a word in her vocabulary – it had taken her over a decade in the business to notch up such self-confidence, but after that length of time she had surely paid her dues and was deserving of the praise she heaped upon herself.

The track was written by Ester Dean, a hit-maker famous for her work with Rihanna, Britney Spears, Katy Perry, Nicole Scherzinger and Beyoncé to name but a few. Yet while she had teamed up with Beyoncé, she had also experimented beyond the pop genre, having written 'Superbass' for Nicki Minaj and worked on various tracks for Tinie Tempah. In Kelly's eyes, Ester's experience could provide just the crossover theme she was looking for.

Of course, the studio sessions weren't all about boastful bravado and sizzling sex appeal. There were a few serious tracks to balance things out, too. 'Turn It Up' is the candid tale of a woman driven to the bottle by a lover who's already attached elsewhere. Her solution to the pain he's caused? Another round of drinks.

Then there was 'Grown Woman', which saw Kelly look back at her past and reflect on the adult she has become. The new Kelly is cool, calm and confident, someone who hasn't got time to play childish games and won't let her rage get the better of her. In fact, as she icily informs her detractors, they aren't worth breaking a nail over.

Perhaps the darkest song of all was 'Rose-Colored Glasses', a track which Kelly confessed had made her cry so much that her vocal chords had become swollen. "The song is about relationships – the good, the bad and the ugly," she elaborated to *I Heart Radio*. "It made me think of all the relationships where I had to wear rose-coloured glasses… It's just so nice to express that emotion and get it all out there because everyone out there, I'm sure you guys can relate to the pain of feeling like a complete idiot, when everybody's laughing at you, when you're getting played by the person in your life at the time – and you just need to take off your rose-coloured glasses."

She'd also found a title. With a strong collection of tracks now complete, by early 2010 Kelly believed she had enough material to release her third album. Her marriage of dance and R&B music was partly modelled on Janet Jackson's own crossover experiments on her eponymously titled album *Janet*, so, in honour of how the songstress had inspired her, Kelly resolved simply to call the album *Kelly Rowland*. That decision was the biggest hint so far that her album would be the most representative yet of how Kelly was as a person. Yet fans – especially American ones – had a little longer to wait before they could hear her new sound.

The first setback was with 'Commander'. Capitalising on the success of her dance tracks in European markets, she released the track as a single internationally on May 18, 2010 – hitting radio everywhere but North America.

Kelly's aim for the song was to combine a feel-good dance track with a soulful vibe that would melt listeners' hearts at the same time, but most of all, she wanted it to carry a serious message – one of female empowerment. "I hope to see women singing the song like they're in charge," Kelly told *The Daily Star*. "It's important to know that we're commanders who have the power to shape our own destiny."

The accompanying video explored that theme, seeing Kelly standing tall in a bright red bodysuit and a tight, slicked-back ponytail to unleash her inner dominatrix against a black leather cat-suit version of herself, commanding anyone within earshot to get up and dance. Dramatic scenes of smashing glass end the video. What's more, it's an all-night occupation - she calls her driver to ensure he won't collect her any earlier than 8 a.m.

The song even opened the Miss Universe 2010 event in Las Vegas, empowering the beauties present to take the driving seat in their careers and indeed their lives, using their sex appeal to their best advantage along the way.

The track was an instant hit, making the Top 10 in the UK and even reaching the number one spot on the dance chart. Plus, with a 16-week reign in the Top 40, it was one of Kelly's longest-running singles on British shores yet.

However, her big comeback was partially blighted by the ill-timed arrival of Beyoncé's 'Why Don't You Love Me?' in the charts, appearing just before 'Commander' hit the airwaves. A visually arresting video accompanied the song, featuring Beyoncé in bright red lipstick and stockings – a move that was guaranteed to take some of the heat off Kelly. While Kelly came across as feisty, the poster child for an almost militant brand of feminism, Beyoncé's stance in the rival video was – in stark contrast – irresistibly feminine, and her more classically beautiful appearance was raising the heat for male viewers.

The timing couldn't have been worse, sending the "sisters" into direct competition with one another – and yet Kelly took the scheduling mishap in her stride. "[The media is] making too much of a big deal out of it," Kelly would later exclaim, "and trying to create a feud where it doesn't exist... I think there's room for everybody [and] I love her till our dying days and that's all that counts."

To prove that there was no bad feeling, Kelly invited Beyoncé's mother, Tina, to the launch party of her new non-profit charity initiative I Heart My Girlfriends. Also joining them would be tennis giant Serena Williams, and – in a clear message that Kelly was now no-one's puppet – ex-band mate LeToya Luckett, allegedly an arch-enemy of the Knowles family, was also present. Rumours were rife that Kelly's open-armed acceptance of LeToya infuriated Mathew, in particular. "Mathew saw the rekindled friendship as an insult and a betrayal after all he's done for her and her career – it was like a slap in the face to him, especially someone as strict as he is," an anonymous source claimed.

However, with Mathew already estranged from Tina due to an extra-marital affair, the truth about Kelly's forgiveness of LeToya and the reception of it in the Knowles family remained uncertain. For Kelly's part, she was at pains to point out she was at loggerheads with no-one. "Obviously the world likes a feud because the world likes a little tension," Kelly related to *Singers Room*. "As far as Beyoncé and I are concerned, we came from a group. It's a cliché that girl groups don't get along and they hate each other. The press would love for us to fight and bicker and bite each other's heads off. For me, I feel like there's space for everybody and the press pit us against each other. If there's great music, why can't we love it all? You don't have to choose."

In fact, sisterhood and female togetherness – loving instead of fighting – was at the heart of Kelly's charity. With the slogan "educate a girl, empower a woman", it promoted good morals, feminist ideals, education, self-worth and mutual friendship. The idea was that by building girls' self-esteem and helping them to realise their own value, they could grow into empowered, confident women. Another message at the heart of the campaign was for girls to turn their envy at their friends' achievements into inspiration.

"There's a little stigma set on women that when we meet each other, we size each other up," Kelly groaned, "and there's no reason for that. You possess something that I am probably weak at, period. And I think all women possess something that another one might be weak at, but we can always look to you to be strong and ask you about it instead of being insecure about it. Females rule the world, period. I love the fact that we have more power than we know about. I Heart My Girlfriends is all about putting that to good use."

By encouraging girls to stay together instead of becoming embroiled in bitching and backstabbing, Kelly inspired listeners, too. "Fans tried so hard to make you have beef with Beyoncé, but you never did," one girl wrote on the charity's Facebook page, "and that motivates me to keep my bond with my girlfriends strong."

While Kelly claimed she'd made a conscious decision not to include Beyoncé on her third album so that she could stand alone, she insisted there was no friction between the pair – and that sentiment seemed to be setting a standard for women worldwide.

The charity would go on to hold fund-raising events for specific causes such as women with disabilities, but for the time being Kelly's focus had returned to her career. For the first time since 2002's 'Stole' she was hotting up in UK territory as a solo artist – and she was loving the attention.

However, she didn't instantly fit in with British audiences. For example, in interviews, when asked to name her favourite book, she responded "The Bible". In the ultra-religious state of Texas where she was raised, no-one would have blinked an eyelid – in fact, she might have expected a few nods of approval. Yet the UK's secular culture left fans bewildered by her public passion for God – and they weren't sure it sat well with her new raunchy image. That said, the controversy kept the rumour mill turning and the gossip columns flowing – all publicity that Kelly could relish.

Cheered on by the success in the UK and Europe, she announced the album's lead single in North America would be 'Shake Them Haters Off'. The song had been penned by Ne-Yo, who had also written for fellow divas Rihanna and Beyoncé, and served as a defiant war cry against the "miserable people" who criticised her. Hot on the heels of her appearance in 50 Cent's video 'Baby By Me', the lyrics seemed to have been inspired by one of the rapper's earlier tracks, 'Hustler's Ambition'. In his song, 50 taunts that his rivals' hatred provides the adrenalin rush of anger he needs to push him forwards in his career and that, like a fire that feeds on their oxygen, he won't burn unless the haters are there.

Kelly launches an equally caustic attack on her own detractors, groaning that they never seemed to take a break, but also claiming that they only motivate her to succeed and prove them wrong.

As an established household name among American music fans, with a track record of number one hits with other artists and several top-selling albums of his own, Ne-Yo seemed like a safe bet for her US lead single. However, suddenly and without explanation, 'Shake Them Haters Off' was withdrawn just before its release, only to be replaced by two new singles.

'Grown Woman' was released to urban radio while 'Rose-Colored Glasses' targeted the pop market – and both hit the radio waves on June 29. This approach gave US audiences a taste of the familiar urban flavour they knew and loved from her previous albums, breaking them in gently when it came to her show-stopping new sound, while the pop track aimed to expand her usual audience – how could it fail?

There were two eye-catching videos as well. 'Grown Woman' saw

Kelly reminiscing over old photos from her Destiny's Child days, before realising just how much she had grown, while 'Rose-Colored Glasses' – which depicted her encircled by doves and butterflies – revealed Kelly breaking through a wall to move on from a negative situation. The message was clear – Kelly had returned to the music scene a new woman.

However, her transformation was falling on deaf ears. The American public didn't seem to be listening. Both tracks flopped, failing to reach the *Billboard* Top 100 and her best performance globally was a measly number 25 in Slovakia.

Subsequent single 'Forever And A Day', released on September 20, didn't fare much better. Bloggers denounced it as an "unremarkable track devoid of the kick-ass attitude we're used to seeing from Kelly", while even hardcore fans seemed to see it as a poor replacement for her long-awaited – and still elusive – third album.

At a listening party for the press in New York in June, Kelly had confidently promised a September release date for the album, but after the disastrous performance of the two new singles, she called for a rethink. Publicly, she insisted the delay was down to a combination of uncertainty over the album's name and a desire to collaborate with more producers such as Bryan-Michael Cox and Jermaine Dupri. Notably, however, neither of these writers would make it on to the finished product. The project had crashed and burned and, when the rescheduled release date of mid-October came and went, fans began to fear the album wouldn't ever see the light of day.

However, Kelly hadn't given up – behind closed doors, she was reworking her tracks in earnest and had even recorded a new song, 'Down For Whatever'. She'd teamed up with super-producer Red One, who counted himself responsible for taking Lady Gaga to the top.

When he first met the 'Born This Way' singer, she was a frustrated artist moonlighting as a stripper – someone whose music had been relegated to low-key releases on the underground scene. Gaga's wealthy father, who back then had disapproved of her avant garde ambitions, had vowed to cut off her financial support completely if she didn't prove her antics were profitable and make a name for herself in the music business fast. As opposed as she was to the notion of getting a 'proper' job, with the clock ticking fast, she'd almost begun to lose hope.

Enter Red One, someone she credited with changing her life. He produced her breakthrough single 'Just Dance', which saw her rise out of obscurity and become a number-one-selling songstress around the world. Perhaps he could give Kelly a new lease of life too – someone who already had a fully-fledged career and just needed an injection of sass to revive it?

'Down For Whatever' proved to be just as dance-orientated as his early work with Gaga, sporting an irresistibly catchy club beat and slightly huskier than usual vocals from the velvety voiced Kelly. What was more, its sexy lyrics and dancefloor beat had her UK team rubbing their hands together, dollar signs in their eyes, and predicting a number one hit.

"It was a party from the moment that [Red One and I] met," Kelly reminisced to MTV later. "I was just so excited about the record, and the UK Universal team heard it and they were like, 'That's our first single!'"

And while Kelly had identified tracks like 'Motivation' and 'Lay It On Me' as contenders to break through and appease the fickle US urban market, she resolved to remove chart failures 'Grown Woman' and 'Rose Colored Glasses' from the US edition of the album altogether.

Kelly now believed she had a marketing formula fit for both sides of the Atlantic – but she hadn't finished yet. To raise her profile, she also began to release collaborations with other artists who were already key players on the music scene.

She started with Tinie Tempah, a huge hit on the UK's urban scene. Tracks like 'Pass Out' and 'Frisky' were regular additions to playlists, blaring out of the speakers of seemingly every self-respecting nightclub in the country. Yet a slightly younger Tinie had been inspired by Kelly's music growing up and vowed to pay tribute to her on 'Invincible'. The track, which saw Kelly on guest vocals, had an accompanying video in which Tinie went back in time to reflect on his early influences such as Destiny's Child. The tune was released on December 27.

Just a few days later, on January 4, 2011, Kelly appeared as a guest star on Nelly's 'Gone', which was lyrically a sequel to 'Dilemma'. In the lyrics, Nelly warns the world that the girl who'd once lived up the street from him is back – and better than ever.

Being in the charts with both Nelly and Tinie simultaneously was all part of Kelly's plan to rekindle her success in America, while continuing to nurture her new-found popularity in Britain. Meanwhile, by March, the anthemic dance track 'What A Feeling' by Alex Gaudino had hit radio, again featuring Kelly's vocals. It was to be a huge hit in the European market when it was officially released in April.

Kelly was rebuilding her career brick by brick and making a name for herself outside of Destiny's Child, all as a build-up to her third album. Before long, she had become so confident in her abilities that – despite a cameo in 'Party', a Beyoncé track featuring Outkast's Andre 3000 – Kelly was adamant that Beyoncé wasn't going to feature on her own album. She no longer needed her as an emotional crutch.

"I finally realised I wanted more for me," she explained to *The Glasgow Evening Times*. "I had been thinking as a team for so long that I carried it over to my solo career, but with all due respect, as much as I love my sisters, I should have been thinking about me more, rather than the 'we, we, we'."

She would later add, "I want people to hear me for me. Not Kelly from Destiny's Child, but Kelly Rowland... With this album, I want to stand on my own."

With that in mind, what to call the album wasn't a mystery any more; in fact what she'd been racking her brains to find was right in front of her. It was destined to be *Here I Am*.

Chapter 11

Down For Whatever

Kelly's confidence wasn't misplaced – when her US lead single, 'Motivation', finally hit the airwaves, it sailed quickly to number one. What was more, the track was her first ever number one in the US as a lead solo artist – it might have been a long time coming, but she finally felt on top of her game.

Not only was the sound fresh and unexpected, but Kelly felt she had finally become a fully fledged woman – and the public couldn't help but notice. While Kelly had been a goody-two-shoes in her 20s, someone who played it safe, now that she had hit 30, she was displaying sizzling sex appeal with few of her previous inhibitions.

In the video, while Lil' Wayne let loose innuendo after innuendo, a once demure Kelly was writhing expertly and flicking her hair as if it was a Cupid-sent weapon of mass destruction designed to shoot down every man watching. Some fans could scarcely believe this was the same girl who once cowered nervously in the back of Destiny's Child's videos, sneaking fearful glances at the camera over God-fearing Beyoncé's shoulder. Now, Kelly was giving the teenage nymphets of the music world a run for their money, truly living up to the legend of 'dirty 30'.

Following the song's April 8 release, American audiences bought the song in their droves. By May 23, it had hit the number one spot – and it was still there when she performed the track live at the BET Awards on June 26, storming on stage in the middle of Trey Songz's track 'Love Faces'. As Kelly soaked up the attention from a throng of half-naked male dancers and shared a playful kiss with Trey, audiences gave her a standing ovation, which MTV claimed was "one of the loudest of the night". Within minutes, her name was trending on Twitter. The public wasn't accustomed to this side of Kelly – but they clearly liked it.

"I think 'Motivation' opened up a different chapter for me," Kelly told the press at the award ceremony. "I was dreaming about performing on the BET Awards stage. I would dream and pray about it. When you ask God for it, he'll deliver."

While Twitter buzzed with praise for Kelly's most sexually charged, electrified performance yet, the *Baltimore Sun* added: "If this isn't the year's hands-down sexiest song thus far, it has to be in the discussion. Rowland, whose sultry voice could get a priest hot, weaving in and out of the minimal beat and setting the table for Lil' Wayne's stuttering after-hours guest verse. Stack the pieces together and it's an understated knockout that gets sexier with each spin."

Unfortunately, not everyone agreed – and some of Kelly's detractors were a little too close for comfort. Jeff Bhasker, who produced three tracks on Beyoncé's album *4*, took to Twitter to confound the praise for her awards performance by sneering: "How can this KR song with the weakest beat and melody of all time be the #1 song on urban?! Oh yeah. Wayne."

A furious backlash began from Kelly's fans, who retweeted his comment in indignation. Jeff then gave the track a second appraisal, adding: "I just listened to 'Motivation' again to see if I was too harsh in my critique. I wasn't. The lyrics are horrid as well."

Not only had Jeff produced for Beyoncé, but he'd also worked on the Alicia Keys tracks 'Try Sleeping With A Broken Heart' and 'Wait Til You See My Smile'. Ironically, perhaps he had also borrowed some of his straight-talking tactics from outspoken rapper Kanye West, with whom he worked on the latter's 2008 album *808s And Heartbreak*. Kanye was no stranger to controversy – he infamously charged on stage at the VMAs to intercept Taylor Swift's acceptance speech and declare she didn't deserve her award because Beyoncé had released one of the best videos of all time. Now his producer seemed to be taking a leaf out of his book – although the consensus among many tweeters was that he was launching his attack as little more than a publicity stunt to promote himself.

Kelly simply shrugged it off, explaining: "Opinions are like assholes, everybody's got one. He's made wonderful music with my sister and other artists. There's no reason for me to say anything negative… I won't tell you the thought that's really in my head. I'll just kill 'em with kindness."

Plus, while Bhasker might have worked with plenty of artists she admired, 'Motivation' producer Jim Jonsin had an equally impressive CV. He too had worked with Beyoncé and Kanye, as well as collaborating with Eminem on his best-selling album *Recovery* and artists including Nelly, Kid Cudi and Usher. He was even responsible for signing B.O.B., who shot to the number one spot in the UK due to a guest slot on Jessie J's 'Price Tag'.

In further support for Kelly's single, it had been remixed several times featuring the vocals of celebrity fans R Kelly, Mario, the Dream and Busta Rhymes. However, Kelly herself was a million miles away from all the controversy: she had just been selected, along with Gary Barlow, Tulisa Contostavlos and Louis Walsh, to form part of the *The X-Factor*'s UK judging panel. Kelly had taken time out from her promotional schedule to attend auditions and aid the search for Britain's next big global talent.

The schedule started off in Glasgow, where Kelly hit headlines for her diva demands, including booking a golf buggy to carry her from her dressing room to the stage. She later explained away what might have seemed the height of laziness by defending that she and Tulisa had been wearing razor-thin six-inch pin heels and could barely hobble a few footsteps, let alone walking a mile. "Don't get me wrong, I've spent two hours on stage in heels, but it was like a mile from the dressing rooms to the stage and we had six-inch heels on!" she exclaimed to *The Sun*.

However, wearing perilously high Fendi stilettos didn't prevent her from joining three teenage dancers and a man brandishing bagpipes when they serenaded her outside the studio and attempted to teach her the Highland fling. She later raved to her bemused fellow judges that she wanted a repeat performance – but this time she wanted to be kitted out in traditional Scottish costume herself.

As the judges toured the UK, Kelly, who confessed to a soft spot for British men, found herself overcome with lust by the talent she saw – and it wasn't always the musical kind. When one contestant slaughtered the Whitney Houston ballad 'I Have Nothing', Kelly grimaced. "My darling, I must admit I love your abs a little bit more than your voice," she teased. "It's going to be a no from me, but I'm going to be dreaming about those abs!" Of another contestant, she joked, "[He] was so cute I almost gave him my Blackberry Messenger PIN!"

Even Louis didn't escape Kelly's wandering eye. "I can't stop touching Louis' butt!" she revealed to *The Sun*. "I literally touch his butt every time I see him – he has the cutest little booty."

Yet it wasn't all light-hearted fun: Kelly wasn't afraid to work "13-hour days" and was committed to finding the next big thing. Yet finding an English star wasn't enough – to Kelly, Britain was just a tiny island. "All I've looked for is a global star," she insisted. "Me and Tulisa will differ. I heard Tulisa say, 'We're looking for that next big UK star,' and I said, 'Well, I'm looking for the next international star because you can't just put someone in a box, you give them everything they deserve. That's what they're here for, they're here for international success. I want them to be better than me, better than Gaga and better than Beyoncé. Each generation is meant to be better."

To some nervous contestants, her determination was formidable. She didn't hold back with her criticism, dismissively telling one would-be star: "That was a pitchy, weak vocal" and later groaning to *Vibe*, "Some people's vocals are hard to deal with! They come in and conjure up the dead!"

Yet her straight-talking, no-nonsense attitude was nothing Kelly hadn't already endured herself in the boot-camp-style early days of her own career. Labelled the "sensitive one" of the group, manager

Mathew's bully-boy tactics – which had been shrugged off by all the others – had regularly left Kelly humiliated and in floods of tears. Yet she came to believe that the hardship had been in her best interests, as it had taught her discipline and pushed her to succeed. "I've had no's in my career since the age of 13," she told the *Daily Mail*. "Signed, dropped, signed, dropped. I know what it feels like."

As Kelly had practised round the clock throughout her childhood, she was wise to the sob stories and took claims that contestants had been working themselves into the ground with a pinch of salt. "I've heard so many kids explain how hard they've worked," she told *The Sun*. "Even their parents will tell me, 'She practised, so don't be mean.' But I've been in that exact same situation and have been turned down many times… auditioning in front of a record label, doing showcases over and over again, the possibility of being signed by a label or production company… It felt like every year we were being rejected until we were finally signed. So when people say I don't know what they're going through, let me tell you – I know it all!"

Kelly also brought a wealth of more recent experience to the panel. She had learned a hard lesson due to the failed singles of the previous year. While some of her songs had flopped in the US, they had been a hit in the UK and she had to adapt to releasing different tracks in different countries. She had struggled to make her songs sell on both sides of the Atlantic simultaneously – and the challenge had been to find hits that were relatable globally.

Therefore when she saw a contestant on *The X-Factor*, she wasn't just looking for talent, but evidence that they could find a multinational platform. "The first thing I think is, 'Can they cross over?'" she explained. "The UK has had artists from the Beatles to Adele who have done that and been successful both here and in the States." She added, "To be in the business for 17 years and pick up so much knowledge, you've just got to give it back."

In fact, Kelly was so passionate about pioneering the acts she believed in that she personally intervened, storming off stage on one occasion to persuade a sobbing singer to return. Chrissie Pitt's group, Twisted, had received the thumbs down from the judges, but Chrissie stood out to

Kelly. Yet, racked with guilt at betraying the friends she'd auditioned with, Chrissie had fled backstage and was refusing the judges' pleas to come out and perform solo.

Kelly ran backstage to confront her, demanding: "What are you doing with these doo-wop singers? You don't need them, you're a stand-alone singer… this is your *opportunity*!"

After nearly half an hour, she convinced Chrissie to return to the stage, where she made it through to the next round. For some, the drama was an eye-opening introduction to the cut-throat world of showbiz. A distraught girl was encouraged to double-cross her friends who had been dismissed as talentless and inferior to her for a piece of national TV entertainment. To succeed, it seemed that sometimes loyalty and friendship had to take second place to cold-blooded, single-minded and ruthless ambition. Kelly had had a lesson in single-mindedness herself that year, when she decided to keep Beyoncé off her album to ensure she'd be judged on her own merit. It was about striking a balance between sisterhood and selfishness and, by now, she had had more than enough practice.

Kelly might have seemed to be a tough cookie but, underneath the exterior was a soft, sweet caramel filling. "I want to be constructive," she insisted to *The Sun*. "I'm not here to crush anybody's dreams."

As the auditions continued, and Kelly judged one anxious contestant after another as gently as possible, she had her own heart-in-mouth dilemma to contend with: the release of her new album.

Scheduled to hit the shelves on July 22, it was tipped for success, but nothing was certain. 'Motivation' and 'Commander' had been huge, whereas 'Rose Colored Glasses' and 'Grown Woman' had flopped. Not only that but she had suffered a few other recent failures, too. Her collaboration with Pitbull for his sixth album, *Planet Pit*, 'A Castle Made Of Sand', only charted in New Zealand, where it took the number 37 spot. Pitbull's popularity had increased dramatically that year and his album featured top names like Nelly, Sean Paul, Enrique Iglesias and Ludacris – yet somehow his collaboration with Kelly had missed most of the charts altogether.

Then there was 'Favor', a track released by Lonny Bereal to which she contributed her vocals. Released on May 17, it had barely scraped the number 85 spot on the US Hip Hop chart before fading into oblivion.

Reactions to her new material had been far from consistent, so it was near impossible to predict the public's attitude to the album. Would fans have tired of waiting for a release that had constantly been pushed back? It also came years after *Ms Kelly* – would the music world have forgotten about her? America had new vocal icons to watch – Katy Perry, Nicki Minaj and Lady Gaga to name just a few.

The speculation ended when the album debuted at number one on America's R&B and Hip Hop Albums chart and number three on the mainstream *Billboard* chart. The result was the highest début position yet of her entire solo career.

However, Kelly had no time to celebrate – it was now time to film a video for her next single, 'Lay It On Me'. Swathed in a skintight white dress, she looked like the cat that got the cream as she cavorted in a sandwich of topless male models. The choreography was simple yet striking, with Kelly grinding and gyrating her hips whilst surveying the eye candy around her. It was more than just a predictable display of sex appeal, though – a baby elephant named Suzie was joining her on stage too. Along with a slinky she rubbed over her body, perhaps its trunk was a phallic symbol to join the abundance of other sexual metaphors. Bizarrely, Kelly had tweeted afterwards that her animal companion had been "a good listener".

The single, which was released on August 16, was a moderate success, just missing the Top 40 in the US R&B and Hip Hop charts, and reaching number 19 in the UK singles chart and number 69 in Japan.

As it made playlists worldwide, Kelly struggled to juggle her work commitments to "promote the hell out of" her new number one album with her obligations to *The X-Factor*. In fact, just a day after auditions ended, she was jetting off to North America as a support act for Chris Brown – and she wouldn't be returning until three weeks later, just days before the live shows aired.

However, Kelly's decision, based on her enthusiasm to be part of the shamed singer's comeback after he narrowly avoided a jail sentence for battering ex-lover Rihanna, was met with horror and derision by some. The tour announcement sparked debate over whether it was irresponsible for female role models in the industry to be glorifying Chris by joining him, in case it silently condoned his behaviour. Domestic violence campaigners felt it minimised or ignored what he had done, setting a bad example to impressionable young women yet to find their identity, who might look to Kelly to shape their own behaviour. Could her actions lead them to see violence as acceptable and ultimately forgivable?

The heat rose further as comments from love-struck teenagers appeared on Twitter, claiming, "I'd let Chris Brown beat me any day."

"It's dangerous for girls to see him publicly getting another chance," one anonymous blogger claimed. "What if an abuse victim sees that happen and decides to give her own partner another chance – and next time he batters her to death?!"

However, amid rumours that rapper Jay-Z was disappointed by her decision to join the tour, Kelly's affection for Chris remained intact. She admired the way that, like her, he combined different genres of music – from the urban-flavoured 'Look At Me Now' to the dance-influenced 'Beautiful People'.

Plus, on the Choice Breakfast Show, she sounded positively enamoured with him. "I think he should be given a second chance," she told the host. "I love my Chrissy boo. He's a really sweet young man." Claiming that the altercation between Chris and Rihanna had been behind closed doors and was "none of our business", she added, "Everybody should just chill out."

As the fury towards Chris raged on, the tour – which began on September 12 – made its way through America. During his hit single 'Take Me Down', Chris was even filmed giving Kelly an onstage lap dance one night, leading to rumours that they were dating.

In between concert dates with Chris, Kelly – who had already been assigned the girls' category on *The X-Factor* – was rushed to her marble-floored Miami mansion where she would mentor the eight hopefuls who were battling it out for a place on the show's live episodes. She wasn't alone – not only was she joined by a stream of interviewers and press photographers, but US singer and actress Jennifer Hudson – who'd been in the film *Dreamgirls* alongside Beyoncé – was on hand to help her choose who would be in her final four.

There had already been some nerve-racking moments: 24-year-old Sian Phillips, who was tipped by production staff as a dead cert for the finals, had a criminal past and her 10-day jail sentence for affray banned her from travelling to America. Another girl, who had narrowly missed out on the Judges' Houses stage of the camp, was drafted in to replace her. Kelly had selected her final four: flame-haired Irish songstress Janet Devlin, rock chick Amelia Lily, Adele sound-a-like Sophie Habibis, and troubled but talented teenager Misha Bryan. Now they would battle with Gary's boys, Louis' over 26s and Tulisa's groups to win the show and the coveted price of a £1-million recording contract.

Before the live shows had even begun, Louis had branded Kelly the "biggest diva" he'd ever seen, claiming that she had the largest entourage in the history of *The X-Factor*. "She has six people in her entourage that the viewers don't see," he revealed to *The Mirror*. "Every time she moves, there are two assistants down at her feet fixing her shoes. She has a hairstylist running after her everywhere she goes putting every strand of hair back in place as soon as she moves from one part of the set to the other. There are even people on hand to give her a massage as soon as she feels a bit tense. She's a full-on diva!" Kelly would later retort of her entourage, "I need them if I haven't slept for four days!"

There was no doubt that she was set to look her very best on stage. But it wasn't all about extravagant showbiz demands: she also had her competitive face on for her girls and she was desperate to win. Backstage, life for the contestants was about as far from the archetypal fame fantasy of sex, drugs and rock 'n' roll as it was possible to get. To heighten the girls' chances against their rivals, Kelly had compiled a list of restrictions so stringent that it might have made even a highly disciplined Olympic athlete groan.

There'd be no alcohol, no smoking and no sex. They would work long hours, sacrifice their social lives and replace boozy nights out with beauty sleep. In the event that they did venture out to check out the nightlife, they had been instructed not to shout over the music, lest it weaken their vocal chords. That meant no drinks and no conversation – a pretty miserable night out by many people's definition. Yet Kelly's defence was that stardom wasn't easy and didn't come cheap. "I didn't go out until I was at least 22 and I didn't party until two years ago," she revealed to *The Mirror*. "I've always been strict. I don't drink a lot, I don't smoke – I want to succeed… Don't let anybody affect your focus – anything, anyone – or you will lose everything."

Not only was she ruling her own contestants with an iron fist, but she reportedly came to blows with fiery North Londoner Tulisa by barging into her dressing room and giving her advice on how to mentor her own acts. Silently furious, Tulisa declined and Kelly soon found herself talking to a closed door. She had allegedly boasted that she knew the music industry like the back of her hand, was more experienced than "baby" Tulisa and was there to help in the show's best interests.

Archetypally American and full of self-belief and bravado, Kelly felt this was no moment for modesty – and she had the approval of TV's very own Mr Nasty, Simon Cowell, to be as outspoken as she pleased. "He basically told me not to be shy about my success: he knows how successful Destiny's Child were and he just said, use your experience at the very top to help the contestants," Kelly explained simply to *People*. "It was great advice because without it, I would probably be wary about being overconfident."

However, she hadn't bargained for single-minded Tulisa, who wasn't impressed with her advice at all. She was mortified that, as she saw it, Kelly was trying to assert superiority over her. On the other hand, Kelly was offended that her offer of help had been shunned. Knowing she had the show's boss in her corner, she made no apologies. "Dude, I'm nobody's puppet!" she told *The Mirror*. "I have a smart mouth... When Simon gave me the job, he liked the fact I stood by my word."

Kelly had come a long way from the shy, quiet pre-teen rehearsing in Beyoncé's backyard and she had trod the line between confidence and arrogance for several years now. She felt she had paid her dues and that conquering the struggles of her earlier career entitled her to a bit of self-belief. "If you don't know your worth, if you don't know your value, if you don't know how fantabulous you are, it's going to be hard for other people to see it," Kelly had warned in *Essence* magazine. "Being appreciative of self is beauty to me."

Of course, it wasn't quite so beautiful to Tulisa. During auditions, the two had bonded – affectionately naming each other LuLu and Booboo – but their friendship seemed to be short-lived. Kelly had warned *UnrealityTV*: "Let's not forget what we're here for, because I know once the competition starts, things will get competitive!"

Perhaps it hadn't helped that Gary had been stirring up trouble in his own way, revealing to *The Graham Norton Show* that he'd "done the typical man thing" by buttering up both girls. He had visited their dressing rooms separately to comfort them, telling each that the other was to blame. While Gary was enjoying his role as a ladies' man, Louis was forecasting a storm – and this time in public. "There is no way Tulisa and Kelly are going to get through the series without a major row... and they won't have to fake it," he chuckled to *The Mirror*. "It will be real. It will be box office gold!"

By that point, backstage it was a "No shit, Sherlock!" conclusion. There was already an icy silence between the two girls, which constantly threatened to spill over into outright hostility. Audiences were waiting for the moment Louis had predicted – and, when Tulisa accused Kelly's protégé Misha of bullying her contestants, it quickly came.

Tulisa hit out when Misha was at her most vulnerable – standing in the bottom two and waiting with bated breath to hear whether she had been eliminated or granted a reprieve. Tulisa claimed her caustic remarks that she was the best and destined to outdo the others in the final had left some contestants in tears. Kelly was outraged, claiming that what went on behind closed doors was irrelevant and that Misha should be judged purely on her singing ability.

Was the complaint a cheap stunt intended to make a popular rival contestant fall out of favour with the public? If so, it indicated that the hopefuls were being used as pawns, their dreams exploited for the sake of TV entertainment. Either way, Kelly was furious.

Tulisa's position was that she was simply giving the kind of constructive criticism that Kelly usually advocated, helping Misha to become more diplomatic – and hence more likeable – in the future. She added that she related to Misha's bolshiness, believing it was driven by insecurity, fear and defensiveness.

Having grown up on a tough council estate in a violent inner-city neighbourhood, Tulisa had adopted the mentality of "kill or be killed", where getting in the first defensive blow was vital in order to survive. Misha had admitted to suffering a traumatic childhood herself, estranged from her heroin-addicted mother with just an aunt to care for her, while Tulisa had a mother with severe bipolar disorder.

Misha seemed to graciously accept Tulisa's explanation, but Kelly was hearing no excuses – and, according to media reports, they instantly stopped speaking. Some saw Kelly's reaction as extreme, but she refused to apologise. "If I'm passionate about something, I put my heart and soul into it," she told *Planet Notion*. "If it means getting my point across and being a bitch about it, then so be it!"

Soon afterwards, tragedy struck again. Kelly had briefly returned to America, where she was struck down with a mystery throat virus – one so severe she could barely swallow. She was absent from the judging panel that weekend, replaced by former *X-Factor* winner Alexandra Burke. Two of her girls formed the bottom two, which some claimed was due to Kelly's absence and inability to mentor them that week.

The night that Sophie and Misha went head to head, with the former being sent home, Kelly made a croaky phone call to the studios, sparking rumours that she was feigning illness, or that perhaps she was leaving the show altogether in indignation at how she had been treated by her younger rival. Once she'd recovered, Kelly was furious. "Someone said that I had to fake being sick," she told *GQ*. "I don't want anybody to feel the way I felt. I wouldn't wish that upon an enemy, I couldn't swallow my own saliva. I've never experienced pain the way I experienced pain with my throat. All [my jawline] was swollen. I looked like a frickin' linebacker. I didn't want to look in the mirror. I was like, 'This is an awful, really unattractive human being that I'm looking at right now!'"

When TV shows began to mock her, labelling it "the worst impression of an ill person" they had ever heard, a furious Kelly retaliated by calling it "a slap in the face".

However, the following week, on returning to the nation's TV screens, she'd broken the ice a little with Tulisa. She even developed a soft spot for her group Little Mix, whom she predicted could be "the next big girl group to come out of Britain". However, her outspoken antics weren't over yet – and next in the firing line was Louis.

Hapless teenage tearaway Frankie Cocozza, who was said to model himself on Pete Doherty and was better known for his shambolic performances, tight trousers and big hair than his singing voice, had been attempting to pull off a version of the Black Eyed Peas song 'I Gotta Feeling'.

The audience watched in horror. There had been loud whispers from both viewers and the media alike that he had been chosen for the show due to his flamboyant personality rather than any artistic merit – and this performance, like many of his others, had only seemed to confirm that. Frankie had the names of sexual conquests tattooed across his buttocks, and – despite promising he would settle down and find a girlfriend as soon as he'd racked up 100 notches on his bedpost – for now he was a notorious womaniser.

At large, the nation enjoyed his antics but saw him as more of a comedy act than a credible voice of the future - like an unrealistic drag queen with hairy legs trying to blend in with a pageant full of beauty queens – and this wasn't lost on Louis. Once the disastrous rendition was over, he let loose. "That was like really bad karaoke and I don't know why you're still here," he exclaimed. "You're not a rock star, you'll never be a rock star and the only thing that's big about you is your hair!"

His comments sparked anger from Kelly, who blasted: "You're out of line for telling someone what they'll never be." Louis responded with a low blow, retorting: "At least I'm here every week!"

It was an embarrassing Achilles-heel moment for Kelly. Back in her Destiny's Child days, she had prided herself on her focus and had even labelled former bandmate Farrah unprofessional for letting a gastric virus prevent her from fulfilling work commitments. She told the press that if she could attend concerts with a broken foot, then Farrah should have risen above adversity too. Yet now Kelly herself had succumbed to illness – the type that wasn't taking no for an answer.

Blushes aside, Kelly maintained that Louis' attitude to Frankie had been unfair. If he didn't have what it took to be a star, why had he been allowed to take part? Was humiliating him to entertain the nation and boost TV viewing figures unethical? Plus, aside from that, hadn't Louis put comedy act Wagner through to the live shows the previous year? With that track record, one the nation had ridiculed, was he really in a position to criticise other people's acts?

"I just strongly disagreed with what Louis said," Kelly vented to *Star*. "You don't tell someone what they'll never do and that struck a chord with me as someone has told me I'll never do something before." She added: "Some of the contestants are rather young and it's important to choose your words carefully. There is a way to be constructive when giving criticism. I'm not downing Louis' perspective, but it really, really got under my skin."

If it had made Kelly wince – an international star with no shortage of self-confidence – what might it have done to Frankie? Viewers divided themselves on the issue, with some believing it was gratuitous bullying and others insisting it was all par for the course when it came to live TV. Some felt it was not just pointless but counter-productive to bolster Frankie's ego out of kindness and lead him on with false hope. Yet soon the debate would be over altogether, when Frankie crashed out of the show for cocaine use.

Kelly's shock and sympathy turned to delight when she realised it meant one of her eliminated contestants stood a chance of returning. Earlier in the competition, judges had been invited to choose which one of their four acts to eliminate initially. In previous years, this had been decided by viewer vote, but this time the onus was on Kelly to bite the bullet and she had axed crowd favourite Amelia Lily. Now Amelia, along with Tulisa's group Two Shoes, Louis' act Jonjo Kerr and Gary's act James Michael were in the running to replace Frankie. With an overwhelming majority of viewer votes, it was announced that Amelia – whose rendition of Michael Jackson's 'Billie Jean' had seen her defeated before – had won a second chance.

Stories began circulating that there was hostility between Kelly and Amelia, with the latter holding a grudge that she had been eliminated prematurely and accusing her mentor of giving preferential treatment to Misha. However, the pair looked nothing less than thrilled to be reunited on the night.

Meanwhile, if Misha and Kelly did have an extra-special bond, perhaps it was because they both shared the raw trauma of unresolved childhood abandonment. It came to a head on the November 20 episode *of The X-Factor* when, backstage, Kelly and Misha comforted each other as they sat embracing on the dressing room floor in floods of tears.

Misha was struggling to come to terms with her mother abandoning her when she was three months old – she'd been a heroin addict who'd served a 21-month prison sentence – while Kelly still felt the pain an absent father had left her with. Misha's estranged mother, who had left her in the care of her aunt, had written an open letter in the press to the daughter she had never known. "When I heard you say on *The X-Factor* that you don't know your real mum or why she abandoned you, I felt all the heartbreak from when I parted with you 19 years ago come flooding back," it had begun.

Misha, who read the message just a couple of days before that episode of the show, was beside herself in a whirlwind of emotions. Any relief or comfort she might have felt at her mother reaching out was doubtless underscored by the question of why, if she cared so much, she hadn't been in touch sooner. Was she sincere or simply jumping on the bandwagon of gold-diggers, ready to exploit her estranged daughter's new-found fame? After all, she'd had nearly two decades to contact her – to forge a friendship if nothing else.

These were tricky questions that Kelly had to ask herself, too. Her father had recently got in touch by giving his story to *The Mirror* and urging her to call him. He'd left it even longer to break the ice – 23 years. How could she trust his motives?

Yet, as she advised a sobbing Misha, a blood connection was a blood connection. "It's really important to just forgive my father," she told her. "I want to meet him this Christmas because now is the time, because nothing's promised to us. It's important to forgive people and move on, we have to. The pain is there, of course it will be there, but it's important to know that forgiveness is the first step towards healing it all."

When Kelly had seen the photographs of her father in a newspaper, she'd been incredulous – not just that he had reached out in such a public way, but that when she saw his face looking back at her from the pages, she hadn't recognised him. Something had instinctively made her look twice, murmuring under her breath: "Who is this guy?" When she got her answer, she began hyperventilating with shock and found herself being comforted in the arms of her assistant. For that reason, Kelly could relate to the intense emotions of the teenager who sat beside her. "When it comes to parents, I truly, truly understand," she reassured her. "You'll get through this with flying colours... This is the exact same position I'm in, so I completely get it."

A couple of weeks later, it was Kelly's turn to strike out against adversity. While she mentored her girls, she was hearing 'Down For Whatever' on every radio station and, by November 28, the international edition of *Here I Am* was released. The first 12 tracks were the same as the deluxe edition released earlier in the year, but they were also accompanied by 'When Love Takes Over', 'Rose Colored Glasses', the Diplo remix of 'Motivation', 'Forever And A Day' and her collaboration with Alex Gaudino, 'What A Feeling'. Not only that, but those who had only purchased the standard edition when it was released the first time round also benefitted from two bonus tracks – 'Heaven And Earth' and 'Each Other'.

Kelly celebrated the album's release by singing latest single 'Down for Whatever' live on *The X-Factor* followed by a repeat performance on the German version of the show in Cologne two days later.

Then it was the weekend of *The X-Factor* final. Misha had been defeated in the semi-finals – which some speculated was down to Tulisa branding her a bully – and now it was just Amelia Lily competing against Little Mix and Gary's act Marcus Collins.

Despite a well-liked duet with Kelly of Tina Turner's 'River Deep Mountain High', Amelia was the first of the three to leave the competition – and the eventual winners were Little Mix. Kelly might not have won, but she hadn't regretted taking part: she saw it as just another stage in her evolution.

And Kelly had certainly evolved. With *Here I Am* more representative

of who she was than ever before, she had started to come into her
sexuality. Earlier that year, she'd had a "friends with benefits" situation
with a Londoner. She had also posed topless and taken part in countless
sexually exploratory photo shoots – something which would never have
got past Mathew Knowles's eagle-eyed gaze.

Now she was free to explore that side of herself without fearing
his disapproval – and interviews with her proved that. "I love going
commando!" she randomly revealed to *The Sun* during one interview.
"Don't you ever just like to wear a dress and that's it? It just makes you
feel yummy."

What was more, it sounded like making underwear optional was a
Rowland family tradition. "One thing my grandmother told me is you
should feel sexy without anything on," she added.

She even told the press that, late at night, away from the paparazzi's
prying eyes, she made secret visits to sex shops. Clearly she was no
longer shy.

Little by little, going solo had seen Kelly move away from the
restrictions of the strict moral compass that had directed her as part
of Destiny's Child. While, like Beyoncé, she was still a Christian, she
didn't agree with the stance of some hard-line, religious zealots on
topics like homosexuality. Amid protests that same-sex marriage should
be outlawed and that gay relationships were against God, Kelly told
Frontiers LA that she had no such prejudices. "I remember having this
discussion with my grandmother," she explained. "She said that we love
who we love – we all should just have an expression of love and that
doesn't matter whether it's male-female, male-male, female-female –
everybody should definitely have their expression of love, period. And
I agree with her."

This was one debate, however, that might have separated her
brand of spirituality from Beyoncé's. While Kelly regularly partied
in gay nightclubs and insisted she didn't have a homophobic bone in
her body, Beyoncé had been accused of the exact opposite. She had
told *The Face* – a now-defunct fashion and culture magazine – that
she could never contemplate kissing another woman, as the Bible
condemned it.

Kelly, on the other hand, had blushingly confessed to gay-rights blogger Clay Cane that she wasn't immune from a couple of celebrity girl crushes. "I just love how confident they are," she praised. "I love how happy Drew Barrymore is all the time. Angelina Jolie has just got that confident beauty thing going for her – she is absolutely stunning."

There'd been another specific episode, before the split of Destiny's Child, which had led onlookers to believe Beyoncé was homophobic. In 2003, to celebrate the 20th year of MTV's VMAs, organisers had decided to bring in the ultimate crowd-pleaser – some suggestive lesbian action.

First, Madonna's then pre-teen daughter Lourdes appeared dressed as a flower girl at a wedding, before Britney Spears and Christina Aguilera jumped out of a giant cake wearing wedding dresses. The pair serenaded Madonna with her hit 'Like A Virgin', provoking her to jump out from the cake herself, dressed as the groom. Madonna, then 45, played the "butch" lesbian cougar, turning to kiss each of her feminine companions on the lips.

While the camera cut to Britney's ex Justin Timberlake, whose usually immaculate face was contorted with grimaces of disapproval, an MTV producer voiced what many viewers might have been thinking. "It was sensational, but I wonder what the good folk in places like Provo, Utah State would make of it. Middle America is not going to let this one go lightly."

As the Madonna of the contemporary music world, in the true sense of the word, neither was Beyoncé. She was quoted as saying, "I have standards. There are things I will not do." *The Sun* printed a headline about her reading "God Let Me Strip On Stage, But Not Kiss Girls". A horrified Beyoncé, whose openly gay uncle had died of an AIDS-related illness, claimed that her comments had been taken out of context. However, she'd made her message clear – same-sex kisses were against her religious beliefs.

Kelly had kept a dignified silence while in the group, but years later, she contradicted it, telling *Bang Showbiz*: "My gay fans are the reason I'm here… The gay community provides so much strength and I really say this from the heart. There is so much unconditional love… When I went to G.A.Y. [to perform] I was so overwhelmed with the love that I almost teared up!"

Whether it was her TV career, her music, her love life or her beliefs, it seemed a newly liberated Kelly was fully living up to her promise that she was 'Down For Whatever' – and, with plans for many more albums yet, the pace shows no signs of slackening.

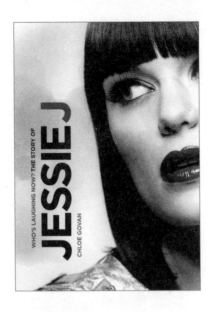

WHO'S LAUGHING NOW
THE JESSIE J STORY
By Chloë Govan

This extraordinary biography tells how Jessica Ellen Cornish from Ilford in north east London overcame being 'not really that good at anything' to reinvent herself as Jessie J and record one of the biggest selling albums of 2011.

Success came in the face of extraordinary setbacks. Childhood bullying, an irregular heartbeat, a serious fall from the stage and a minor stroke at the age of 18 all threatened the health and career of the BRIT school student who first pursued fame through dance and the musical theatre.

Author Chloe Govan has interviewed record producers, school classmates, friends, dance tutors and many others to unearth the real stories behind Jessie J's improbable road to fame.

Chloë Govan has written about travel, lifestyle and music for a variety of publications around the world including Travel Weekly, The Times *and* Real Travel, *where she has a monthly column. She is also the author of* Katy Perry: A Life of Fireworks *and* Rihanna: Rebel Flower, *also published by Omnibus Press.*

ISBN: 978.1.78038.313.2
Order No: OP54505

CRAZY IN LOVE
THE BEYONCE KNOWLES BIOGRAPHY
By Daryl Easlea

Crazy In Love explores the life and astonishing career trajectory of Beyoncé Knowles, the Texan teenager who rose from performing in her hometown backyards to headlining shows all over the world. Daryl Easlea's biography details her time with Destiny's Child – the troubled group that launched her – and her subsequent spectacular rise to a particularly modern kind of fame.

Beyoncé now spans movies, albums, product endorsements and the obligatory celebrity marriage. Hitched to Jay-Z, she kept changing her hairstyles and was accused of changing her complexion to a lighter shade for a L'Oréal commercial. She even changed her name to Sasha Fierce for one album. Making sense of the chameleonic career that prompted Michelle Obama to declare Beyoncé 'one of my favorite performers on the planet' the author has produced a biography that is both exciting and revealing.

Daryl Easlea was the deputy editor at Record Collector, to which he remains a regular contributor. His work can be found in Mojo *and* bbc.co.uk; *and has appeared in* The Guardian, Uncut, Dazed & Confused *and* The Independent. *He is the author of the critically acclaimed* Everybody Dance: CHIC & The Politics of Disco *and* The Story Of The Supremes.

ISBN: 978.085712.723.5
Order No: OP53988